GAMES AND SONGS

OF

AMERICAN CHILDREN

COLLECTED AND COMPARED BY

WILLIAM WELLS NEWELL

WITH A NEW INTRODUCTION AND INDEX BY

CARL WITHERS

DOVER PUBLICATIONS, INC.

NEW YORK

Published in Canada by General Publishing Company, Ltd., 30 Lesmill Road, Don Mills, Toronto, Ontario.

Published in the United Kingdom by Constable and Company, Ltd.

This Dover edition, first published in 1963, is an unabridged republication of the second (1903) edition of the work first published by Harper and Brothers in 1883. This edition also contains the Editor's Note from the first edition and a new Introduction and Index especially prepared for this edition by Carl Withers.

International Standard Book Number: ***0-486-20354-9***

Library of Congress Catalog Card Number: 63-3347

Manufactured in the United States of America
Dover Publications, Inc.
180 Varick Street
New York, N. Y. 10014

INTRODUCTION TO DOVER EDITION (1962).

"There is no intellectual interest which folklore does not touch; the poet and the artist, the historian and the philologist, the student of mores and the student of religions, each finds in it a different attraction."—William Wells Newell, *Journal of American Folklore II*, (1889), 158.

William Wells Newell's *Games and Songs of American Children* is filled with games that have delighted many generations of youngsters, and it will charm everyone capable of enchantment by "the bright poetry" of childhood. It was first published nearly eighty years ago, by a poet and literary scholar who had a naturalist's accurate eye for detail and the rigorous mind of a scientist. It is a beautifully written book that reflects great learning and is full of warm humanity.

The author gathered the melodies, formulas, rules, and prescribed movements of the games both from the memories of adults and by observing and interviewing the children who played them. He set them down with tenderness and extraordinary sensitivity to the imaginative qualities of childhood and with a surprising amount of surrounding social circumstance to illuminate their use. His children come alive. Who could forget the pictures he evokes of little Cornish boys dancing in May Day file behind a leader playing imaginary music on a wooden flute? of New England girls bewildering a dull brother and uninstructed elders with the gibberish of "Hog Latin"? of a little Negro girl giving him the words and tune of a ballad (Child 155) in her cabin near Central Park, New York City? He accompanied his descriptions of children's pastimes with many literary and other testimonies to the antiquity and tenacity of childhood tradition. Since Newell believed—somewhat wrongly—that the games were vanishing so rapidly in "a general ruin" of popular traditions that they would soon be wholly extinct, the book conveys an elegiac quality of lament. We can hardly read it today without nostalgia for our own childhood and for a time when the whole world, or so it seemed to the author, was more childlike and poetical.

The book is also an important pioneer study in the field of American folklore, one that is still very valuable to folklorists. It was the first systematic large-scale gathering and presentation of the games and game songs of English-speaking children. More important still, it was the first annotated, comparative study which showed conclusively that these games and their texts were part of an international body of data. As his bibliography on pages 267–269 shows, Newell had familiarized himself with previous collections of children's games, rhymes, and songs in many countries. He had also searched through literature, from the Greek and Roman classics through later times, for accounts of children's play. As a result, he related the games of American children not only to those of their British cousins, but to similar diversions of children in many other European countries, over hundreds of years. He showed that games and even songs and rhymes (for all their difficulty of translation) move as easily as folktale or legend across language barriers. Viewing the traditional lore of children as "straws on the surface" of more important historical "currents of thought," and as transmitted from children to children with minimal adult mediation or interference, Newell considered the subject as especially appropriate for historical comparative study.

Games and Songs of American Children was first published in 1883. Twenty years later, in 1903, Newell enlarged and reissued the book as it appears here (except that the brief Editor's Note to the first edition, which he dropped from the 1903 edition, has now been restored). Newell added the present Preface and Chapter XVI, entitled "Aftermath," containing thirty new items (Nos. 161–190) with appropriate comparative notes, and the last seven bibliographical titles listed on page 269. These were collections of children's games that had appeared in the meantime. The most important of them was Mrs. A. B. Gomme's *The Traditional Games of England, Scotland, and Ireland* (2 vols., London, 1894 and 1898).* Her great collection contained few games that

* Mrs. Gomme arranged her collection of games alphabetically. Newell's attempt to arrange his games in categories of use (e.g., "Love-Games," "Playing at Work," "Guessing-Games," etc.) was a remarkable and imaginative pioneer thrust toward what was later to be called "functionalism." I am greatly indebted to my friend Herbert Halpert for this observation and for various other details of fact and insight embraced in this Introduction.

Newell had not reported, though many more variants, and thus testified to the thoroughness of his pioneer research. It corroborated Newell's main viewpoints about the distribution and diffusion of children's games and songs, and it enabled him to correct a mistaken belief that they had survived better in the New World than in the mother country.

How well have these games survived among children today? Like most other folklore collectors, Newell was impressed by the paradox of conservatism and evanescence. He saw children preserving verbal formulas so old as to have lost all reasonable meaning; he also saw them substituting new words for old in traditional rhymes and songs, and inventing brand-new games out of their environment. To the folklorist in the field, however rich the harvest of older lore, new items often seem to be pushing the older ones into oblivion, and collectors tend to develop a feeling of urgency: to gather the old before it is too late. Newell felt this urgency keenly, about every branch of popular tradition and folkways. Yet folklore is very durable—it changes more readily than it disappears. The games and songs printed here have lasted better than Newell predicted. In general it is the most ancient and widespread of the nonsinging games that still live on, and with least change, in childhood tradition. But many of the singing games are still popular, and most of them can be found *somewhere* among American and other English-speaking children. In the United States they have lasted better as truly traditional games among less privileged children—for example, in Harlem, or in the Appalachians—than among middle-class children, whose playtime has become almost as completely organized and supervised as their study time. Teachers and other supervisors of youngsters often teach singing games from printed books; but folklore transmitted by books, records or other mass media is no longer, strictly speaking, "traditional." There was, in fact, more adult mediation in transmitting these games eighty years ago than Newell believed—by older youth, teachers, parents, and grandparents. The life of children had not yet been rigidly confined to extremely narrow age grades. Teachers often taught their pupils a "new" old game and joined in its playing. Grandparents still had valued roles as human beings, and one role was to transmit such traditional amusements as riddles, rhymes, and games to children. Living in a time of organized "togetherness" and commercialized entertainment, it is increasingly difficult for us to picture the intimacies of family, neighborhood, and community three generations ago. There was more neighborhood life, even in the largest cities, and most Americans then lived in small towns or on farms.

So many collections of children's games and songs have been published in the present century that it would require many pages merely to list their titles. Two important American collections should be mentioned: Paul G. Brewster's *American Nonsinging Games* (Norman, Okla., 1953) and his "Children's Games and Rhymes," in N. I. White, ed., *The Frank C. Brown Collection of North Carolina Folklore*, I (Durham, N.C., 1952). Both contain long bibliographies of collections and other relevant studies. The two Western European collections most useful to the student are F. M. Böhme's *Deutsches Kinderlied und Kinderspiel* (Leipzig, 1897) and S. T. Thyregod's *Danmarks Sanglege* (Copenhagen, 1931); each gives much comparative material from English and other languages. Folklorists have expanded Newell's pioneer work with many additional games and comparisons, but only a few have added significantly to his method. One who has developed important new methods of research is Brian Sutton-Smith, who studies the lore of children in terms of historical changes and of its psychological and sociological function. His book *The Games of New Zealand Children* (Berkeley, Calif., 1959) contains references to other valuable studies he has made. His work suggests research in many fruitful directions.

The most original recent approach to the study of children's folklore has been made by Iona and Peter Opie in Great Britain. Their book *The Lore and Language of Schoolchildren* (London, 1959; New York, 1960) is both a literary delight and a masterpiece of research on the mental life of children. It treats a folklore which is indeed wholly transmitted from one generation of children to the next with slight notice and still less encouragement from the surrounding adult world, and with only such influences from it as the children themselves adopt and adapt to their own uses. This lore embraces a vast array of rhymes, riddles and jokes, repartee, nicknames and epithets, jeers, tricks and pranks, magical beliefs, and many other categories of knowledge and behavior fascinating to children. Another important book by the Opies, *The Oxford Dictionary of Nursery Rhymes* (London, 1951), treats exhaustively and comparatively the great body of rhyme and verbal rigmarole that children receive almost entirely from nurses, parents, and other adults, often (or usually) by the aid of printed compilations.

The present book represents only one facet of William Wells Newell's activity and productivity. A hunter of only one kind of quarry in the forests of knowledge would be easier to describe systematically. Those who knew him spoke of him as "a many-sided man" with great personal charm, marked intellectual enthusiasm and wide-ranging interests. Yet there is a tantalizing lack of published detail about his life. *The Dictionary of American Biography* and *The Cyclopaedia of American Biography* print brief biographies and the former lists several obituaries which give some additional information. He was born in Cambridge, Massachusetts, the son of a minister, January 24, 1839, and died January 21, 1907, just before his sixty-eighth birthday. He graduated from Harvard College in 1859 and from Harvard Divinity School in 1863. He spent the next seven or eight years at various occupations: he was briefly (and in turn) assistant to Edward Everett Hale, Minister of the South Congregational Church in Boston; a war-time employee of the Sanitary Service of the War Department in Washington; minister of a Unitarian church in Germantown, Pennsylvania; and tutor in philosophy at Harvard. About 1870 he opened a school in New York, at which "he was very successful." Early in the 1880's he gave up teaching, traveled and studied "a year or two" in Europe, and returned to Cambridge for "the pleasant life of the private scholar." He never married. While living in New York, he began observing and collecting children's street games and he "was closely in touch with artistic circles." He is also said to have "acquired during his stay abroad a number of canvases . . . which later found their way into the Metropolitan Museum in New York and other public and private collections."

Throughout his life as a writer, he interspersed purely literary work with important scientific and theoretical (but none the less literary) contributions to folklore. His publications, which did not begin until he was well into his forties, show that he had well utilized his earlier years in acquiring a varied and profound learning in languages, literature, religion, and all branches of folklore. He is said to have read "as many as forty languages and dialects." He was also a poet, and his first book was *King Œdipus: The Œdipus Tyrannus of Sophocles Rendered into English Verse* (1881). He later translated *The Sonnets and Madrigals of Michelangelo Buonarroti* (1900), and published a volume of his own poems, *Words for Music* (1895, reprinted 1904). Readers of the present book will note the skill and charm with which, for illustration and ornament, he has turned into English verse children's rhymes and songs from European countries, a long and delightful passage from Froissart, and fragments from Homer and the songs of troubadour and minnesinger.

A major literary-folklore interest and occupation of Newell's during many years was the Arthurian legend, about which he wrote three books. His *King Arthur and the Table Round* (1897) is a version of the stories surrounding Arthur that he considered more illustrative of their earlier forms than Malory's fifteenth-century *Morte d'Arthur*, which too much harmonized the legends with British tradition. *The Legend of the Holy Grail and the Perceval of Crestien of Troyes* (1902) was a collection of papers in which he examined historically the widespread European relationships of the Arthurian stories. Tracing them through many countries and languages, he concluded that they had been developed largely on the European continent, before their importation into Britain, by professional poets and narrators, for the entertainment of noble audiences in palace and castle. He chided contemporary literary scholars who considered them to any great extent as a detritus of Celtic history and myth, or a product of the uneducated sector of the folk. A further study of the "matter of Arthur," *Isolt's Return*, was published posthumously in 1907.

But Newell's greatest influence in the field of folklore was in connection with the American Folklore Society, founded in 1888 by five anthropologists and five literary scholars who were the leading folklore scholars in America. Among them, besides Newell, were Franz Boas, the founder of modern anthropological science, and Francis J. Child, famed for his definitive compilation of English and Scottish ballads.

Folklore collection had begun much earlier in Europe than in America. The publication of the Grimms' *Kinder und Hausmärchen* (the "Household Tales" of German peasants) in 1812–15 stimulated the collection of oral traditions in many countries. Before the century ended great quantities of folklore had been gathered, and published or archived, from Finland to Italy and from Russia to the British Isles. In European countries sentiments of nationality or linguistic identity stimulated its collection and enhanced its value. (From such sentiments, incidentally, have arisen the two diseases of folklore—sentimentality, and national or regional chauvinism—hindering its growth as a branch of social science.)

In America the only truly autochthonous, or native, folklore was that of the American Indians. All else was imported, mainly from Europe and Africa, and newly rooted in this continent. The American Folklore Society recognized these facts in formulating its main purposes: to foster the gathering, publication, and study of (1) the relics of Old English ballads, tales, superstitions, dialect, etc., in North America; (2) Negro lore in the South; (3) the lore of North American Indian tribes; and (4) the lore of French Canada, Mexico, etc.

With energy and "contagious enthusiasm" Newell took over the chief task of encouraging and carrying out these aims. He edited the first thirteen volumes of *The Journal of American Folklore* (1888–1900), official organ of the Society, and its first nine book-length *Memoirs*.* He remained Executive Secretary of the Society till his death in 1907.

During these years Newell added new recruits to the ranks of field researchers; he printed in the *Journal* the first traditional Anglo-American folktales and songs to be published in America; he contributed many folklore items he had personally collected to books by Bergen, Child and others; he extended the stated aims of the Society by encouraging collection of folklore from Pennsylvania and Canadian Germans, Louisiana French, Spanish Americans and (after the Spanish-American War), native tribes of the Philippine Islands. He contributed many original articles to the *Journal*, besides a large quantity of commentary, signed and unsigned, on folklore news and developments throughout the world. He also, for many years, reviewed in the *Journal* nearly every important new book, appearing in Europe or America, on folklore or related fields. No complete bibliography of Newell's writing exists. The most extensive, accompanying an article about him by A. F.

* These covered an amazing range of subject matter: African folktales from Angola; Louisiana-French folktales; Bahama songs and stories; a Mexican folk play; a volume each of traditions from the Navaho, the Pawnee and the Thompson River Indians of Canada; and F. D. Bergen's *Current Superstitions* and *Animal and Plant Lore*, chiefly from the tradition of English-speaking folk.

Chamberlain in *The American Anthropologist*, IX (1907), 366 ff., lists over sixty books and articles, but omits scores of important book reviews.

Newell's reviews—charming in style and scintillating with learned citation—form a body of brilliant critical and theoretical discussion that is still significant and useful. He reviewed books as varied in kind and scope as Bolton's *Counting Out Rhymes of Children*, Frazer's *Golden Bough*, Pitré's Sicilian collections, Child's *English and Scottish Popular Ballads*, Charles C. Jones's *Negro Tales From the Georgia Coast*, Kittredge's *The Old Farmer and His Almanac*, Chatelain's *Folktales of Angola*—and the great new collections of American Indian folktales, myths, and rituals which Boas and others had just begun to gather.

Each review showed Newell's understanding of the material treated, of its theoretical implications, and of new field research necessary to create sound theories through the inductive study of data. With amusing wit he rebuked the armchair mythologists of his time who with few threads of fact were weaving elaborate fabrics of pseudo-theory regarding the "origin" of folktales and legends in early sun myths and their "survival" into the modern world from civilized man's "savage past." What flabbergasted his poetical, literary, sane, scientific mind even more was the widely held "theory" going even farther back into the unknowable past—that man had created myths from a "disease of language," by a sequence of imagined prehistoric events related to puns, displaced word meanings, and personifications. In regard to the European preoccupation with problems of "origin" he wrote: "Go back as far as we may, we never arrive at origins, or at simple and natural opinions; we find only artificial and complicated systems of belief and worship, built on the ruins of antecedent systems, extending farther than the eye can reach." Against the influential contemporary theories of Max Müller and Andrew Lang, Newell insisted that valid thinking about folklore and mythology could come only from the study and comparison of carefully collected field data and authentic historical documents. "One fact," he said, "is worth a thousand theories." He praised every new publication which showed accurate, responsible gathering in every field of folklore.

Perhaps his greatest praise went to the volumes of American Indian traditions which he reviewed. In these he saw folktales, rituals, new mythological worlds as complicated as Old World religious systems, still functioning meaningfully in the daily life of "alien races with which the Anglo-Americans had lived for three centuries without penetrating further than the surface of their mentality."

In *The Journal of American Folklore*, IX (1896), 75–79, Newell reviewed Franz Boas' *Indian Stories of the Northwest Coast* (published in German). He ended the review with a parable:

"In Herculaneum was once exhumed a library consisting of about 1800 volumes, of which modern skill has deciphered a number. Unluckily it was a philosophical and theological collection, and up to the present time has proved nearly worthless. What would classical students give for a library of Greek and Roman traditions? But such a collection of volumes would relatively be no more precious than five centuries hence would be a library of a thousand volumes like the present."

If men do in fact inhabit the earth in the year 2396, having still survived the further "ruins of antecedent systems," and among them are some who are interested in examining past traditions, they will be lucky indeed if they are able to exhume and possess a thousand volumes as precious and illustrative of life in our to them ancient era as *Games and Songs of American Children.*

CARL WITHERS

New York City
August, 1962

PREFACE TO SECOND EDITION (1903).

The gleaning now reprinted from plates is subject to imperfections perhaps pardonable in a survey of unexplored territory. Two decades ago, quite by accident, my attention was drawn to the existence of material for the most part unrecorded on either side of the Atlantic; after brief inquiry, I was surprised to find myself in possession of matter which I thought as interesting as it was novel. If the presentation shows an idyllic tinge, enthusiasm must be my excuse; indeed, admitting a basis of primitive barbarism, the songs belong to a period in which the crude ore had been so successfully refined that, even from a literary point of view, some of the rhymes will continue to be esteemed as a treasure of the language.

Eleven years later, the abundant and admirable gathering of Mrs. Gomme furnished means for comparison; it then appeared that between British and American usages of play existed a correspondence approaching identity. Contrary to the relation indicated by previous knowledge, it became apparent that the stream of childish tradition continued to flow abundantly in England; Mrs. Gomme, aided by competent collaborators, was able by direct observation to describe the movement and action of the games more perfectly than had been possible for myself, who had been obliged to depend chiefly on the reminiscence of grown persons. On the other hand, to this very manner of record was due a measure of freedom from recent vulgarity, while some important songs are better preserved in American variants, or even are altogether unknown in the mother country; accordingly, in order to understand English custom, it will always be necessary to include the tradition of the New World.

In the general remarks of the Introduction I find little to recant. As between English and Continental usage, I explained similarity as due to constant intercommunication. In England, at the time of writing, it was usual to consider such correspondences as owing either to common inheritance or parallel invention. It is now known that West European ballads and tales are no more than local versions of a general West European stock; the relation is the same with games; in investigation of origins, it is necessary to take into account the entirety of the tradition.

The history of the game-rhyme is included in that of the ballad. Rhymed ballads were introduced into England, doubtless after Romance models, at a period not precisely to be specified, but certainly antedating the eleventh century. For a long time the new form of composition appealed to intelligent minds, and was favored in the castle even more than in the cottage. Wherever such songs were chanted existed an ardent fancy, a disposition to welcome novelty; minstrels acquainted with many lands were able to translate lays which by oral repetition soon wore away traces of foreign descent; archaic verse continually passed into oblivion, and was superseded by new rhymes, often similarly motived, but always more attractively expressed.

About the fifteenth century education came to establish between the different ranks of society intellectual differences which had previously been non-existent. Superior minds came to entertain for the old type of song a distaste which was enforced by the advent of printing; ballads in the ancient manner were composed only in rural districts, or left to the lips of "the vulgar," on which they acquired a rustic accent. With game-songs the process has corresponded, save that owing to the absence of print such change was postponed.

In tracing diffusion from country to country, regard should be had to the law that transmission usually proceeds from above to below. When superior culture comes in contact with inferior, the former, itself but little affected, remodels the latter. Illustrations need hardly be offered, seeing that civilization itself is an example. With habits of play the principle holds; thus in America the African, even where in great majority, has abandoned his native custom to accept that of his white masters. In this manner negroes adopt old English rounds, which they repeat with every variation of accuracy, from perfect correctness to unintelligible confusion. The case is similar in bilingual districts in Scotland, where children of Gaelic descent acquire English rhymes; a process which exemplifies what took place when Celts of Gaul came in contact with Roman culture. Mediæval England has ever borrowed its fashions from France, and it is likely that popular respect led to the imitation of French game-songs; indeed, such history is sufficiently proved by the character of the chants, fragrant with the courtesy of that new civilization which Europe owes to the land of Charlemagne.

If mediæval dances have been better preserved in Great Britain, the superiority is chiefly referable to insular conservatism, retentive of habits which had gone out of use across the Channel. A similar relation has existed between Great Britain and her American colonies; costume and manners were maintained in the new England after they had ceased to be fashionable in old England. A curious example is found in the continuance of the custom which entitled a lady, even on a first introduction, to honor with a kiss any favored gentleman. In family letters I find that my great-grandfather, an Englishman, after the Revolution, rather to his disgust, found the practice obligatory in Massachusetts; he complains that the frequency of undesired salutations had trained him to cursory performance, and that by the habitual substitution of "a peck" he had forgotten how to make a genuine kiss. Yet three generations later the usage had so completely disappeared that, in my own circle, it had vanished even from children's play. The ladies of the Infanta, who at the time of the Restoration were shocked by English freedom, were not aware that such liberty only kept up a manner of greeting which in the twelfth century had belonged also to the court of France.

In any country childish play is subject to an exchange which causes rapid integration between province and province. In England general circulation has been attained by game-rhymes which are not a century old, while in America has arisen a separate tradition, sometimes more faithful to old-English usage. In the Introduction reference is made to the secret languages of children; it has lately come to my notice that a simple form, which has lasted at least a generation, and which consists in spelling each letter of a word with a modified alphabet, is still common, with dialectic variation as between Pennsylvania and Minnesota. The silent diffusion answers to that of new slang, which is suddenly found on all lips, while its origin can seldom be traced.

Childish play is, of course, co-operative. It is not long since the introduction of rural delivery. In my neighborhood, a boy of six years, who had taken lessons in "sloyd," undertook to manufacture a toy barn.

It occurred to a comrade a year older that the construction might be utilized for a post-box; corresponding change was made, with imitation of slit, signal, and attachment. Hence a performance, in which a postman approached, and was watched through the window of the house. It is easy to see that in a few years such an amusement might extend through a wide territory. The process answers to that by which all inventions are produced and adapted; it does not appear necessary to devise separate psychology for games, any more than for other branches of folk-lore.

As the book was originally intended to exhibit a selection rather than a complete record, so the "Aftermath" now appended by no means shows the totality of later gathering. Under the several numbers I have added explanatory remarks; but limitations of time and space forbid these observations from being extended beyond the English material. The comparative history of the dances I hope hereafter to examine.

Thanks are due to the kindness of friends who have rendered indispensable assistance. Mr. Henry E. Krehbiel, who has consented to edit the additional melodies, has also permitted me to use material printed in the New York *Tribune.* Mr. William H. Babcock allows citation from a collection of games played by Washington children, published in the *American Anthropologist.* To Miss Anne Weston Whitney I owe melodies from Maryland. Other contributions are acknowledged in the Notes.

The time for collection has not yet entirely passed. I shall be grateful for information which may tend to complete or improve this record.

EDITOR'S NOTE TO FIRST EDITION (1883).

The existence of any children's tradition in America, maintained independently of print, has hitherto been scarcely noticed. Yet it appears that, in this minor but curious branch of folk-lore, the vein in the United States is both richer and purer than that so far worked in Great Britain. These games supply material for the elucidation of a subject hitherto obscure: they exhibit the true relation of ancient English lore of this kind to that of the continent of Europe; while the amusements of youth in other languages are often illustrated by American custom, which compares favorably, in respect of compass and antiquity, with that of European countries.

Of the two branches into which the lore of the nursery may be divided —the tradition of children and the tradition of nurses—the present collection includes only the former. It is devoted to formulas of play which children have preserved from generation to generation, without the intervention, often without the knowledge, of older minds. Were these— trifling as they often are — merely local and individual, they might be passed over with a smile; but being English and European, they form not the least curious chapter of the history of manners and customs. It has therefore been an essential part of the editor's object to exhibit their correspondences and history; but, unwilling to overcloud with cumbrous research that healthy and bright atmosphere which invests all that really belongs to childhood, he has thought it best to remand to an appendix the necessary references, retaining in the text only so much as may be reasonably supposed of interest to the readers in whom one or another page may awaken early memories.

He has to express sincere thanks to the friends, in different parts of the country, whose kind assistance has rendered possible this volume, in which almost every one of the older states is represented; and he will be grateful for such further information as may tend to render the collection more accurate and complete.

The melodies which accompany many of the games have been written from the recitation of children by S. Austen Pearce, Mus. Doc. Oxon.

CONTENTS.

PAGE

INTRODUCTORY.

I. LOVE-GAMES.

II. HISTORIES.

III. PLAYING AT WORK.

IV. HUMOR AND SATIRE.

V. FLOWER ORACLES, ETC

VI. BIRD AND BEAST.

VII. HUMAN LIFE.

VIII. THE PLEASURES OF MOTION.

IX. MIRTH AND JEST.

X. GUESSING-GAMES.

XI. GAMES OF CHASE.

XII. CERTAIN GAMES OF VERY LITTLE GIRLS.

XIII. BALL, AND SIMILAR SPORTS.

XIV. RHYMES FOR COUNTING OUT.

XV. MYTHOLOGY.

XVI. AFTERMATH.

APPENDIX.

GAMES AND SONGS

OF

AMERICAN CHILDREN.

INTRODUCTORY.

I.

THE DIFFUSION AND ORIGIN OF AMERICAN GAME-RHYMES.

"The hideous Thickets in this place* were such that Wolfes and Beares nurst up their young from the eyes of all beholders in those very places where the streets are full of Girles and Boys sporting up and downe, with a continued concourse of people."—"Wonder-working Providence in New England," 1654.

"The first settlers came from England, and were of the middle rank, and chiefly Friends. * * * In early times weddings were held as festivals, probably in imitation of such a practice in England. Relations, friends, and neighbors were generally invited, sometimes to the amount of one or two hundred. * * * They frequently met again next day; and being mostly young people, and from under restraint, practised social plays and sports."—Watson's "Account of Buckingham and Solebury" (Pennsylvania; settled about 1682).

A majority of the games of children are played with rhymed formulas, which have been handed down from generation to generation. These we have collected in part from the children themselves, in greater part from persons of mature age who remember the usages of their youth; for this collection represents an expiring custom. The vine of oral tradition, of popular poetry, which for a thousand years has twined and bloomed on English soil, in other days enriching with color and fragrance equally the castle and the cottage, is perishing at the roots; its prouder branches have long since been blasted, and children's song, its humble but longest-flowering offshoot, will soon have shared their fate.

It proves upon examination that these childish usages of play are almost

* Boston.

entirely of old English origin. A few games, it is true, appear to have been lately imported from England or Ireland, or borrowed from the French or the German; but these make up only a small proportion of the whole. Many of the rounds still common in our cities, judging from their incoherence and rudeness, might be supposed inventions of "Arabs of the streets;" but these invariably prove to be mere corruptions of songs long familiar on American soil. The influence of print is here practically nothing; and a rhyme used in the sports of American children almost always varies from the form of the same game in Great Britain, when such now exists.

There are quarters of the great city of New York in which one hears the dialect, and meets the faces, of Cork or Tipperary. But the children of these immigrants attend the public school, that mighty engine of equalization; their language has seldom more than a trace of accent, and they adopt from schoolmates local formulas for games, differing more or less from those which their parents used on the other side of the sea. In other parts of the town, a German may live for years, needing and using in business and social intercourse no tongue but his own, and may return to Europe innocent of any knowledge of the English speech. Children of such residents speak German in their homes, and play with each other the games they have brought with them from the Fatherland. But they all speak English also, are familiar with the songs which American children sing, and employ these too in their sports. There is no transference from one tongue to another, unless in a few cases, when the barrier of rhyme does not exist. The English-speaking population, which imposes on all new-comers its language, imposes also its traditions, even the traditions of children.

A curious inquirer who should set about forming a collection of these rhymes, would naturally look for differences in the tradition of different parts of the Union, would desire to contrast the characteristic amusements of children in the North and in the South, descendants of Puritan and Quaker. In this he would find his expectations disappointed, and for the reason assigned. This lore belongs, in the main, to the day before such distinctions came into existence; it has been maintained with equal pertinacity, and with small variations, from Canada to the Gulf. Even in districts distinguished by severity of moral doctrines, it does not appear that any attempt was made to interfere with the liberty of youth. Nowhere have the old sports (often, it is true, in crude rustic forms) been more generally maintained than in localities famous for Puritanism. Thus, by a natural law of reversion, something of the music, grace, and gayety of an earlier period of unconscious and natural living has been preserved to sweeten the formality, angularity, and tedium of an otherwise beneficial religious movement.

It is only within the century that America has become the land of motion and novelty. During the long colonial period, the quiet towns, less in communication with distant settlements than with the mother-country itself, removed from the currents of thought circulating in Europe, were under those conditions in which tradition is most prized and longest maintained. The old English lore in its higher branches, the ballad and the tale, already belonging to the past at the time of the settlement, was only sparingly existent among the intelligent class from which America was peopled; but such as they did bring with them was retained. Besides, the greater simplicity and freedom of American life caused, as it would seem, these childish amusements to be kept up by intelligent and cultivated families after the corresponding class in England had frowned them down as too promiscuous and informal. But it is among families with the greatest claims to social respectability that our rhymes have, in general, been best preserved.

During the time of which we are writing, independent local usages sprang up, so that each town had oftentimes its own formulas and names for children's sports; but these were, after all, only selections from a common stock, one place retaining one part, another another, of the old tradition. But in the course of the last two generations (and this is a secondary reason for the uniformity of our games in different parts of the country) the extension of intercourse between the States has tended to diffuse them, so that petty rhymes, lately invented, have sometimes gained currency from Maine to Georgia.

We proceed to speak of our games as they exist on the other side of the sea. A comparison with English and Scotch collections shows us very few games mentioned as surviving in Great Britain which we cannot parallel in independent forms. On the other hand, there are numerous instances in which rhymes of this sort, still current in America, do not appear to be now known in the mother-country, though they oftentimes have equivalents on the continent of Europe. In nearly all such cases it is plain that the New World has preserved what the Old World has forgotten; and the amusements of children to-day picture to us the dances which delighted the court as well as the people of the Old England before the settlement of the New.*

To develop the interest of our subject, however, we must go beyond the limits of the English tongue. The practice of American children enables us to picture to ourselves the sports which pleased the infancy of Froissart and Rabelais.† A dramatic action of the Virginia hills preserves the usage of Färöe and Iceland, of Sweden and Venice.‡ We discover that it is an unusual thing to find any remarkable childish sport on the European continent which failed to domesticate itself (though now perhaps forgotten) in England. It is thus vividly and irresistibly forced upon our notice, that the traditions of the principal nations of Europe have differed little more than the dialects of one language, the common tongue, so to speak, of religion, chivalry, and civilization.

A different explanation has been given to this coincidence. When only the agreement, in a few cases, of English and German rhymes was noticed, it was assumed that the correspondence was owing to race-migration; to the settlement in England of German tribes, who brought with them national traditions. The present volume would be sufficient to show the untenability of such an hypothesis. The resemblance of children's songs in different countries, like the similarity of popular traditions in general, is owing to their perpetual diffusion from land to land; a diffusion which has been going on in all ages, in all directions, and with all degrees of rapidity. But the interest of their resemblance is hardly diminished by this consideration. The character of some of these parallelisms proves that for the diffusion in Europe of certain games of our collection we must go back to the early Middle Age; § while the extent of the identity of our American (that is, of old English) child's lore with the European is a continual surprise.‖

Internal evidence alone would be sufficient to refer many of the sports to a mediæval origin, for we can still trace in them the expression of the life of that period.

* See Nos. 40 and 58. † See No. 21. ‡ See No. 2. § See No. 1.

‖ More than three fourths of all children's games in the German collections are paralleled (it may be in widely varying forms) in the present volume. Allowing for the incompleteness of collections, the resemblance of French games is probably nearly as close. The case is not very different in Italy and Sweden, so far at least as concerns games of any dramatic interest. Not till we come to Russia, do we find anything like an independent usage. Taken altogether, our American games are as ancient and characteristic as any, and throw much light on the European system of childish tradition.

We comprehend how deeply mediæval religious conceptions affected the life of the time, when we see that allusions to those beliefs are still concealed in the playing of children. We find that the tests which the soul, escaped from the body, had, as it was supposed, to undergo—the scales of St. Michael, the keys of St. Peter, and the perpetual warfare of angels and devils over departed souls—were familiarly represented and dramatized in the sports of infants.* Such allusions have, it is true, been excluded from English games; but that these once abounded with them can be made abundantly evident. We see that chivalric warfare, the building and siege of castles, the march and the charge of armies, equally supplied material for childish mimicry. We learn how, in this manner, the social state and habits of half a thousand years ago unconsciously furnish the amusement of youth, when the faith and fashion of the ancient day is no longer intelligible to their elders.

It will be obvious that many of the game-rhymes in this collection were not composed by children. They were formerly played, as in many countries they are still played, by young persons of marriageable age, or even by mature men and women. The truth is, that in past centuries all the world, judged by our present standard, seems to have been a little childish. The maids of honor of Queen Elizabeth's day, if we may credit the poets, were devoted to the game of tag,† and conceived it a waste of time to pass in idleness hours which might be employed in that pleasure, with which Diana and her nymphs were supposed to amuse themselves. Froissart describes the court of France as amusing itself with sports familiar to his own childhood; and the *Spectator* speaks of the fashionable ladies of London as occupied with a game which is represented in this series.‡

We need not, however, go to remote times or lands for illustration which is supplied by New England country towns of a generation since. In these, dancing, under that name, was little practised; it was confined to one or two balls in the course of the year on such occasions as the Fourth of July, lasting into the morning hours. At other times, the amusement of young people at their gatherings was "playing games." These games generally resulted in forfeits, to be redeemed by kissing, in every possible variety of position and method. Many of these games were *rounds;* but as they were not called dances, and as mankind pays more attention to words than things, the religious conscience of the community, which ob-

* See Nos. 150–153. † Barley-break. See No. 101. ‡ No. 90.

jected to dancing, took no alarm. Such were the pleasures of young men and women from sixteen to twenty-five years of age. Nor were the participants mere rustics; many of them could boast as good blood, as careful breeding, and as much intelligence, as any in the land. Neither was the morality or sensitiveness of the young women of that day in any respect inferior to what it is at present.

Now that our country towns are become mere outlying suburbs of cities, these remarks may be read with a smile at the rude simplicity of old-fashioned American life. But the laugh should be directed, not at our own country, but at the by-gone age.* In respectable and cultivated French society, at the time of which we speak, the amusements, not merely of young people, but of their elders as well, were every whit as crude. The suggestion is so contrary to our preconceived ideas, that we hasten to shelter ourselves behind the respectable name of Madame Celnart, who, as a recognized authority on etiquette, must pass for an unimpeachable witness.† This writer compiled a very curious "Complete Manual of Games of Society, containing all the games proper for young people of both sexes," which seems to have gained public approbation, since it reached a second edition in 1830. In her preface she recommends the games of which we have been speaking as recreations for *business men:*

"Another consideration in favor of games of society: it must be admitted that for persons leading a sedentary life, and occupied all day in writing and reckoning (the case with most men), a game which demands the same attitude, the same tension of mind, is a poor recreation. * * * On the contrary, the varying movement of games of society, their diversity, the gracious and gay ideas which these games inspire, the decorous caresses which they permit—all this combines to give real amusement. These caresses can alarm neither modesty nor prudence, since a kiss in honor given and taken before numerous witnesses is often an act of propriety."

* It must be remembered that in mediæval Europe, and in England till the end of the seventeenth century, a kiss was the usual salutation of a lady to a gentleman whom she wished to honor. The Portuguese ladies who came to England with the Infanta in 1662 were not used to the custom; but, as Pepys says, in ten days they had "learnt to kiss and look freely up and down." Kissing in games was, therefore, a matter of course, in all ranks.

† Mme. Elisabeth-Félicie Bayle-Mouillard, who wrote under this pseudonym, had in her day a great reputation as a writer on etiquette. Her "Manuel Complet de la Bonne Compagnie" reached six editions in the course of a few years, and was published in America in two different translations—at Boston in 1833, and Philadelphia in 1841.

She prefers "rounds" to other amusements: "All hands united; all feet in cadence; all mouths repeating the same refrain; the numerous turns, the merry airs, the facile and rapid pantomime, the kisses which usually accompany them—everything combines, in my opinion, to make rounds the exercise of free and lively gayety."

We find among the ring-games given by our author, and recommended to men of affairs, several of which English forms exist in our collection, and are familiar to all children.*

We are thus led to remark an important truth. It is altogether a mistake to suppose that these games (or, indeed, popular lore of any description) originated with peasants, or describe the life of peasants. The tradition, on the contrary, invariably came from above, from the intelligent class. If these usages seem rustic, it is only because the country retained what the city forgot, in consequence of the change of manners to which it was sooner exposed. Such customs were, at no remote date, the pleasures of courts and palaces. Many games of our collection, on the other hand, have, it is true, always belonged to children; but no division-line can be drawn, since out of sports now purely infantine have arisen dances and songs which have for centuries been favorites with young men and women.†

* See Nos. 10 and 36.

† See No. 154, and note.

II.

THE DANCE, THE BALLAD, AND THE GAME.

Entre Paris et Saint-Denis
Il s'élève une danse;
Toutes les dames de la ville
Sont alentour qui dansent.

Toutes les dames de la ville
Sont alentour qui dansent;
Il n'y a que la fille du roi
D'un côté qui regarde.

Canadian Round.

GAMES accompanied by song may be divided into ballads, songs, and games proper.

By the term ballad is properly signified a dance-song, or dramatic poem sung and acted in the dance. The very word, derived through the late Latin * from the Greek, attests that golden chain of oral tradition which links our modern time, across centuries of invasion and conflict, with the bright life of classic antiquity.

Still more pleasantly is a like history contained in another name for the same custom. The usual old English name for the round dance, or its accompanying song, was *carol*, which we now use in the restricted sense of a festival hymn. Chaucer's "Romaunt of the Rose" describes for us the movement of the "karole," danced on the "grene gras" in the spring days. He shows us knights and ladies holding each other by the hand, in a flowery garden where the May music of mavis and nightingale blends with the "clere and ful swete karoling" of the lady who sings for the dancers. This sense of the word continued in classic use till the sixteenth century, and has survived in dialect to the present day. Many of the

* *Ballad, ballet, ball,* from *ballare,* to dance.

games of our series are such rounds or carols, "love-dances" in which youths and maidens formerly stood in the ring by couples, holding each other's hands, though our children no longer observe that arrangement. Now the word *carol* is only a modernized form of *chorus*. Thus childish habit has preserved to the present day the idea and movement of the village ring-dance, the chorus, such as it existed centuries or millenniums before another and religious form of the dance accompanied by song had received that technical name in the Greek drama.

Very little was needed to turn the ballad into a dramatic performance, by assigning different parts to different actors. It is natural also for children to act out the stories they hear. We find, accordingly, that ancient ballads have sometimes passed into children's games. But, in the present collection, the majority of the pieces which can be referred to the ballad are of a different character. In these the remainder of the history is reduced to a few lines, or to a single couplet. These *historiettes* have retained the situation, omitting the narration, of the ancient song. We can understand how youthful or rustic minds, when the popular song had nearly passed out of mind, should have vaguely maintained the upshot of the story:

Here sits the Queen of England in her chair;
She has lost the true love that she had last year.

It is the tragedy told in a line; and what more is needed, since an excuse is already provided for the kiss or the romp?*

Of lyric song we have scarce anything to offer. The fifteenth and sixteenth centuries gave birth, all over Europe, to popular lyric poesy, modelled on literary antecedents, and replacing in general estimation the ancient dramatic ballad. Shakespeare, who merely refers to the ballad proper, makes frequent use of the popular song of his day. In many countries this taste has penetrated to the people; the power of lyric composition has become general, so that a collection of popular songs will contain many sweet and pleasing pieces. The ballad has thus passed into the *round*. An inconsequent but musical babble, like that of a brook or a child, has replaced the severe accents of the ancient narration. But in English—why, we will not pause to inquire—it is not so. Whatever of this kind once existed has passed away, leaving but little trace. All that is poetical or pretty is the relic of past centuries; and when the ancient

* See Nos. 12–17.

treasure is spent, absolute prose succeeds. The modern soil is incapable of giving birth to a single flower.

Our rhymes, therefore, belong almost entirely to the third class—the game proper. But though less interesting poetically, and only recorded at a late period, it does not follow that they have not as ancient a history as the oldest ballads; on the contrary, it will abundantly appear that the formulas used in games have an especially persistent life. As the ballad is a dramatic narrative, so the game is a dramatic action, or series of actions; and the latter is as primitive as the former, while both were employed to regulate the dance.

Most modern dances, silently performed in couples, are merely lively movements; but in all ancient performances of the sort the idea is as essential as the form. Precisely as the meaningless refrains of many ballads arise from a forgetfulness of intelligible words, dances which are only motion grew out of dances which expressed something. The dance was originally the dramatized expression of any feature of nature or life which excited interest. Every department of human labor—the work of the farmer, weaver, or tradesman; the church, the court, and the army; the habits and movements of the animals which seem so near to man in his simplicity, and in whose life he takes so active an interest; the ways and works of the potent supernatural beings, good or evil, or, rather, beneficent or dangerous, by whom he believes himself surrounded; angel and devil, witch and ogre—representations of all these served, each in turn, for the amusement of an idle hour, when the labor which is the bitterness of the enforced workman is a jest to the free youth, and the introduction of spiritual fears which constitute the terror of darkness only adds an agreeable excitement to the sports of the play-ground. All this was expressed in song shared by the whole company, which was once the invariable attendant of the dance, so that the two made up but one idea, and to "sing a dance" and "dance a song" were identical expressions.

The children's rounds of to-day, in which each form of words has its accompanying arrangement of the ring, its significant motion and gesture, thus possess historic interest. For these preserve for us some picture of the conduct of the ballads, dances, and games which were once the amusement of the palace as of the hamlet.

The form of the verses used in the games also deserves note. These usually consist either of a rhyming couplet, or of four lines in which the second and fourth rhyme; they are often accompanied by a refrain, which may be a single added line, or may be made up of two lines inserted into the stanza; and in place of exact consonance, any assonance, or similarity of sound, will answer for the rhyme. Above all, they possess the freedom and quaintness, the tendency to vary in detail while preserving the general idea, which distinguish a living oral tradition from the monotonous printed page; in these respects, our rhymes, humble though they be, are marked as the last echo of the ancient popular poetry.

There is especial reason why an Englishman, or the descendants of Englishmen, should take pride in the national popular song.* European mediæval tradition was, it is true, in a measure a common stock; but, though the themes may often have been thus supplied, the poetic form which was given to that material in each land was determined by the genius of the language and of the people. Now, among all its neighbors, the English popular poesy was the most courtly, the most lyric, the most sweet. So much we can still discern by what time has spared.

The English ballad was already born when Canute the Dane coasted the shore of Britain; its golden age was already over when Dante summed up mediæval thought in the "Divina Commedia;" its reproductive period was at an end when Columbus enlarged the horizon of Europe to admit a New World; it was a memory of the past when the American colonies were founded; but even in its last echoes there lingers we know not what mysterious charm of freshness, poetic atmosphere, and eternal youth. Even in these nursery rhymes some grace of the ancient song survives. A girl is a "red rose," a "pretty fair maid," the "finest flower," the "flower of May." The verse itself, simple as it is, often corrupted, is a cry of delight in existence, of satisfaction with nature; its season is the season of bloom and of love; its refrain is "For we are all so gay." It comes to us, in its innocence and freshness, like the breath of a distant and inaccessible garden, tainted now and then by the odors of intervening city streets. But the vulgarity is modern, accidental; the pleasure and poetry are of the original essence.

We cannot but look with regret on the threatened disappearance of these childish traditions, which have given so much happiness to so many generations, and which a single age has nearly forgotten. These songs

* Yet there is no modern English treatise on the history of the ballad possessing critical pretensions. It is to the unselfish labors of an American—Professor Francis J. Child, of Harvard University—that we are soon to owe a complete and comparative edition of English ballads.

have fulfilled the conditions of healthy amusement, as nothing else can do. The proper performance of the round, or conduct of the sport, was to youthful minds a matter of the most serious concern—a little drama which could be represented over and over for hours, in which self-consciousness was absorbed in the ambition of the actors to set forth properly their parts. The recital had that feature which distinguishes popular tradition in general, and wherein it is so poorly replaced by literature. Here was no repetition by rote; but the mind and heart were active, the spirit of the language appropriated, and a vein of deep though childish poetry nourished sentiment and imagination. It seems a thousand pities that the ancient tree should not continue to blossom; that whatever may have been acrid or tasteless in the fruit cannot be corrected by the ingrafting of a later time. There is something so agreeable in the idea of an inheritance of thought kept up by childhood itself, created for and adapted to its own needs, that it is hard to consent to part with it. The loss cannot be made good by the deliberate invention of older minds. Children's amusement, directed and controlled by grown people, would be neither childish nor amusing. True child's play is a sacred mystery, at which their elders can only obtain glances by stealth through the crevice of the curtain. Children will never adopt as their own tradition the games which may be composed or remodelled, professedly for their amusement, but with the secret purpose of moral direction.

We do not mean, however, to sigh over natural changes. These amusements came into existence because they were adapted to the conditions of early life; they pass away because those conditions are altered. The taste of other days sustained them; the taste of our day abandons them. This surrender is only one symptom of a mighty change which has come over the human mind, and which bids fair to cause the recent time, a thousand years hence, to be looked back upon as a dividing-mark in the history of intelligence. If it should turn out that the childhood of the human intellect is passing gradually into the "light of common day"—if the past is to be looked back upon with that affectionate though unreasoning interest with which a grown man remembers his imaginative youth—then every fragment which illustrates that past will possess an attraction independent of its intrinsic value.

III.

MAY GAMES.

All lovers' hearts that are in care
To their ladies they do repair,
In fresh mornings before the day,
Before the day;
And are in mirth aye more and more,
Through gladness of this lovely May,
Through gladness of this lovely May.
Old Song.

CHILDREN'S rhymes and songs have been handed down in two principal ways. First, they have been used for winter amusements, particularly at the Christmas season,* as has from time immemorial been the case in northern countries; and, secondly, they have been sung as rounds and dances, especially during summer evenings, upon the village green or city sidewalk. The latter custom is fast becoming extinct, though the circling ring of little girls "on the green grass turning" may now and then be still observed; but a generation since the practice was common with all classes. The proper time for such sports is the early summer; and many of our rounds declare themselves in words, as well as by sentiment, to be the remainder of the ancient May dances. To render this clear, it will be necessary to give some account of the May festival; but we shall confine ourselves to customs of which we can point out relics in our own land. These we can illustrate, without repeating the descriptions of English writers, from Continental usage, which was in most respects identical with old English practice.

It was an ancient habit for the young men of a village, on the eve of the holiday, to go into the forests and select the tallest and straightest tree

* In the country, in Massachusetts, *Thanksgiving* evening was the particular occasion for these games.

which could be found. This was adorned with ribbons and flowers, brought home with great ceremony, and planted in front of the church, or at the door of some noted person, where it remained permanently to form the centre of sports and dances. The May-pole itself, the songs sung about it, and the maiden who was queen of the feast, were alike called *May*. In the absence of any classic mention, the universality of the practice in mediæval Europe, and the common Latin name, may be taken as proof that similar usages made part of the festival held about the calends of May—the *Floralia* or *Majuma*.

Notwithstanding all that has been said about the license of this festival in the days of the Empire, it is altogether probable that the essential character of the feast of Flora or Maia was not very different from its mediæval or modern survival. The abundance of flowers, the excursions to the mountains, the decoration of houses, and the very name of Flora, prove that, whatever abuses may have introduced themselves, and whatever primitive superstitions may have been intermingled—superstitions to an early time harmless and pure, and only in the decline of faith the source of offence and corruption—the population of ancient Italy shared that natural and innocent delight in the season of blossom which afterwards affected to more conscious expression Chaucer and Milton.

This "bringing home of summer and May" was symbolic; the tree, dressed out in garlands, typifying the fertility of the year. As in all such rites, the songs and dances, of a more or less religious character, were supposed to have the power of causing the productiveness which they extolled or represented.* These practices, however, were not merely superstitious; mirth and music expressed the delight of the human heart, in its simplicity, at the reappearance of verdure and blossom, and thanksgiving to the generous Bestower, which, so long as man shall exist on earth, will be instinctively awakened by the bright opening of the annual drama. Superstition has been the support about which poetry has twined: it is a common mistake of investigators to be content with pointing out the former, and overlooking the coeval existence of the latter. Thus the natural mirth and merriment of the season blended with the supposed efficacy of the rite; and the primitive character of the ring-dance appears to be the circle about the sacred tree in honor of the period of bloom.

A relic, though a trifling one, of the ancient custom, may be seen in

* The feast of *Flora*, says Pliny, in order that everything should *flower*.

some of our cities on the early days of the month. In New York, at least, groups of children may then be observed carrying through the streets a pole painted with gay stripes, ribbons depending from its top, which are held at the end by members of the little company. These proceed, perhaps, to the Central Park, where they conduct their festivities, forming the ring, and playing games which are included in our collection. Within a few years, however, these afternoon expeditions have become rare.

The May-pole, as we have described it, belonged to the village; but a like usage was kept up by individuals. It was the duty of every lover to go into the woods on the eve or early morn of May-day, and bring thence boughs and garlands, which he either planted before the door of his mistress, or affixed thereto, according to local custom. The particular tree, or *bush* (this expression meaning no more than bough), preferred for the purpose was the hawthorn, which is properly the tree of May, as blooming in the month the name of which it has in many countries received. A belief in the protective influence of the *white-thorn*, when attached to the house-door, dates back to Roman times. The May-tree, whatever its species, was often adorned with ribbons and silk, with fruit or birds, sometimes with written poems. The lover brought his offering at early dawn, and it was the duty of his mistress to be present at her window and receive it; thus we have in a song of the fifteenth or sixteenth century from the Netherlands—

> Fair maiden, lie you still asleep,
> And let the morning go?
> Arise, arise, accept the May,
> That stands here all a-blow.

An English carol alludes to the same practice—

> A branch of May I bring to you,
> Before your door it stands.*

The custom was so universal as to give rise to proverbial expressions. Thus, in Italy, "to plant a May at every door" meant to be very susceptible; and in France, to "esmayer" a girl was to court her.

Some of our readers may be surprised to learn that an offshoot of this

* So in Southern France—

> "Catherine, ma mie—reveille-toi, s'il vous plaît;
> Regarde à ta fenêtre le mai et le bouquet."

usage still exists in the United States; the custom, namely, of hanging "May baskets." A half-century since, in Western Massachusetts, a lad would rise early on May-morning, perhaps at three o'clock, and go into the fields. He gathered the trailing arbutus (the only flower there available at the season), and with his best skill made a "basket," by the aid of "winter-green" and similar verdure. This he cautiously affixed to the door of any girl whom he wished to honor. She was left to guess the giver. The practice is still common in many parts of the country, but in a different form. Both boys and girls make "May baskets," and on May-eve attach them to each other's doors, ringing at the same time the house-bell. A pursuit follows, and whoever can capture the responsible person is entitled to a kiss. We do not venture to assert that the latter usage is entirely a corruption of the former.*

The term "May-baskets" is no doubt a modernized form of the old English word "May-buskets," employed by Spenser.† *Buskets* are no more than *bushes*—that is, as we have already explained, the flowering branches of hawthorn or other tree, picked early on the May-morn, and used to decorate the house. It seems likely that a misunderstanding of the word changed the fashion of the usage; the American lad, instead of attaching a bough, hung a basket to his sweetheart's door.

A French writer pleasantly describes the customs of which we are speaking, as they exist in his own province of Champagne: "The hours have passed; it is midnight; the doors of the young lads open. Each issues noiselessly. He holds in his hand branches and bouquets, garlands and crowns of flowers. Above the gate of his mistress his hand, trembling with love, places his mysterious homage; then, quietly as he came, he retires, saying, 'Perhaps she has seen me.' . . . The day dawns. Up! boys and girls! up! it is the first of May! up, and sing! The young

* "On May-day eve, young men and women still continue to play each other tricks by placing branches of trees, shrubs, or flowers under each other's windows, or before their doors."—Harland, "Lancashire Folk-lore."

† The "Shepheards Calender" recites how, in the month of May,

> Youngthes folke now flocken in every where,
> To gather *May-buskets* and smelling brere;
> And home they hasten the postes to dight,
> And all the kirk-pillours eare day-light,
> With hawthorn buds, and sweete eglantine,
> And girlonds of roses, and soppes in wine.

"Sops in wine" are said to be pinks.

men, decked out with ribbons and wild-flowers, go from door to door to sing the month of May and their love."

Of the morning song and dance about the "bush," or branches of trees planted as we have described, we have evidence in the words of American rhymes. Thus—

As we go round the *mulberry-bush*,
All on a frosty morning.

In one or two instances, a similar refrain figures in the childish sports of little girls, who have probably got it by imitation; in others, it is the sign of an old May game.* An English writer of the sixteenth century alludes to the morning dance in a way which proves that these songs really represent the practice of his time.†

The playing of May games was by no means confined to the exact date of the festival. The sign of a country tavern in England was a thorn-bush fixed on a pole, and about this "bush" took place the dance of wedding companies who came to the tavern to feast, whence this post was called the *bride's stake.* Whether the thorn-bush was introduced into the "New English" settlements we cannot say; but the dancing at weddings was common, at least among that portion of those communities which was not bound by the religious restraint that controlled the ruling class. There were, as a French refugee wrote home in 1688, "all kinds of life and manners" in the colonies. In the Colony of Massachusetts Bay, 7th May, 1651, the General Court resolved, "Whereas it is observed that there are many abuses and disorders by dauncinge in ordinaryes, whether mixt or unmixt, upon marriage of some persons, this court doth order, that henceforward there shall be no dauncinge upon such occasion, or at other times, in ordinaryes, upon the paine of five shillings, for every person that shall so daunce in ordinaryes." While youth in the cities might be as gay as elsewhere, in many districts the Puritan spirit prevailed, and the very name of dancing was looked on with aversion. But the young people met this emergency with great discretion; they simply called their amusements *playing games*, and under this name kept up many of the rounds which were the time-honored dances of the old country.

* See Nos. 23, 26, and 160.

† "In summer season howe doe the moste part of our yong men and maydes in earely rising and getting themselves into the fieldes at dauncing! What foolishe toyes shall not a man see among them!"—"Northbrooke's Treatise," 1577.

The French writer whom we have already had occasion to quote goes on to speak of the customs of the younger girls of his province—the *bachelettes*, as they are called. "On the first of May, dressed in white, they put at their head the sweetest and prettiest of their number. They robe her for the occasion: a white veil, a crown of white flowers adorn her head; she carries a candle in her hand; she is their queen, she is the *Trimouzette.* Then, all together, they go from door to door singing the song of the *Trimouzettes;* they ask contributions for adorning the altar of the Virgin, for celebrating, in a joyous repast, the festival of the Queen of Heaven."

This May procession, which has been the custom of girls for centuries, from Spain to Denmark, existed, perhaps still exists, in New England. Until very recently, children in all parts of the United States maintained the ancient habit of rising at dawn of May-day, and sallying forth in search of flowers. The writer well remembers his own youthful excursions, sometimes rewarded, even in chilly Massachusetts, by the early blue star of the hepatica, or the pink drooping bell of the anemone. The maids, too, had rites of their own. In those days, troops of young girls might still be seen, bareheaded and dressed in white, their May-queen crowned with a garland of colored paper. But common-sense has prevailed at last over poetic tradition; and as an act of homage to east winds, a hostile force more powerful at that period than the breath of Flora, it has been agreed that summer in New England does not begin until June.

These May-day performances, however, were originally no children's custom; in this, as in so many other respects, the children have only proved more conservative of old habit than their elders. There can be no doubt that these are the survivals of the ancient processions of Ceres, Maia, Flora, or by whatever other name the "good goddess," the patroness of the fertile earth, was named, in which she was solemnly borne forth to view and bless the fields. The queen of May herself represents the mistress of Spring; she seems properly only to have overlooked the games in which she took no active part.*

A writer of the fifteenth century thus describes the European custom of his day: "A girl adorned with precious garments, seated on a chariot

* As I have seen the lady of the May
Set in an arbour (on a holy-day)
Built by the May-pole.
—Wm. Browne.

filled with leaves and flowers, was called the queen of May; and the girls who accompanied her as her handmaidens, addressing the youths who passed by, demanded money for their queen. This festivity is still preserved in many countries, especially Spain." The usage survives in the dolls which in parts of England children carry round in baskets of flowers on May-day, requesting contributions.

Of this custom a very poetical example, not noticed by English collectors, has fallen under our own observation. We will suppose ourselves in Cornwall on May-day; the grassy banks of the sunken lanes are gay with the domestic blooms dear to old poetry; the grass is starry with pink and white daisies; the spreading limbs of the beech are clad in verdure, and among the budding elms of the hedge-rows "birds of every sort" "send forth their notes and make great mirth." A file of children, rosy-faced boys of five or six years, is seen approaching; their leader is discoursing imitative music on a wooden fife, to whose imaginary notes the rest keep time with dancing steps. The second and third of the party carry a miniature ship; its cargo, its rigging, are blooms of the season, bluebells and wall-flowers; the ship is borne from door to door, where stand the smiling farmers and their wives; none is too poor to add a penny to the store. As the company vanishes at the turn of the lane, we feel that the merriment of the children has more poetically rendered the charm of the season than even the song of the birds.

There is in America no especial song of the festival, though children at the May parties of which we have spoken still keep up the "springing and leaping" which mediæval writers speak of as practised by them at this occasion. Popular songs are, however, still remembered in Europe, where their burden is, May has come! or, Welcome to May! Pleasing and lyric is the song of the "Trimazos," the lay of the processions of girls to which we have alluded, though its simplicity becomes more formal in our version of the provincial French:

It is the merry month of May, Winter has taken flight;
I could not keep my heart at home that bounded for delight:
And as I went, and as I came, I sang to the season gay,
It is the May, the merry May, the merry month of May!

E'en as I came the meadows by, the wheat-fields have I seen,
The hawthorn branches all a-flower, the oat-fields growing green;
O Trimazos!
It is the May, the merry May, the merry month of May!

Madam, I thank you for your coin, and for your courtesy;
It is for Mary and her Babe, and it is not for me:
But I will pray the Child for you to whom your gift is given,
That he return it you again more royally in heaven.

So, in the Vosges, young girls fasten a bough of laurel to the hat of a young man whom they may meet on the way, wishing

That God may give him health and joy,
And the love that he loves best:
Take the May, the lovely May.

They ask a gift, but not for themselves:

It shall be for the Virgin Mary,
So good and so dear:
Take the May, the lovely May.

Corresponding to the French song from which we have quoted is the English May carol, similarly sung from dwelling to dwelling:

Rise up the mistress of this house, with gold along your breast,
For the summer springs so fresh, green, and gay;
And if your body be asleep, we hope your soul's at rest,
Drawing near to the merry month of May.

God bless this house and harbor, your riches and your store,
For the summer springs so fresh, green, and gay;
We hope the Lord will prosper you, both now and evermore,
Drawing near to the merry month of May.

The frequent allusions of the earlier English poets to "doing May observance," or the "rite of May," show us how all ranks of society, in their time, were still animated by the spirit of those primitive faiths to which we owe much of our sensibility to natural impressions. Milton himself, though a Puritan, appears to approve the usages of the season, and even employs the ancient feminine impersonation of the maternal tenderness and bounty of nature, invoking the month:

The flow'ry May, who from her green lap throws
The yellow cowslip and the pale primrose.
Hail, bounteous May, that dost inspire
Mirth and youth, and warm desire;

Woods and groves are of thy dressing,
Hill and dale doth boast thy blessing.
Thus we salute thee with our early song,
And welcome thee, and wish thee long.

Time, and the changes of taste, have at last proved too strong for the persistency of custom; the practices by which blooming youth expressed its sympathy with the bloom of the year have perished, taking with them much of the poetry of the season, and that inherited sentiment which was formerly the possession of the ignorant as well as of the cultivated class.

IV.

THE INVENTIVENESS OF CHILDREN.

In the days of childhood new,
When Time had years and ours were few,
Here on grassy fields at play,
Ran we this, the other way;
On this very meadow-ground
First violets found,
Where the cattle graze to-day.

Minnesinger, 13*th Century.*

THE student of popular traditions is accustomed to recognize the most trifling incidents of a tale, or the phrases of a song, as an adaptation of some ancient or foreign counterpart, perhaps removed by an interval of centuries. It is the same with rhymes of the sort included in this collection, in which formulas of sport, current in our own day and in the New World, will be continually found to be the legacy of other generations and languages. Should we then infer that childhood, devoid of inventive capacity, has no resource but mechanical repetition?

We may, on the contrary, affirm that children have an especially lively imagination. Observe a little girl who has attended her mother for an airing in some city park. The older person, quietly seated beside the footpath, is half absorbed in revery; takes little notice of passers-by, or of neighboring sights or sounds, further than to cast an occasional glance which may inform her of the child's security. The other, left to her own devices, wanders contented within the limited scope, incessantly prattling to herself; now climbing an adjoining rock, now flitting like a bird from one side of the pathway to the other. Listen to her monologue, flowing as incessantly and musically as the bubbling of a spring; if you can catch enough to follow her thought, you will find a perpetual romance unfolding itself in her mind. Imaginary personages accompany her footsteps; the properties of a childish theatre exist in her fancy; she sustains a conversation in three or four characters. The roughnesses of the ground, the hasty passage of a squirrel, the chirping of a sparrow, are occasions sufficient to suggest an exchange of impressions between the unreal figures with which her world is peopled. If she ascends, not without a stumble, the artificial rockwork, it is with the expressed solicitude of a mother who guides an infant by the edge of a precipice; if she raises her glance to the waving green overhead, it is with the cry of pleasure exchanged by playmates who trip from home on a sunshiny day. The older person is confined within the barriers of memory and experience; the younger breathes the free air of creative fancy.

A little older grown, such a child becomes the inventor of legend. Every house, every hill in the neighborhood, is the locality of an adventure. Every drive includes spots already famous in supposed history, and passes by the abodes of fancied acquaintances. Into a land with few traditions the imagination of six years has introduced a whole cycle of romance.

If the family or vicinity contains a group of such minds, fancy takes outward form in dramatic performance. The school history is vitalized into reality; wars are waged and battles performed in a more extended version, while pins and beans signify squadrons and regiments. Romances are acted, tales of adventure represented with distribution of rôles. Thus, in a family of our acquaintance, the children treasured up wood-engravings, especially such as were cut from the illustrated journals: runaway horses, Indian chiefs, and trappers of the wilderness were at an especial premium. These they stored in boxes, encamped in different corners of the room, and performed a whole library of sensational tales. A popular piece set forth the destruction of the villain of the story by a shark, while navigating a *catamaran*. The separated beds of the sleeping-room represented the open planks of the raft; the gentlest and most compliant character personified the malefactor; and the shark swam between the bedsteads.

Where sports require or allow such freedom, the ingenuity of children puts to shame the dulness of later years, and many a young lady of twenty would find it impossible to construct the dialogue which eight summers will devise without an effort. It was a favorite amusement of two girls just entering their teens to conduct a boarding-school. The scholars and the teachers of the imaginary school were all named, and these characters were taken in dialogue by the little actors, each sustaining several perfectly well-defined parts. The pupils pursued their pleasures and their studies according to their several tastes; while their progress, their individual accomplishments and offences, were subsequently gravely discussed by the instructors, and the condition, prospects, and management of the institution talked over. Thus, hour after hour, without hesitation or weariness, the conversation proceeded, with the duo of friends for actors and audience!

Oftentimes, with young children, an outward support is required for fancy, an object to be mentally transformed. One set of little girls collected in the fall birch-leaves, changed to yellow, out of which alone they created their little nursery. Another party employed pins, which they inserted in a board, and called pin-fairies. By the aid of these, long dramatizations were performed, costumes devised, and palaces decorated, under regulations rigidly observed.

Such exercises of imagination are usually conducted in strict privacy, and unremarked, or not understood, by parents; but when the attention of the latter is directed to these performances, they are often astonished by the readiness they disclose, and are apt to mistake for remarkable talent what is only the ease of the winged fancy of youth, which flies lightly to heights where later age must laboriously mount step by step.

As infancy begins to speak by the free though unconscious combination of linguistic elements, so childhood retains in language a measure of freedom. A little attention to the jargons invented by children might have been serviceable to certain philologists. Their love of originality finds the tongue of their elders too commonplace; besides, their fondness for mystery requires secret ways of communication. They therefore often create (so to speak) new languages, which are formed by changes in the mother-speech, but sometimes have quite complicated laws of structure, and a considerable arbitrary element.

The most common of these, which are classified by young friends under the general name of *gibberish*, goes in New England by the name of "Hog Latin." It consists simply in the addition of the syllable *ery*, preceded by the sound of hard *g*, to every word. Even this is puzzling to older persons, who do not at first perceive that "Wiggery youggery goggery wiggery miggery" means only "Will you go with me!" Children sometimes use this device so perpetually that parents fear lest they may never recover the command of their native English. When it ceases to give pleasure, new dialects are devised. Certain young friends of ours at first changed the termination thus—"Withus yoovus govus withus meevus?" which must be answered, "Ivus withus govus withus yoovus;" the language, seemingly, not admitting a direct affirmative. The next step was to make a more complicated system by prefixing a *u* (or *oo*) sound with a vowel suffix. Thus, "Will you go with me to lunch?" would be "Uwilla uoa ugoa uwitha umea utoa uluncha?" But this contrivance, adopted by all the children of a neighborhood,* was attended with variations incapable of reduction to rule, but dependent on practice and instinct. The speech could be learned, like any other, only by experience; and a little girl assured us that she could not comprehend a single word until, in the course of a month, she had learned it by ear. She added, in regard to a particular dialect, that it was much harder than French, and that her brother had to think a great deal when he used it. The application of euphonic rules was more or less arbitrary. Thus, *understand* would be *uery-uinste.* The following will answer for a specimen of a conversation between a child and a nurse who has learned the tongue: "Uery uisy uemy uity?" "Up-stairs, on the screen in your room." The child had asked, "Where is my hat?"

A group of children living near Boston invented the *cat language*, so called because its object was to admit of free intercourse with cats, to whom it was mostly talked, and by whom it was presumed to be comprehended. In this tongue the cat was naturally the chief subject of nomenclature; all feline positions were observed and named, and the language was rich in such epithets, as Arabic contains a vast number of expressions for *lion.* Euphonic changes were very arbitrary and various, differing for the same termination; but the adverbial ending *ly* was always *osh; terribly, tirriblosh.* A certain percentage of words were absolutely independent, or at least of obscure origin. The grammar tended to Chinese or infantine simplicity; *ta* represented any case of any personal pronoun. A proper name might vary in sound according to the euphonic requirement of the different Christian-names by which it was preceded. There were two dialects, one, however, stigmatized as *provincial.*

This invention of language must be very common, since other cases have fallen under our notice in which children have composed dictionaries of such.

It would be strange if children who exhibit so much inventive talent did not contrive new games; and we find accordingly that in many families

* In Cincinnati.

a great part of the amusements of the children are of their own devising. The earliest age of which the writer has authentic record of such ingenuity is two and a half years.

Considering the space which our Indian tribes occupy in the imagination of young Americans, it is remarkable that the red man has no place whatever in the familiar and authorized sports. On the other hand, savage life has often furnished material for individual and local amusements.

Near the country place of a family within our knowledge was a patch of brushwood containing about forty acres, and furnishing an admirable ground for savage warfare. Accordingly, a regular game was devised. The players were divided into Indians and hunters, the former uttering their war-cry in such dialect as youthful imagination regarded as aboriginal. The players laid ambushes for each other in the forest, and the game ended with the extermination of one party or the other. This warfare was regulated by strict rules, the presentation of a musket at a fixed distance being regarded as equivalent to death.

In a town of Massachusetts, some thirty years since, it was customary for the school-girls, during recess, to divide themselves into separate tribes. Shawls spread over tent-poles represented Indian lodges, and a girl always resorted to her allotted habitation. This was kept up for the whole summer, and carried out with such earnestness that girls belonging to hostile tribes, though otherwise perfectly good friends, would often not speak to each other for weeks, in or out of school.

In the same town was a community of "Friends," or "Quakers." It was the custom for children of these to play at meeting. Sitting about the room on a "First-day" gathering, one of them would be moved by the spirit, rise, and exhort in the sing-song tone common to the meeting-house. There was a regular formula for this amusement—a speech which the children had somewhere heard and found laughable: "My de-ar friends, I 've been a thinking and a thinking and a thinking; I see the blinking and the winking; pennyroyal tea is very good for a cold."

A young lady of our acquaintance, as a child, invented a game of pursuit, which she called Spider and Fly. The Flies, sitting on the house-stairs, buzzed in and out of the door, where they were exposed to the surprise of the Spider. The children of the neighborhood still maintain the sport, which is almost the exact equivalent of a world-old game whose formula is given in our collection.

We need not go on to illustrate our thesis. But it remains true that the great mass of the sports here presented are not merely old, but have existed in many countries, with formulas which have passed from generation to generation. How are we to reconcile this fact with the quick invention we ascribe to children?

The simple reason why the amusements of children are inherited is the same as the reason why language is inherited. It is the necessity of general currency, and the difficulty of obtaining it, which restricts the variation of one and of the other. If a sport is familiar only to one locality or one set of children, it passes away as soon as the youthful fancy of that region grows weary of it. Besides, the old games, which have prevailed and become familiar by a process of natural selection, are usually better adapted to children's taste than any new inventions can be; they are recommended by the quaintness of formulas which come from the remote past, and strike the young imagination as a sort of sacred law. From these causes, the same customs have survived for centuries through all changes of society, until the present age has involved all popular traditions, those of childhood as of maturity, in a general ruin.

V.

THE CONSERVATISM OF CHILDREN.

Here, as girl's duty is, Timarete lays down her cymbals,
Places the ball that she loved, carries the net of her hair;
Maiden, and bride to be, her maids* to maid Artemis renders,
And with her favorites too offers their various wardrobe.

Greek Anthology.

As the light-footed and devious fancy of childhood, within its assigned limits, easily outstrips the grave progress of mature years, so the obedience of children is far more scrupulous not to overstep the limits of the path. It is a provision of nature, in order to secure the preservation of the race, that each generation should begin with the unquestioning reception of the precepts of that which it follows. No deputy is so literal, no nurse so Rhadamanthine, as one child left in charge of another. The same precision appears in the conduct of sports. The formulas of play are as Scripture, of which no jot or tittle is to be repealed. Even the inconsequent rhymes of the nursery must be recited in the form in which they first became familiar; as many a mother has learned, who has found the versions familiar to her own infancy condemned as inaccurate, and who is herself sufficiently affected by superstition to feel a little shocked, as if a sacred canon had been irreligiously violated.

The life of the past never seems so comprehensible, and the historic interval never so insignificant, as when the conduct and demeanor of children are in question. Of all human relations, the most simple and permanent one is that of parent and child. The loyalty which makes a clansman account his own interests as trifling in comparison with those of his chieftain, or subjects consider their own prosperity as included in their sovereign's, belongs to a disappearing society; the affection of the sexes is dependent, for the form of its manifestation, on the varying

* The same Greek word, *kora,* signifies *maiden* and *doll.*

usages of nations; but the behavior of little children, and of their parents in reference to them, has undergone small change since the beginnings of history. Homer might have taken for his model the nursery of our own day, when, in the words of Achilles' rebuke to the grief of Patroclus, he places before us a Greek mother and her baby—

Patroclus, why dost thou weep, like a child too young to speak plainly,
A girl who runs after her mother, and cries in arms to be taken,
Catching hold of her garment, and keeping her back from her errand,
Looking up to her tearful, until she pauses and lifts her?

And the passage is almost too familiar to cite—

Hector the radiant spoke, and reached out his arms for the baby;
But the infant cried out, and hid his face in the bosom
Of his nurse gayly-girdled, fearing the look of his father,
Scared by the gleam of the bronze, and the helmet crested with horse-hair,
Dreading to see it wave from the lofty height of the forehead.

In the same manner, too, as the feelings and tastes of children have not been changed by time, they are little altered by civilization, so that similar usages may be acceptable both to the cultivated nations of Europe and to the simpler races on their borders.

It is natural, therefore, that the common toys of children should be world-old. The tombs of Attica exhibit dolls of classic or ante-classic time, of ivory or terra-cotta, the finer specimens with jointed arms or legs. Even in Greece, as it seems, these favorites of the nursery were often modelled in wax; they were called by a pet name, indicating that their owners stood to them in the relation of mamma to baby; they had their own wardrobes and housekeeping apparatus. The Temple of Olympian Zeus at Elis contained, says Pausanias, the little bed with which Hippodamia had played. But the usage goes much further back. Whoever has seen the wooden slats which served for the cheaper class of the dolls of ancient Egypt, in which a few marks pass for mouth, nose, and eyes, will have no difficulty in imagining that their possessors regarded them with maternal affection, since all the world knows that a little girl will lavish more tenderness on a stuffed figure than on a Paris doll, the return of affection being proportional to the outlay of imagination.

When Greek and Roman girls had reached an age supposed to be superior to such amusements, they were expected to offer their toys on the altar of their patroness, to whatever goddess might belong that function, Athene or Artemis, Diana or Venus Libitina. If such an act of devotion was made at the age of seven years, as alleged, one can easily understand that many a child must have wept bitterly over the sacrifice. To this usage refers the charming quatrain, a version of which we have set as the motto of our chapter.

Children's rattles have from the most ancient times been an important article of nursery furniture. Hollow balls containing a loose pebble, which served this purpose, belong to the most ancient classic times. These "rattles," however, often had a more artistic form, lyre-shaped with a moving plectrum; or the name was used for little separate metallic figures—"charms," as we now say—strung together so as to jingle, and worn in a necklace. Such were afterwards preserved with great care; in the comic drama they replace the "strawberry mark" by which the father recognizes his long-lost child. Thus, in the "Rudens" of Plautus, Palæstra, who has lost in shipwreck her casket, finds a fisherman in possession of it, and claims her property. Both agree to accept Dæmones, the unknown father of the maiden, as arbiter. Dæmones demands, "Stand off, girl, and tell me, what is in the wallet?" "Playthings."* "Right, I see them; what do they look like?" "First, a little golden sword with letters on it." "Tell me, what are the letters?" "My father's name. Then there is a two-edged axe, also of gold, and lettered; my mother's name is on the axe. . . . Then a silver sickle, and two clasped hands, and a little pig, and a golden heart, which my father gave me on my birthday." "It is she; I can no longer keep myself from embracing her. Hail, my daughter!"

In the ancient North, too, children played with figures of animals. The six-year-old Arngrim is described in a saga as generously making a present of his little brass horse to his younger brother Steinolf; it was more suitable to the latter's age, he thought.

The weapons of boys still preserve the memory of those used by primitive man. The bow and arrow, the sling, the air-gun, the yet more primeval club or stone, are skilfully handled by them. Their use of the top and ball has varied but little from the Christian era to the present day. It is, therefore, not surprising that many games are nearly the same as when Pollux described them in the second century.† Yet it interests us to discover that not only the sports themselves, but also the words of

* *Crepundia;* literally, *rattles.*

† See Nos. 105 and 108.

the formulas by which they are conducted, are in certain cases older than the days of Plato and Xenophon.*

We have already set forth the history contained in certain appellations of the song and dance. If the very name of the *chorus* has survived in Europe to the present day, so the character of the classic round is perpetuated in the ring games of modern children. Only in a single instance, but that a most curious one, have the words of a Greek children's round been preserved. This is the "tortoise-game," given by Pollux, and we will let his words speak for themselves:

"The *tortoise* is a girl's game, like the *pot;* one sits, and is called *tortoise.* The rest go about asking:

> "O torti-tortoise, in the ring what doest thou?"

She answers:

> "I twine the wool, and spin the fine Milesian thread."

The first again:

> "Tell us, how was it that thy offspring died?"

To which she says:

> "He plunged in ocean from the backs of horses white."

Our author does not tell us how the game ended; but from his comparison to the "pot-game"† we conclude that the tortoise immediately dives into the "ocean" (the ring) to catch whom she can.

This quaint description shows us that the game-formulas of ancient times were to the full as incoherent and obscure as those of our day frequently are. The alliterative name of the tortoise,‡ too, reminding us of the repetitions of modern nursery tales, speaks volumes for the character of Greek childish song.

Kissing games, also, were as familiar in the classic period as in later time; for Pollux quotes the Athenian comic poet Crates as saying of a coquette that she "plays kissing games in rings of boys, preferring the handsome ones."

It must be confessed, however, that we can offer nothing so graceful

* See Nos. 91, 92, and 93.

† "The *pot-game*—the one in the middle sits, and is called a *pot;* the rest tweak him, or pinch him, or slap him while running round; and whoever is caught by him while so turning takes his place." We might suppose the disconnected verse of the "tortoise-game" to be imitated, perhaps in jest, from the high-sounding phrases of the drama.

‡ "Cheli-chelone," *torti-tortoise.*

as the cry with which Greek girls challenged each other to the race, an exclamation which we may render, "Now, fairies!" *—the maidens assuming for the nonce the character of the light-footed nymphs of forest or stream.

Coming down to mediæval time, we find that the poets constantly refer to the life of children, with which they have the deepest sympathy, and which they invest with a bright poetry, putting later writers to shame by comparison. That early period, in its frank enjoyment of life, was not far from the spirit of childhood. Wolfram of Eschenbach represents a little girl as praising her favorite doll:

None is so fair
As my daughter there.

The German proverb still is "Happy as a doll."

It has been remarked how, in all times, the different sex and destiny of boys and girls are unconsciously expressed in the choice and conduct of their pleasures. "Women," says a writer of the seventeenth century, "have an especial fondness for children. That is seen in little girls, who, though they know not so much as that they are maids, yet in their childish games carry about dolls made of rags, rock them, cradle them, and care for them; while boys build houses, ride on a hobby-horse, busy themselves with making swords and erecting altars."

Like causes have occasioned the simultaneous disappearance of like usages in countries widely separated. In the last generation children still sang in our own towns the ancient summons to the evening sports—

Boys and girls, come out to play,
The moon it shines as bright as day;

and similarly in Provence, the girls who conducted their ring-dances in the public squares, at the stroke of ten sang:

Ten hours said,
Maids to bed.

But the usage has departed in the quiet cities of Southern France, as in the busy marts of America.

It is much, however, to have the pleasant memory of the ancient rules which youth established to direct its own amusement, and to know that

* "Phitta Meliades."

our own land, new as by comparison it is, has its legitimate share in the lore of childhood, in considering which we overleap the barriers of time, and are placed in communion with the happy infancy of all ages. Let us illustrate our point, and end these prefatory remarks, with a version of the description of his own youth given by a poet of half a thousand years since—no mean singer, though famous in another field of letters—the chronicler Jean Froissart. He regards all the careless pleasures of infancy as part of the unconscious education of the heart, and the thoughtless joy of childhood as the basis of the happiness of maturity; a deep and true conception, which we have nowhere seen so exquisitely developed, and which he illuminates with a ray of that genuine genius which remains always modern in its universal appropriateness, when, recounting the sports of his own early life,* many of which we recognize as still familiar, he writes:

In that early childish day
I was never tired to play
Games that children every one
Love until twelve years are done;
To dam up a rivulet
With a tile, or else to let
A small saucer for a boat
Down the purling gutter float;
Over two bricks, at our will,
To erect a water-mill;
And in the end wash clean from dirt,
In the streamlet, cap and shirt.
We gave heart and eye together
To see scud a sailing feather;

* Froissart's account of the school he attended reminds us of the American *district school,* and his narration has the same character of charming simplicity as his allusion to playing *with the boys of our street.*

After I was put to school,
Where ignorance is brought to rule,
There were girls as young as I;
These I courted, by-and-by,
Little trinkets offering—
A pear, an apple, or glass ring;
For their favor to obtain
Seemed great prowess to me then,
And, sober earnest, so it is.

And now and then it pleased us well
To sift dust through a piercèd shell
On our coats; or in time ripe,
To cut out a wheaten pipe.
In those days for dice and chess
Cared we busy children less
Than mud pies and buns to make,
And heedfully in oven bake
Of four bricks; and when came Lent,
Out was brought a complement
Of river-shells, from secret hold,
Estimated above gold,
To play away, as I thought meet,
With the children of our street;
And as they tossed a counter, I
Stood and shouted, "Pitch it high!"
When the moon was shining bright
We would play in summer night
Pince-merine; and time so passed,
I was more eager at the last
Than outset, and I thought it shame
When I was made to stop my game.
  More to tell, we practised too
The sport entitled *Queue loo loo*,*
Hook, *Trottot Merlot*, *Pebbles*, *Ball;*
And when we had assembled all,
Pears, swiftly running; or were lief
To play at *Engerrant the Thief.*
Now and then, for a race-course,
Of a staff we made a horse,
And called him *Gray;* or, in knight's guise,
We put our caps on helmet-wise;
And many a time, beside a maid,
A mimic house of shells I made.
Upon occasions we would choose
The one who hit me I accuse,
Take Colin off; and by-and-by
Selected *King who does not lie*,
Ring, *Prison-bars;* or were content,
When in-doors, with *Astonishment*,

* For the games here mentioned, compare note in Appendix.

Oats, *Scorn*, or *Riddles;* nor forget
Replies, and *Grasses*, *Cligne-musette*,
Retreat, and *Mule*, and *Hunt the Hare;*
Leaping and *Palm-ball* had their share,
Salt Cowshorn, and *Charette Michaut;*
And oftentimes we chose to throw
Pebbles or pence against a stake;
Or small pits in the ground would make,
And play at nuts, which he who lost,
His pleasure bitterly was crossed.
To drive a top was my delight
From early morning until night;
Or to blow, single or double,
Through a tube a bright soap-bubble,
Or a batch of three or four,
To rejoice our eyes the more.
Games like these, and more beside,
Late and early have I plied.
  Followed a season of concern;
Latin I was made to learn;
And if I missed, I was a dunce,
And must be beaten for the nonce.
So manners changed, as hands severe
Trained me to knowledge and to fear.
Yet lessons done, when I was free,
Quiet I could never be,
But fought with my own mates, and thus
Was vanquished or victorious;
And many a time it was my fate
To come home in a ragged state
And meet reproof and chastisement;
But, after all, 'twas pains misspent;
For, let a comrade come in sight,
That moment I had taken flight,
And none could hinder; in that hour
Pleasure unto me was power,
Though oft I found, as I find still,
The two inadequate to my will.
  Thus I did the time employ—
So may Heaven give me joy—
That all things tended to my pleasure,

Both my labor and my leisure,
Being alert and being still;
Hours had I at my own will.
Then a wreath of violets,
To give maids for coronets,
Was to me of more account
Than the present of a count,
Twenty marks, would be to-day;
I had a heart content and gay,
And a soul more free and light
Than the verse may well recite.
So, to fashion form and feature,
Co-operated Love and Nature:
Nature made the body strong,
And forces that to Love belong,
Soft and generous the heart;
Truly, if in every part
Of the body soul did live,
I should have been sensitive!
Not a splendor upon earth
I esteemed so seeing-worth
As clustered violets, or a bed
Of peonies or roses red.
When approached the winter-time,
And out-of-doors was cold and rime,
No loss had I what to do,
But read romances old and new,
And did prefer, the rest above,
Those of which the theme was love,
Imagining, as on I went,
Everything to my content.
Thus, since infantine delight
Oft inclines the heart aright,
After his own living form
Love my spirit did inform,
And pleasure into profit turned;
For the fortitude I learned,
And the soul of high emprise,
Hath such merit in my eyes,
That its worth and preciousness
Words of mine cannot express.

GAMES AND SONGS OF AMERICAN CHILDREN

I

LOVE-GAMES.

— Many a faire tourning,
Upon the grene gras springyng.
The Romaunt of the Rose.

No. 1.

Knights of Spain.

THIS ancient and interesting, now nearly forgotten, game was in the last generation a universal favorite in the United States, imported, no doubt, by the early settlers of the country; and was equally familiar, in numerous variations, through England and Scotland. It is not, however, the exclusive property of English-speaking peoples, but current under a score of forms throughout Europe—from Latin France, Italy, and Spain, to Scandinavian Iceland, from the Finns of the Baltic coast to the Slavs of Moravia. Its theme is courtship; but courtship considered according to ancient ideas, as a mercantile negotiation. To "buy" a bride was the old Norse expression for marriage, and in a similar sense is to be understood the word "sold" in our rhyme. The frankly mercenary character of the original transaction ceasing to be considered natural, it was turned into a jest or satire in Sweden and Scotland. The present song assumed all the grace and courtesy characteristic of the mediæval English ballad, while a primitive form survived in Iceland; and a later outgrowth (our No. 3) represented the whole affair as one of coquetry instead of bargaining, substituting, for the head of the house or the mother, the bride herself as the negotiator.

Our first version shows the form of the game as played in New York in the early part of the century.

On a sofa, or row of chairs, a mother, with her daughters on either side, seated. Advance three suitors.

"Here come three lords out of Spain,
A-courting of your daughter Jane."

"My daughter Jane is yet too young,
To be ruled by your flattering tongue."

"Be she young, or be she old,
'Tis for the price she may be sold.

"So fare you well, my lady gay,
We must turn another way."

"Turn back, turn back, you Spanish knight,
And scour your boots and spurs so bright."

"My boots and spurs they cost you nought,
For in this land they were not bought.

"Nor in this land will they be sold,
Either for silver or for gold.

"So fare you well, my lady gay,
We must turn another way."

"Turn back, turn back, you Spanish knight,
And choose the fairest in your sight."

"I'll not take one nor two nor three,
But pray, Miss [Lucy], walk with me."

The Spanish knight takes the girl named by the hand, and marches off with her. Walking round the room, he returns, saying,

"Here comes your daughter safe and sound,
In her pocket a thousand pound,

"On her finger a gay gold ring—
I bring your daughter home again."

In Philadelphia the game had a peculiar ending, which, however, as we shall see, preserved, though in a corrupt form, an ancient trait:

"Here comes your daughter safe and sound,
In her pocket a thousand pound,

"On her finger a gay gold ring:
Will you take your daughter in?"

"No!"

The girl then runs away, the mother pursuing her. The Spanish knight catches her, and brings her back, saying,

"Here comes your daughter safe and sound,
In her pocket *no* thousand pound,

On her finger *no* gay gold ring,
Will you take your daughter in?"

"Yes!"

The daughter then once more flies, and the Spanish knight has to catch her.

The following is a New England version:

"We are three brethren from Spain,
Come to court your daughter Jane."

"My daughter Jane is yet too young
To be courted by your flattering tongue."

"Be she young, or be she old,
It is for gold she must be sold.

Then fare ye well, my lady gay,
I must return another day."

"Come back, come back, you Spanish knight,
Your boots and spurs shine very bright."

"My boots and spurs they count you nought,
For in this town they were not bought."

"Come back, come back, you Spanish knight,
And choose the fairest in your sight."

"This is too black, and that is too brown,
And this is the fairest in the town."

The only part of the country, so far as we know, in which the game now survives is the neighborhood of Cincinnati, where it is still played in a reduced but original form:

"Here comes a knight, a knight of Spain,
To court your daughter, lady Jane."

"My lady Jane, she is too young,
To be controlled by flattering tongue."

"Be she young or be she old,
Her beauty's fair, she must be sold."

"Go back, go back, you Spanish man,
And choose the fairest in the land."

"The fairest one that I can see,
Is [Annie Hobart] to walk with me."

The game now proceeds, "Here come two knights," then with three, four, etc., till all the players are mated.*

It will be proper to add some account of the comparative history of this curious game. The English and Scotch versions, though generally less well preserved, correspond to our American. But we find a more primitive type in Iceland, where it is, or a few years ago was, an amusement of winter evenings, played not by children, but by men and women, in a form which indicates a high antiquity. The women ask the men, as these advance, what they desire? The latter reply, "a maid," that is, wife. The inquiry now is, what will they give? It is answered, *stone.* This tender is scornfully refused, and the suitors retire in dudgeon, but return to raise their offer, and at last proffer *gold*, which is accepted, and the controversy ends in a dance.†

* The game, half a century since, was played by boys as well as girls. New England variations are numerous; thus for the last line of verse 4, "I'll turn my face another way." For verse 7, "Go through the kitchen and through the hall, and choose the fairest one of all" A New York variety puts the last words into the mouth of the bride: "I'm so happy that I could sing."

† So in an English variety:

"I will give you pots and pans, I will give you brass,
I will give you anything for a pretty lass."

"No."

"I will give you gold and silver, I will give you pearl,
I will give you anything for a pretty girl."

"Take one, take one, the fairest you may see."

Halliwell, "Nursery Rhymes."

Curiously enough, modern Scotland retains this song in nearly all the rude simplicity of the Icelandic just referred to; though the negotiation, instead of being taken as a matter of course, is turned into a satire, being treated as the endeavor of a rich old bachelor to purchase a wife.

In the stewartry of Kirkcudbright, says Chambers, *Janet jo* is a dramatic entertainment among young rustics on winter evenings. A youth, disguised as an old bachelor, enters the room bonnet in hand, bowing, and declaring that "he has come to court Janet jo." The goodwife then demands, "What'll ye gie for Janet jo?" He responds, a "peck of siller," but is told, "Gae awa', ye auld carle!" He retires, but soon returns, and increases his offer, which is less scornfully rejected, until he proffers "three pecks of gowd," which is accepted with the words—

"Come ben beside Janet jo,
Janet jo, Janet jo,
Ye're welcome to Janet jo,
Janet, my jo."

The affair then ends in kissing. A comparison of details (such as the diminishing scorn of the bargainer, and chagrin of the suitors at each rejection) leaves no doubt that the Icelandic and Scotch forms of the game were once (but many centuries since) identical.

The German versions are numerous, but corrupt, and less ancient and characteristic. In one of the most spirited the mother assigns as a reason for refusing the suitor, that

Her tresses are not braided,
Her wedding-gown not done.

Similarly, we find in an English fragment,

My mead's not made, my cake's not baked,
And you cannot have my daughter Jane.

There is a French form, not otherwise especially interesting, which resembles our No. 3.*

More striking than the preceding, and abounding in singular correspondences with the first three numbers of our own collection, is the

* The ending is like ours—

"Prenez la plus jolie de toutes."
"Voilà la plus jolie de toute's."

Italian version, as played in Venice. In this game, one of the rows is composed of a boy, who represents the head of the house, and five or six girls who stand at his right and left. The other row is formed by the *ambassador*, whose suite consists of boys and girls. These last advance towards the first row, singing, "The ambassador is come," then, retreating, sing a chorus, "Olà, olà, olà." The conversation then proceeds in a rhythmical way between the two rows as follows:

"What do you wish?" "A maid."
"Which maid?" "The fairest."
"Who is the fairest?" "Nineta bella."
"What husband will you give her?" "A chimney-sweep."
"That will not do." "The king of France."
"That will do well." "What dowry will you give her?"
"A ducat." "It will not do."
"A zechin a day." "That will do well."
"Come and take her." "Here I come and take her."

The "ambassador" advances and takes the girl by the hand; then, as if changing his mind, rejects her, saying as he returns—

"And now I don't want her!"
"Why do you not want her?" "She is too little (or ugly)."
"Is that the trouble?" "Yes, that is the trouble."
"Come, let us make peace." "Peace is made."

The ambassador then takes by the hand the girl, who is presented to him by the head of the house; the two files unite to form a circle, and the bride receives the general congratulations of the company, who clap their hands, courtesy, and sing,* as in the pretty English equivalent—

And the bells will ring, and the birds will sing,
And we'll all clap hands together.

In Spain, the game is known as the "Embassy of the Moorish King." The "King of the Moors" is seated on the ground, with crossed legs, his attendants about him. The "ambassador" makes three steps forward, and

* Eco la Nina al campo—fra tanti suoni e canti;
Eco la Nina al campo—olà, olà, olà.

Faciamo un bel' inchino—profondo al suo rispeto;
Faciamo un bel' inchino—olà, olà, olà.

demands one of his daughters. The king replies, "If I have them, I have them not to give away; of the bread which I eat, they shall eat as well."

The ambassador withdraws angry: "In discontent I go from the king's palace." But the king, repenting, calls after him—

"Turn thee, knight, come, turn thee hither,
The most fair I'll give to thee—
The most lovely and the sweetest,
Sweetest rose upon the tree."

The ambassador crosses hands with one of his train to make a seat, on which the bride is placed in triumph, singing—

"Thus I take her for her marriage,
Spouse and wedded wife to be."

The king addresses them on departure—

"Listen, knight, I do entreat thee,
Use to her all courtesy."

And the ambassadors reply—

"She, on throne of splendor seated,
Shall be shining to behold,
She shall lodge within a palace,
She shall dress in pearls and gold."

It will thus be seen that the three knights originally represent not suitors, but envoys. If we remember that marriage, in some simple countries, is still conducted through intermediaries, whose duty it is to argue, chaffer, and dispute, before coming to the decision all along intended, we shall see reason to believe that from a form representing more or less literally the usages of primitive society have sprung in the course of time a multitude of confused representations, colored by later tastes and feelings.

The spirit and substance of the courteous and chivalric English rhyme cannot be later than the fourteenth century; the identity and primitive rudeness of the song in Iceland, Scotland (and, we shall presently add, Virginia), supposes an earlier date; while even then we have to bridge the gap between these forms and the Italian. We may, therefore, be tolerably sure that the first diffusion of the game in Europe dates far back into the Middle Age.

No. 2.

Three Kings.

This antique rhyme, which comes to us from West Virginia, is a rude and remarkable variety of the preceding game, but quite unlike any English version hitherto printed.

We find a singular and apparently connected equivalent in the Faroe isles. In the form of the dialogue there in use, as in the present game, the suitor is presented in successively higher characters, as a thrall, smith, and so on, until he is finally accepted as a prince. The Italian song has shown us a similar usage. Thus the surf-beaten rocks of the North Atlantic, with their scanty population of fishermen and shepherds, whose tongue is a dialect of the ancient Norse speech, are linked by the golden chain (or network) of tradition with the fertile vales of the Alleghanies, and the historic lagoons of Venice.

The corrupt ending, too, compared with the Philadelphia version already cited, and with the Venetian game, is seen to rest on an ancient basis. The children, having forgotten the happy close, and not understanding the haggling of the suitors, took the "three kings" for bandits.

On one side of the room a mother with her daughters. On the other three wooers, who advance.

"Here come three soldiers three by three,
To court your daughter merrily;
Can we have a lodging, can we have a lodging,
Can we have a lodging here to-night?"

"Sleep, my daughter, do not wake—
Here come three soldiers, and they sha'n't take;
They sha'n't have a lodging, they sha'n't have a lodging,
They sha'n't have a lodging here to-night."

"Here come three sailors three by three,
To court your daughter merrily;
Can we have a lodging," etc.

"Sleep, my daughter, do not wake—
Here come three sailors and they sha'n't take;
They sha'n't have a lodging," etc.

"Here come three tinkers three by three,
To court your daughter merrily;
Can we have a lodging," etc.

"Sleep, my daughter, do not wake—
Here come three tinkers and they sha'n't take;
They sha'n't have a lodging," etc.

"Here come three kings, three by three,
To court your daughter merrily;
Can we have a lodging," etc.

"Wake, my daughter, do not sleep—
Here come three kings, and they *shall* take;
They *shall* have a lodging, they shall have a lodging,
They shall have a lodging here to-night."

(*To the kings*)—

"Here is my daughter safe and sound,
And in her pocket five hundred pound,
And on her finger a plain gold ring,
And she is fit to walk with the king."

(The daughter goes with the kings; but they are villains in disguise: they rob her, push her back to her mother, and sing)—

"Here is your daughter *not* safe and sound,
And in her pocket *not* five hundred pound,
And on her finger no plain gold ring,
And she's not fit to walk with the king."

(The mother pursues the kings, and tries to catch and beat them).

Charlestown, W. Va.

No. 3.

Here Comes a Duke.

This rhyme is only a later development of the same game. The suitor is now made to address himself directly to his mistress, and the mercenary character of the previous transaction is replaced by coquetry. Our New England song loses nothing by comparison with the pretty Scotch.

A company of little girls sit in a row. A little girl from the middle of the room goes dancing up to the first one in the row, singing,

"Here comes a duke a-roving,
Roving, roving,
Here comes a duke a-roving,
With the ransy, tansy, tea!
With the ransy, tansy, tario!
With the ransy, tansy, tea!
Pretty fair maid, will you come out,
Will you come out, will you come out,
To join us in our dancing?"

Little girl answers,

"No."

Suitor steps backward, singing,

"Naughty girl,* she won't come out,
She won't come out, she won't come out,
To join us in our dancing."

Suitor advances as before. The answer now is,

"Yes."

These two now retire, singing together,

"Now we've got the flowers of May,
The flowers of May, the flowers of May,
To join us in our dancing."

They join hands and call out the next one in the row; thus the play goes on until the last is selected, when they form a ring, dance, and sing,

"Now we've got the flowers of May,
The flowers of May, the flowers of May,
To join us in our dancing."

Concord, Mass.

* A New Hampshire fragment has here,

"The *scornful maid,* she won't come out,"

which seems more genuine.

A vulgarized form of the same game is common through the Middle States:

Boys. "We are three *ducks* a-roving, (thrice)
With a ransom dansom dee."
Girls. "What is your good-will, sir?" etc.
Boys. "My good-will is to marry," etc.
Girls. "Which one of us will you have, sir?" etc.
Boys. "You're all too black and blowzy," etc.
Girls. "We are as good as you, sir," etc.
Boys. "Then I will take you, miss," etc.

The pretended quarrel between intermediaries has here become a dispute of the principals.*

Finally, in the streets of New York the dialogue is made unrecognizable—

The Ring. "Forty ducks are riding,
My dilsey dulsey officer;
Forty ducks are riding,
My dilsey dulsey day.
Which of the lot do you like best?"
Child in Centre. "You're all too black and ugly—ugly," etc.
The Ring. "We're not so black as you are," etc.

The child then selects a partner, when the rest sing,

"Open the gates and let the bride out," etc.;

and the couple pass under lifted hands, circle the ring, and similarly re-enter, to the words,

"Open the gates and let the bride in," etc.

We have thus a curious example of the way in which an apparently meaningless game, which might be supposed the invention of the *gamins*

* An English variety, printed a century since in "Gammer Gurton's Garland," has as the first line of the refrain,

My-a-dildin, my-a-daldin;

and as the alternate line,

Lily white and shine-a.

The last phrase comes to us as the fragment of a game in Massachusetts, about 1800. We are reminded of the songs of Autolycus in "A Winter's Tale," "with such delicate burdens of *dildos* and fadings."

of the street, is, in fact, a degenerate form of the ancient poetry, which was brimful of grace, courtesy, and the joy of existence.

For a purpose presently to be mentioned, we must cite the corresponding Scotch rhyme, given by Chambers:

A dis, a dis, a green grass,
A dis, a dis, a dis;
Come all ye pretty fair maids,
And dance along with us.

For we are going a-roving,
A-roving in this land;
We'll take this pretty fair maid,
We'll take her by the hand.

Ye shall get a duke, my dear,
And ye shall get a drake;
And ye shall get a young prince,
A young prince for your sake.

And if this young prince chance to die,
Ye shall get another;
The bells will ring, and the birds will sing,
And we'll all clap hands together.

No. 4.

Tread, Tread the Green Grass.

Tread, tread the green grass,
Dust, dust, dust;
Come all ye pretty fair maids
And walk along with us.

If you be a fair maid,
As I suppose you be,
I'll take you by the lily-white hand
And lead you across the sea.

Philadelphia.

With this musical call to the dance, it was common, a generation since, for girls in this town to begin the evening dances on the green, singing they marched in couples. The "dust" of the rhyme is a corruption. Comparing it with the Scotch song previously quoted, we do not doubt that it represents the Scotch (in other words, old English) *adist*, the opposite of *ayont*, meaning *this way*, come hither. We ought probably therefore to read,

Tread, tread the green grass,
Adist, adist, adist.

This song was no mere dance of rustics; the children at least kept up the usage of the day when a pleasing popular poetry was the heritage of all ranks. The spirit of the strain carries us back to that "carolling" of ladies which was, in the time of Chaucer, no less than the gay green of the meadow or the melody of the birds, an accompaniment of summer.

No. 5.

I'll Give to You a Paper of Pins.

This pretty and interesting, hitherto unprinted, children's song is more or less familiar throughout the Middle States. We have heard it with many variations from persons of all classes and ages. It may often be listened to in the upper part of the city of New York, as it is sung (with a mere apology for a melody) by three or four girls, walking with arms entwined, or crooned by mere infants seated on the casks which, in the poorer quarters, often encumber the sidewalk.

There are also English and Scotch versions, generally inferior as regards poetical merit and antiquity of language. The English form, however, seems to contain the primitive idea, where the wooer appears as a prince, who by splendid presents overcomes the objections of a lady. This mercenary character being repugnant to modern taste, the Scotch rhyme represents the suitor as the Evil One in person; while in the United States the hero is, in his turn, made to cast off the avaricious fair, or else the lady to demand only love for love.

The numerous couplets of the American rhyme are completely in the ballad style. A "paper of pins" is substituted for a "pennorth of pins." The "easy-chair" is modern, but the verse itself ancient, combing golden hair being a world-old occupation of beauties. The gown "trimmed with golden thread," or "set off with a golden crown," refers to the attire of olden times. The mediæval bride wore a crown on the head and flowing hair; a costume also mentioned in old ballads as the usual dress of a demoiselle of rank arrayed for the dance.

"I'll give to you a paper of pins,
And that's the way my love begins;
If you will marry me, me, me,
If you will marry me."

"I don't accept your paper of pins,
If that's the way your love begins;
For I won't marry you, you, you,
For I won't marry you."

"I'll give to you an easy-chair,
To sit in and comb your golden hair.

"I'll give to you a silver spoon,
To feed your babe in the afternoon.

"I'll give to you a dress of green,
To make you look like any queen.*

"I'll give to you the key of my heart,
For you to lock and never to part.

"I'll give to you the key of my chest,
For you to have money at your request."

"I *do* accept the key of your chest,
For me to have money at my request;
And I will marry you, you, you,
And I will marry you."

"Ha, ha, ha, money is all,
And I won't marry you at all;
For I won't marry you, you, you,
For I won't marry you."

This is from a New York child; our next version is from Connecticut:

* Here verses may be improvised at pleasure; for instance, said the little reciter,

"I'll give to you a dress of black,
A green silk apron and a white cap.
If you will marry," etc.

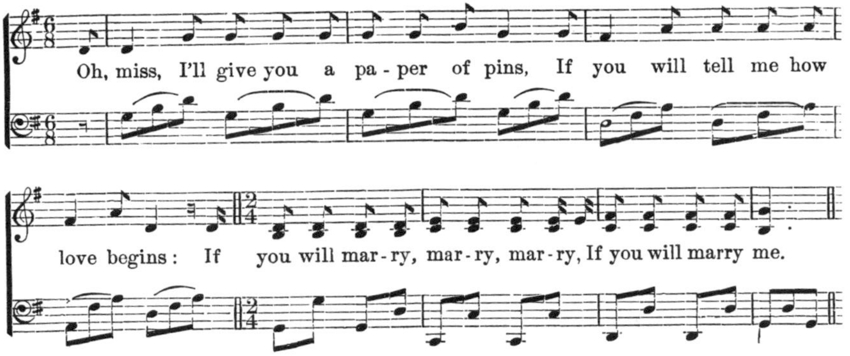

"O miss, I'll give you a paper of pins,
If you will tell me how love begins:
    If you will marry, marry, marry,
    If you will marry me."

"I'll not accept your paper of pins,
And I won't tell you how love begins;
    For I won't marry, marry, marry,
    For I won't marry you."

"O miss, I'll give you a coach and six,
Every horse as black as pitch.

"O miss, I'll give you a red silk gown,
With gold and laces hanging round.

"O miss, I'll give you a little gold bell,
To ring for the waiter* when you are not well.

"O miss, I'll give you the key to my heart,
That we may lock and never part.

"O miss, I'll give you the key to my chest,
That you may have money at your request."

"I will accept the key of your chest,
That I may have money at my request."

"Ah, I see, money is all,
Woman's love is none at all;
    And I won't marry, marry, marry,
    And I won't marry you."

* In the English version "to ring up *your maidens.*"

Finally, we have a variation with a more tender conclusion:

"Will you have a paper of pins?
For that's the way my love begins—
    And will you marry me, me, me,
    And will you marry me?"

"No, I'll not have a paper of pins,
If that's the way your love begins."

"Will you have a little lap-dog,
Who may follow you abroad?

"Will you have a coach and four,
Footman behind and footman before?

"Will you have a dress of red,
All trimmed round with golden thread?

"Will you have a satin gown,
All set off with a golden crown?

"Will you have the key to my chest,
To draw out gold at your request?

"Will you have the key to my heart,
That we may love and never part?"

"Yes, I will have the key to your heart,
That we may love and never part,
    And I will marry you, you, you,
    And I will marry you."

The same idea is contained in a song originally Scotch, but which comes to us (through an Irish medium) from Pennsylvania:

"Will you come to the Highland braes,
    Bonny lassie, Highland lassie?
Will you come to the Highland braes,
    My bonny Highland lassie?"

The reply is, "Na, na, it will not dee, bonnie laddie," etc.: when the wooer gradually increases his offers:

"I will give you a golden comb,
If you will be mine and never roam;"

and finally inquires,

> "Will you go to the kirk with me,
> There to be my wedded wife?"

which is eagerly accepted:

> "*And them's the words away to town,*
> And I will get my wedding-gown."

No. 6.

There She Stands, a Lovely Creature.

This pretty song has been recited to us by informants of the most cultivated class, and, on the other hand, we have seen it played as a round by the very "Arabs of the street," in words identically the same. It is an old English song, which has been fitted for a ring-game by the composition of an additional verse, to allow the selection of a partner.

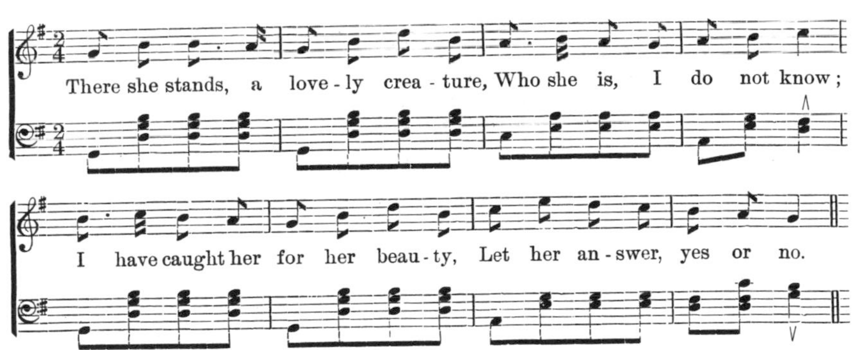

> "There she stands, a lovely creature,
> Who she is, I do not know;
> I have caught her for her beauty,—
> Let her answer, yes or no.

> "Madam, I have gold and silver,
> Lady, I have houses and lands,
> Lady, I have ships on the ocean,
> All I have is at thy command."

"What care I for your gold and silver,
What care I for your houses and lands,
What care I for your ships on the ocean—
All I want is a nice young man."

New York.

No. 7.

Green Grow the Rushes, O!

In former times, the amusements of young people at their winter-evening gatherings consisted almost entirely of "playing games." On such occasions the following rhyme was used (in eastern Massachusetts) about the beginning of the century, to select partners for the ring. Chairs were placed in a circle, and the players of one sex seated, so as to leave alternate vacant places, for which they chose occupants, singing—

"Green grow the rushes, O!
Green grow the rushes, O!
He who will my true love be,
Come and sit by the side of me."

Those waiting to be selected sang,

"Pick and choose, but choose not me,
Choose the fairest you can see."

This dialogue was repeated for each player until all were taken in, which, if the party was numerous, of necessity took a long time.

No. 8.

The Widow with Daughters to Marry.

A child, representing a mother, is followed by a file of daughters, each grasping the frock of the girl in front.

There comes a poor widow from Barbary-land,*
With all her children in her hand;

* Variation: "Here comes an old woman from Sunderland," or "Cumberland."

One can brew, and one can bake,
And one can make a wedding-cake;
  Pray take one,
  Pray take two,
Pray take one that pleases you.*

Philadelphia.

The "poor widow" is also represented as having only one daughter left.

Sister, O Phœbe, how happy we be,
As we go under the juniper-tree!
We'll put on our night-caps to keep our heads warm,
And two or three kisses will do us no harm—
Will do us no harm, Io!
I am a poor widow, a-marching around,
And all of my daughters are married but one;
So rise up my daughter, and kiss whom you please,
And kiss whom you please, Io!

Philadelphia.

Another old version of this round:

I am a rich widow, I live all alone,
I have but one daughter, and she is my own;
Go, daughter, go choose, go choose your one,
Go choose a good one, or else choose you none.

New York.

Finally, we have the modern corruption of the street, which, however, shows us the manner of playing:

A child stands in the ring, as the mother. The daughter reclines as if asleep, her head resting on her hands, till the words, *rise up*.

Here *stands* a poor widow a-walking around,
  Io! Io! Io!

* In Canada the game goes:

J'ai tant d'enfants à marier!
J'ai tant d'enfants à marier!
Grand Dieu! je n' sais comment
  Pouvoir en marier tant.

Mademoiselle, on parle à vous;
On dit que vous aimez beaucoup;
Si c'est vrai que vous aimez,
Entrez dans la danse, entrez!

So put on the night-cap to keep her head warm,
To keep her head warm, Io!
So rise up my daughter, and kiss whom you please,
And kiss whom you please, Io!

New York.

The widow with daughters to marry is a European celebrity. The titles *rich* and *poor*, moreover, in this and the last number, are not meaningless, but show that two independent characters have been united in one. In the original European game, which we have not encountered in an English form, there is both a *rich* and a *poor* mother; the latter begs away, one by one, the daughters of the former, until she has secured all. The present round and the preceding are only reductions, or adaptations to the dance, of this more ancient and dramatic game. Once more, the game of the rich and poor mothers, though centuries old, and existing in many European tongues, is itself but an outgrowth of a still more ancient childish drama, which has given birth to innumerable sports, dances, and songs, exhibiting very different external characteristics all over Europe, but of which primitive and complete versions at present seem to exist only in America.*

No. 9.

Philander's March.

This rhyme has been familiar throughout the New England States. Some of our older readers will remember how the doors of all the apartments of an old-fashioned mansion, with its great chimney in the centre, would be thrown open at an evening party, and the children march through the house, and up and down the staircase, singing the familiar air—

Come, Philanders,† let's be a-marching,
Every one choose from his heartstrings;‡
Choose your true love now or never,
And be sure you choose no other.

* See Note; also No. 154, and Note.

† Usually plural.

‡ Or, dialectically, "every one his true lover *sarching.*"

O, my dear ——, how I do love you!
Nothing on earth do I prize above you!
With a kiss now let me greet you,
And I will never, never leave you.

Plymouth, Mass. (about 1800).

Another version:

Come, Philander, let us be a-marching,
From the ranks there's no deserting,
Choose your own, your own true lover,
See that you don't choose any other;
Now farewell, dear love, farewell,
We're all a-marching, so farewell.

Deerfield, Mass.

Why, of all the names of the Damon and Sylvia class, *Philander*,* which, according to derivation, should mean fondness for the male sex, came to be a proverbial expression for an amorous person, and contributed to the English language a verb (to philander) we cannot say. Children's intelligence made wild work of the word. A New England variation was, "Come, *Lysanders;*" and in Pennsylvania, on the Maryland border, the first line has been ingeniously distorted into "*Cumberland city-town-boys*" marching! Cumberland being a town in the latter state.

No. 10.

Marriage.

(1.) By this name was known in Massachusetts, at the beginning of the century, an elaborate dance (for such, though practised in a Puritan community, it really was) which has a very decided local flavor.

Partners having been chosen, the girl says—

"Come, my dearest partner, and join both heart and hand;
You want you a wife, and I want me a man.
So married we will be, if we can agree,
We'll march down together, so happy are we."

* "Were his men like him, he'd command a regiment of Damons and *Philanders.*"—"Two Faces under One Hood," by Thomas Dibdin.

The partners now separate, the lad saying—

"Now I must part, and leave you alone,
So fare you well, my true love, till I return."

The maid replies—

"I mourn, I mourn, for that is the cry,
I'm left all alone, and I'm sure I shall die."

But, after walking round, rejoins her partner, who welcomes her—

"Oh, here comes my love, and how do you do?
And how have you been since I parted with you?"

The pair then address the row—

"There is a scene secure from all harm,
Please to give us joy by the raising of the arm."

The other players, who stand each lad opposite his lass, raise arms, and the couple walk down under the arch so formed, pausing at the foot—

"Now we are married, and never more to part,
Please to give a kiss from the bottom of the heart."

And the game proceeds with the next couple.

Scituate, Mass. (about 1800).

(2.) No better as respects poetry, but with more evidence of old English origin, is the following game, in which couples circle in a ring about two chairs, from time to time changing partners. We have not been clearly informed of the way of playing, but presume that at the time of the change the youth or girl in the ring must select a mate.

"On the green carpet here we stand,
Take your true love in your hand;
Take the one whom you profess
To be the one whom you love best."

A change of partners.

"Very well done, said Johnny Brown,
Is this the way to London town?
Stand ye here, stand ye there,
Till your true love doth appear."

A mate is finally chosen, and the ring sings—

"Oh, what a beautiful choice you've made!
Don't you wish you'd longer stayed?
[Give her a kiss, and send her away,
And tell her she can no longer stay."*]

Salem, Mass.

The "green carpet" is, of course, the grass, on which the village dance proceeds in the summer-time,† and the remains of an ancient "carol" appear in the corrupt rhyme.

(3.) To the game of *Marriage*, as played in France and Italy, the following closely corresponds:

A boy and girl having been chosen by singing our No. 17, and standing in the centre of the ring, the game proceeds, with imitative motion and gesture—

"Row the boat! Row the boat!
Let the boat stand!
I think —— —— is a handsome young man;
I think —— —— is as handsome as he,
And they shall be married, if they can agree."‡

Such short rhymes are not used independently, but joined to some fragment of a ballad, which they serve to turn into a game, as may be seen in our No. 12.

* From another version.

† As Lodge has it—

Footing it featlie on the grassie ground,
These damsels circling with their brightsome faires—

‡ Fifty years ago the corresponding French game was still played as a "game of society"—

Eh! qui marirons-nous?
Mademoiselle, ce sera vous:
Entrez dans la danse;
J'aimerai qui m'aimera, j'aimerai qui m'aime.

The round then proceeds—

Eh! qui lui donnerons-nous?
Mon beau monsieur, ce sera vous.
Amans, embrassez-vous, etc.

(4.) We take this opportunity to give one or two other familiar examples of kissing rounds:

> Had I as many eyes as the stars in the skies,
> And were I as old as Adam,
> I'd fall on my knees, and kiss whom I please,
> Your humble servant, madam.

In Boston, half a century since, this ran—

> As many *wives as the stars in the skies,*
> And each *as old as Adam,* etc.

In Georgia, at the present day—

> Many, many stars are in the skies,
> And *each as old as Adam,* etc.

(5.) The following is yet more inane, yet it furnishes a curious example of correspondence—

> "—— —— languishes."
> "For whom?"
> "For —— ——."

This is not much more crude than the French equivalent.*

(6.) We may add that the familiar American game, known as "Pillow," or "Pillows and Keys" (why *keys?*), in which a player kneels on a *pillow* and solicits a kiss, is no doubt a descendant of the "Cushion Dance," alluded to by old dramatists.

> * "Qui est-ce qui languira?"
> "Ce sera —— —— qui languira."
> "—— —— la guerira."
> *French game in Cambrai.*

II.

HISTORIES.

A FRESH wreath of crimson roses
  Round my forehead twine will I;
I will wear them for a garland,
  Wear them till the day I die.

I desire that in my coffin
  May be room enough for three;
For my father, for my mother,
  And my love to lie with me.

Afterwards above the coffin
  We will let a flower grow;
In the morning we will plant it,
  In the evening it will blow.

Wayfarers will pause demanding,
  "Whose may be the flower there?"
"'Tis the flower of Rosetina,
  She who died of love's despair."

Round of Girls in Venice.

No. 11.

Miss Jennia Jones.

THIS childish drama has been familiar in the Middle States since the memory of the oldest inhabitant. The Scotch equivalent shows that the heroine's name was originally *Jenny jo.* "Jo" is an old English word for sweetheart, probably a corruption of *joy*, French *joie*, used as a term of endearment. *Jenny my joy* has thus been modernized into Miss Jennia (commonly understood to be a contraction for Virginia) Jones!

The story is originally a love-tale. The young lady, like Rosetina in the Venetian song (a part of which we have translated above) dies of blighted affection and the prohibition of cruel parents. The suitor, in America, is represented by feminine friends. Yet the drama has lived; a proof that in singing and playing love-tales the children rather imitated their elders than followed a necessity of their own nature.

From various versions we select the following:

A mother, seated. Miss Jennia Jones stands behind her chair, or reclines on her lap as if lying sick. A dancer advances from the ring.

"I've come to see Miss Jennia Jones,
 Miss Jennia Jones, Miss Jennia Jones—
I've come to see Miss Jennia Jones,
 And how is she to-day?"

"She's up-stairs washing,
 Washing, washing—
She's up-stairs washing,
 You cannot see her to-day."

The questions are repeated to the same air for every day of the week, and the reply is that Miss Jennia Jones is ironing, baking, or scrubbing. She is then represented as sick, as worse, and finally as dead, which announcement is received with signs of deep grief. The dancers of the ring then discuss the costume in which she shall be buried:

"What shall we dress her in,
 Dress her in, dress her in;
What shall we dress her in—
 Shall it be blue?"

"Blue is for sailors,
 So that will never do."

"What shall we dress her in,
 Shall it be red?"

"Red is for firemen,
 So that will never do."

"Pink is for babies,
 So that will never do."

"Green is forsaken,
 So that will never do."

"Black is for mourners,
So that will never do."

"White is for dead people,
So that will just do."

"Where shall we bury her?
Under the apple-tree."

After the ceremonies of burial have been completed, the ghost of Miss Jennia Jones suddenly arises—

"I dreamt I saw a ghost last night,
Ghost last night, ghost last night—
I dreamt I saw a ghost last night,
Under the apple-tree!"

The ring breaks up, and flies with shrieks, and the one caught is to represent Miss Jennia Jones.

An interesting feature of our game is the symbolism of color. "Each of these colors," says an informant, "which denoted a profession, also typified a feeling. Thus, blue, which is said to be for *sailors*, suggested *constancy*."

In one version of the game, which comes to us from an Irish source, *green* is for *grief*, *red* for *joy*, *black* for *mourning*, and *white* for *death*. In another such version, *white* is for *angels*, and is the chosen color; a reading we would willingly adopt, as probably more ancient, and as expressing the original seriousness of the whole, and the feeling which the color of white symbolized. In more common Irish phrase, *green* is for *Irish*, *yellow* for *Orangemen*. In Cincinnati, *purple* is for *kings* and *queens*, *gray* for *Quakers*. In a Connecticut variation, *yellow* is for *glad folks*.

An English saying corresponds closely to the significance of colors in our game:

Blue is true, yellow is jealous,
Green is forsaken, red is brazen,
White is love, and black is death.

A variation from West Virginia makes the question apply to the dress of the mourners, not of the deceased: "What shall we dress in?" "In our red, in our blue," etc., are rejected, and the decision is, "In our white."

Such imitations of burial ceremonies are not merely imaginative. It was once the custom for the girls of a village to take an active part in the interment of one of their number. In a Flemish town, a generation since, when a young girl died, her body was carried to the church, thence to the cemetery, by her former companions. "The religious ceremony over, and the coffin deposited in the earth, all the young girls, holding in one hand the mortuary cloth, returned to the church, chanting the *maiden's dance* with a spirit and rhythm scarcely conceivable by one who has not heard it. The pall which they carried to the church was of sky-blue silk, having in the middle a great cross of white silk, on which were set three crowns of silver."

The following is a rendering of the "Maiden's Dance:"

In heaven is a dance;
Alleluia!
There dance all the maids;
Benedicamus Domino—
Alleluia!

It is for Amelia;
Alleluia!
We dance like the maids;
Benedicamus Domino—
Alleluia!

Such touching customs show the profound original earnestness underlying the modern child's play, as well as the primitive religious significance of the dance. In England, too, it was the practice for the bearers of a virgin to be maids, as a ballad recites:

A garland fresh and faire
Of lilies there was made,
In signe of her virginity,
And on her coffin laid.
Six maidens, all in white,
Did beare her to the grave.

No. 12.

Down She Comes as White as Milk.

This round is remarkable for being introduced, wherever it occurs, by a stanza with a different melody, whereby the ballad is turned into a game. By this introduction the hero and heroine of the action are selected.

"Little Sally Waters," or "Uncle John," having been first played, the round proceeds about the couple standing in the ring:

He knocks at the door, and picks up a pin,
And asks if Miss —— is in.

She neither is in, she neither is out,
She's in the garret a-walking about.

Down she comes as white as milk,
A rose in her bosom, as soft as silk.

She takes off her gloves, and shows me a ring;
To-morrow, to-morrow, the wedding begins.*

Concord, Mass. (*before* 1800).

* The song exhibits numerous marks of antiquity. "Picks up a pin" was originally, no doubt, "pulls at the pin." The word "garret" here appears to correspond to the Scandinavian "high-loft," the upper part and living room of an ancient house. The third verse is a very ancient ballad commonplace—

Shee's as soft as any silk,
And as white as any milk.

"Ballad of Kinge Adler," in the Percy MS.

Instead of "Water, water, wild-flowers," as printed on the next page, we find in Philadelphia, "*Lily, lily, white-flower,*" which may have been the original, and reminds us of the refrains of certain ballads. In Yorkshire, England, "*Willy, willy, wall-flower.*"

A specimen of the quintessence of absurdity is the following street-song:

Swallow, swallow, weeping
About a willow tree,
All the boys in Fiftieth Street
Are dying down below;
Excepting —— ——
His love he can't deny,
For he loves —— ——
And she loves him beside, etc.

Notwithstanding the vulgarity of these stanzas, and of others which are employed for the same purpose, the practice which they illustrate—namely, the adaptation of a ballad to the dance by uniting with it a game-rhyme—is no doubt ancient. We have other examples in the numbers which follow.

The version now played in New York streets is corrupt, but has a spirited melody:

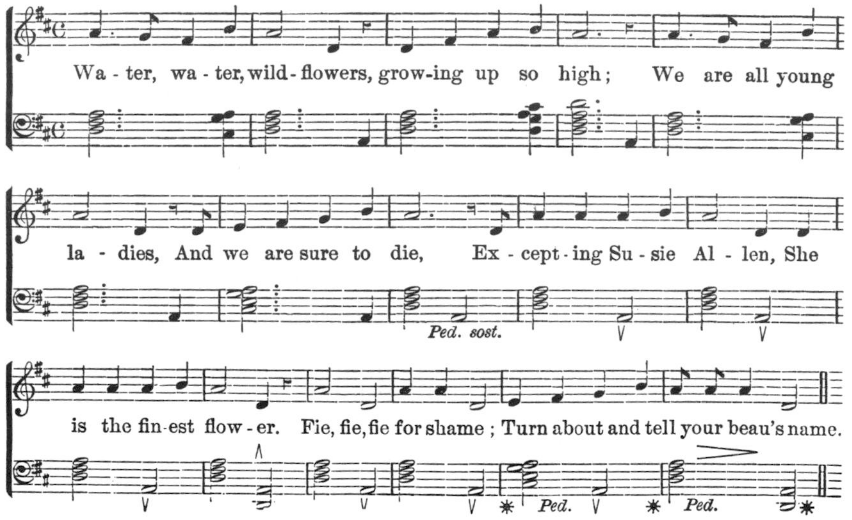

The girl complying, the ballad proceeds—

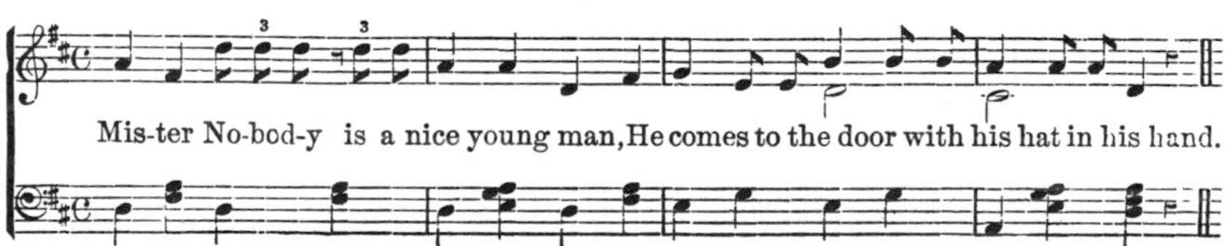

Mr. *Nobody* is a nice young man,
He comes to the door with his hat in his hand.

Down she comes, all dressed in silk,
A rose in her bosom, as white as milk.

She takes off her gloves, she shows me her ring,
To-morrow, to-morrow, the wedding begins.

The song before us furnishes a good example of the persistency of childish tradition. Not only is it still current in New England and the Middle States, with words closely corresponding to those given in our version of almost a century since, but these words are also nearly identical with the language of the round as we are told it is sung at the present day in Ireland.

Of a type similar to the foregoing is an ancient and curious, but unpublished, nursery song,* the first lines of which, at least, will be familiar to some of our readers:

Sing, sparrow, sing!
What shall I sing?
All the boys in our town have gone courting;
All but little Charley,
And he stays at home,
And he says he'll have Mary,
Or else he'll have none.

Row, boat, row!
Where shall I row?
Up to little Mary's door.
Out jumps little Charley in his boots and spurs,
And goes to the door, and pulls at the string—
"Where's little Mary? Is she within?"

"Miss Mary's up-stairs, a-making a cap."
Then down comes Miss Mary, as white as the milk,
All dressed in pink posies and sweet pretty silk,
And goes to the cupboard, and takes up the can,
And drinks to little Charley, a pretty little man.
He takes her in his lap, and pares her nails,†
And gives her a posy of peacock's tails,
And rings and jewels fit for her hand,
And tells little Mary he'll come again.

The mention in this rhyme of the cupboard and the can carries us to a time not so remote indeed in years, but far removed in customs. At the beginning of the century, in the old colonial towns, tumblers were unknown; the silver can stood on the table, and was passed from hand to hand at the meal, the elders drinking first. This usage was accompanied with much ceremony. An informant (born in Salem, Mass.), whose memory goes back almost to the beginning of the century, recollects how, when it came to be his turn to drink, he was obliged to rise

* "Lines told to Lydia Jackson (now Mrs. R. W. Emerson, of Concord, Mass.) by her aunt, Joanna Cotton, in 1806–7–8, in Plymouth."

† Observe how the nursery song differs from the children's dance. The nurse wishes to persuade the little child in her lap that *paring nails* is a mark of great regard and affection, as, while performing that office, she chants the ballad to amuse her charge.

and wipe his lips (the use of the same vessel by a whole family made this habit proper), and repeat the words, while parents and friends laid down knives and forks and looked on, "Duty to Sir and Ma'am, respects to aunt, love to brother and sister, and health to myself." Sometimes, he said, sensitive children would rather "go dry" than endure this ordeal.

No. 13.

Little Sally Waters.

A girl in the centre of the ring, seated, and covering her face with her hands. At the word "rise," she chooses and salutes any one whom she pleases.

Little Sally Waters,
Sitting in the sun,
Crying and weeping,
For a young man.
Rise, Sally, rise,
Dry your weeping eyes,
Fly to the East,
Fly to the West,
Fly to the one you love best.

In the north of England the heroine's name is *Sally Walker:*

Sally Walker, Sally Walker,
 Come spring-time and love—
She's lamenting, she's lamenting,
 All for her young man.

A ballad situation has been united with a dance-rhyme.

No. 14.

Here Sits the Queen of England.

Here sits the Queen of England in her chair,
She has lost the true love that she had last year;
So rise upon your feet, and kiss the first you meet,
 For there's many around your chair.

Georgia.

No. 15.

Green Gravel.

A girl sits in the ring, and turns her head gravely as a messenger advances, while the rest sing to a pleasing air—

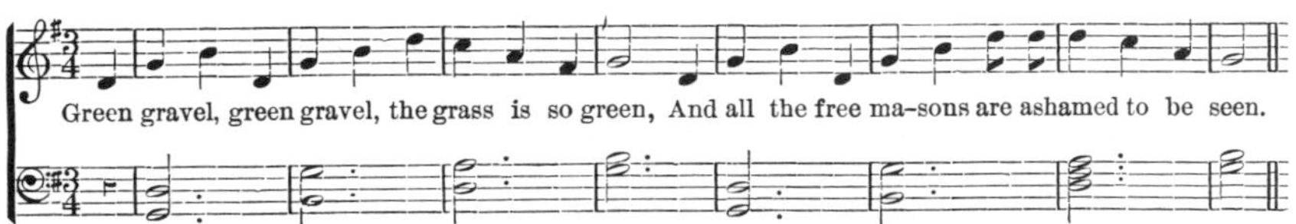

Green gravel, green gravel, the grass is so green,
And all the free *masons* (maidens) are *ashamed* (arrayed?) to be seen;*
O Mary, O Mary, your true love is dead,
The king sends you a letter to turn back your head.†

There are only two lines left of the ballad, or rather reminiscence of one.

A French round begins similarly: "Ah, the bringer of letters! What news is this? Ah, it is news that you must change your love.‡ Must I change my love, I prefer to die; he is not here, nor in France; he is in England, where he serves the gracious king." To this fragment belong the ancient verses which we have set as the motto of Chapter II. of our Introduction. All the other ladies of Paris are at the dance; the king's daughter alone "regarde à coté," "turns her head," looking at a messenger who is approaching; he brings news of her love's unfaithfulness; a rival skilled in magic arts has enchanted him, in the far country where he is warring. There is no more left of the ancient ballad, which, we presume, went on to describe her departure in man's costume, and rescue of her lover. We cannot prove the identity of our fragment, but we see how the child's game may have arisen.

* "It is on a summer's tide, when ladies' hearts are free and gay, when they go arrayed in ermine and silk. The hart strikes his horn against the linden, and the fish leaps in the stream."—*Icelandic Ballad.*

† Some little friends, feeling the unsatisfactoriness of the fragment, added a couplet to the dance—

O Mary, O Mary, your true love's not slain,
The king sends you a letter *to turn round again.*

‡ Eh! la *clinquet* (?) de lettres, que nouvelle est celle-ci?
Eh! ce sont des nouvelles qu'il faut changer d'ami.

No. 16.

Uncle John.

A ring of dancers who circle and sing—

Uncle John is very sick, what shall we send him?
A piece of pie, a piece of cake, a piece of apple-dumpling.*
What shall we send it in? In a piece of paper.
Paper is not fine† enough; in a golden saucer.
Who shall we send it by? By the governor's‡ daughter.
Take her by the lily-white hand, and lead her over the water.

After the words "governor's daughter" all the dancers fall down, and the last down stands apart, selects her confidential friend, and imparts with great mystery the *initials* of some boy in whom she takes an interest. She then returns, and takes her place in the ring with face reversed, while the friend announces the initials, and the dancers sing, using the letters given—

A. B., so they say,
Goes a-courting night and day,
Sword and pistol by his side,
And —— —— to be his bride;
Takes her by the lily-white hand,
And leads her o'er the water—
Here's a kiss, and there's a kiss
For Mr. ——'s daughter.

If the person representing "Uncle John" be a boy, his full name comes first in this rhyme, and the initials of the girl are used.

The choice of the confidante is said to require as much deliberation as the selection of an ambassador of state. *Hartford, Conn.*

This is one of the most familiar of all children's rounds in our country. It is, we see, a love-history; and, thrice vulgarized as it is, bears traces of ancient origin, and may perhaps be the last echo of the mediæval song in which an imprisoned knight is saved from approaching death by the daughter of the king, or soldan, who keeps him in confinement.§

* Or, "Three gold wishes, three good kisses. and a slice of *ginger!*"

† Or, "strong." ‡ Or, "king's daughter," "queen's daughter."

§ See French ballad referred to in the Appendix.

No. 17.

King Arthur was King William's Son.

A row of hats of various sizes, and belonging to both sexes, are placed on the floor. The leader picks up the first hat, and puts it on his own head, marching and singing the verse. He then takes up the next hat, and places it on the head of any one he pleases; the person chosen stands behind him, and they once more march, singing. The process is continued, until all the company are arranged in line:

King Arthur was King William's son,
And when the battle he had won,
Upon his breast he wore a star,
And it was called the sign of war.

Orange, New Jersey.

The following rhyme is exceedingly familiar, throughout the Middle and Southern States, as a kissing-round:

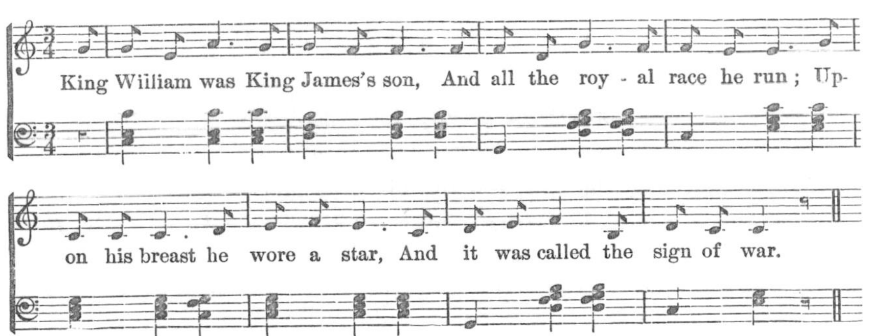

King William was King James's son,*
And all the royal race he run;
Upon his head he wore a star.
Star of the East,
Star of the West,
Star of the one you love the best.
If she's not here don't take her part,
But choose another with all your heart.

* Or, "King *George's* son." For convenience' sake, the last couplet of the first version is printed with the melody.

Down on the carpet you must kneel,
As the grass grows on the field,
Salute your bride, and kiss her sweet,
And rise again upon your feet.

The round is also familiar in Ireland. We learn from an informant that in her town it was formerly played in a peculiar manner. Over the head of a girl, who stood in the centre of a ring, was held a shawl, sustained by four others grasping the corners. The game then proceeded as follows:

King William was King George's son—
From the Bay of Biscay, O!
Upon his breast he wore a star—
Find your way to English schools.

Then followed the game-rhyme, repeated with each stanza, "Go choose you East," etc. King William is then supposed to enter—

The first girl that I loved so dear,
Can it be she's gone from me?

If she's not here when the night comes on,
Will none of you tell me where she is gone?

He recognizes the disguised girl—

There's heart beneath the willow-tree,
There's no one here but my love and me.

"He had gone to the war, and promised to marry her when he came back. She wrapped a shawl about her head, to see if he would recognize her." This was all the reciter could recollect; the lines of the ballad were sung by an old woman, the ring answering with the game-rhyme.

Waterford, Ireland.

The round now in use in the town whence this comes, but where the ballad is not at present known, begins:

King William was King George's son—
From the Bay of Biscay, O!
Upon his breast he wore a star—
Point your way across the sea.

In the year 1287, Folke Algotson, a high-born Swedish youth, carried off to Norway (at that time the refuge of such boldness) Ingrid, a daughter of the "law-man" or judge of East Gothland, who was betrothed to a Danish noble. Popular ballads attached themselves to the occurrence, which are still preserved. The substance of that version of the story with which we are concerned is as follows: A youth loves a maid, who returns his affection, but in his absence her friends have "given" her to another. He rides to the wedding ceremony with a troop of followers. The bride, seeing him approach, and wishing to test his affection, calls on her maidens to "take off her gold crown, and coif her in linen white." But the hero at once recognizes his love, mounts with her on horseback, and flees to Norway.

We cannot believe the resemblance to be accidental, and look upon our rhymes as a branch from the same ancient—but not historical—root.

No. 18.

Little Harry Hughes and the Duke's Daughter.

The writer was not a little surprised to hear from a group of colored children, in the streets of New York city (though in a more incoherent form) the following ballad. He traced the song to a little girl living in one of the cabins near Central Park, from whom he obtained this version. The hut, rude as the habitation of a recent squatter on the plains, was perched on a rock still projecting above the excavations which had been made on either side, preparatory to the erection of the conventional "brown-stone fronts" of a New York street. Rocks flung by carelessly managed explosions flew over the roof, and clouds of dust were blown by every wind into the unswept hovel. In this unlikely spot lingered the relics of old English folk-song, amid all the stir of the busiest of cities. The mother of the family had herself been born in New York, of Irish parentage, but had learned from her own mother, and handed down to her children, such legends of the past as the ballad we cite. A pretty melody gave popularity to the verse, and so the thirteenth-century tradition, extinct perhaps in its native soil, had taken a new lease of existence as a song of negro children in New York.

Under the thin disguise of the heading will be recognized the ballad of "Hugh of Lincoln and the Jew's Daughter," the occasion of which is referred by Matthew Paris to the year 1255. Chaucer, in exquisite verse, has made his Prioress recount the same story: how the child,

> This gemme of chastitè, this emeraude,
> And eek of martirdom the ruby bright,

has his throat cut by "false Jewes," and, cast into a pit, still sings his chant in honor of

> This welle of mercy, Christes moder sweet;

and, when discovered, cannot be buried in peace till the magic grain is removed which "that blissful maiden fre" has laid under his tongue.

The conclusion is, in our version, only implied. In that given by Jamieson the murdered child, speaking from the well, bids his mother prepare the winding-sheet, for he will meet her in the morn "at the back of merry Lincoln;" and the funeral service is performed by angels.

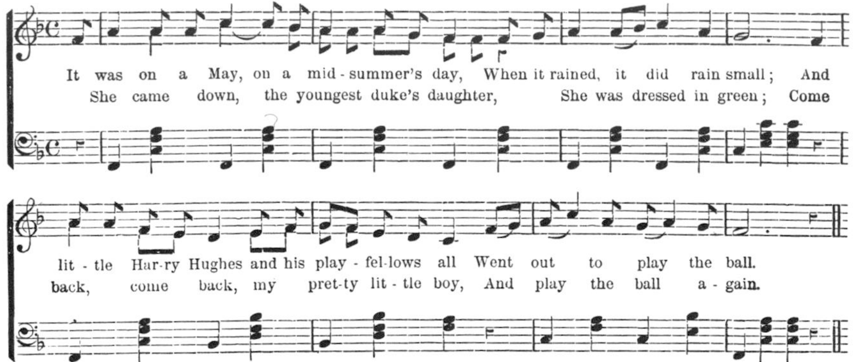

It was on a May, on a midsummer's day,
  When it rained, it did rain small;
And little Harry Hughes and his playfellows all
  Went out to play the ball.

He knocked it up, and he knocked it down,
  He knocked it o'er and o'er;
The very first kick little Harry gave the ball,
  He broke the duke's windows all.

She came down, the youngest duke's daughter,
  She was dressed in green;
"Come back, come back, my pretty little boy,
  And play the ball again."

"I won't come back, and I daren't come back,
  Without my playfellows all;
And if my mother she should come in,
  She'd make it the bloody ball."*

* For if my mother should chance to know,
  She'd make my blood to fall.—*Version of Sir Egerton Brydges.*

She took an apple out of her pocket,
And rolled it along the plain;
Little Harry Hughes picked up the apple,
And sorely rued the day.

She takes him by the lily-white hand,
And leads him from hall to hall,
Until she came to a little dark room,
That none could hear him call.

She sat herself on a golden chair,
Him on another close by;
And there's where she pulled out her little penknife
That was both sharp and fine.

Little Harry Hughes had to pray for his soul,
For his days were at an end;
She stuck her penknife in little Harry's heart,
And first the blood came very thick, and then came very thin.*

She rolled him in a quire of tin,
That was in so many a fold;
She rolled him from that to a little draw-well
That was fifty fathoms deep.

"Lie there, lie there, little Harry," she cried,
"And God forbid you to swim,
If you be a disgrace to me,
Or to any of my friends."

The day passed by, and the night came on,
And every scholar was home,
And every mother had her own child,
But poor Harry's mother had none.†

* And first came out the thick, thick blood,
And syne came out the thin;
And syne came out the bonny heart's blood,
There was nae mair within.
Jamieson.

† When bells were rung, and mass was sung,
And a' the bairns came hame,
When every lady gat hame her son,
The lady Maisry gat nane.
Jamieson.

She walked up and down the street,
  With a little sally-rod* in her hand;
And God directed her to the little draw-well,
  That was fifty fathoms deep.

"If you be there, little Harry," she said,
  "And God forbid you to be,
Speak one word to your own dear mother,
  That is looking all over for thee."

"This I am, dear mother," he cried,
  "And lying in great pain,
With a little penknife lying close to my heart,
  And the duke's daughter she has me slain.

"Give my blessing to my schoolfellows all,
  And tell them to be at the church,
And make my grave both large and deep,
  And my coffin of hazel and green birch.

"Put my Bible at my head,
  My busker† (?) at my feet,
My little prayer-book at my right side,
  And sound will be my sleep."

No. 19.

Barbara Allen.

In the first quarter of the century, this celebrated ballad was still used in New England as a children's game or dance at evening parties. We have here, perhaps, the latest English survival, in cultivated society, of a practice which had once been universal. It is noteworthy that while, in the town of which we speak,‡ the establishment, at the period alluded to, of a children's dancing-school was bitterly opposed, and the children of "church members" were hardly permitted to attend, no such prohibition applied to amusements like this, which were shared in irrespective of sectarian prejudice, by boys as well as by girls.

* Sallow; willow. † In other versions it is "Testament" or "Catechism."
‡ Keene, New Hampshire.

Our informant describes the performers as standing in couples, consisting each of a boy and a girl, facing each other. An elderly lady, who was in particular request at children's parties on account of her extensive stock of lore of the sort, sang the ballad, to which the dancers kept time with a slow metrical movement, balancing without any considerable change of place. At the final words, "Barbara Allen," which end every stanza, a courtesy took the place of the usual refrain. The whole performance is described as exceedingly pretty, stately, and decorous. It cannot be doubted that the version of the ballad sung was traditional, but we have not been able to secure it.

III.

PLAYING AT WORK.

"The king (George III.) danced all night, and finished with the *Hemp-dressers*, that lasted two hours."—*Memoir of Mrs. Delany.*

No. 20.

Virginia Reel.

This dance, which we will not here attempt to describe, is no doubt well known to our readers; but we doubt if any of them has reflected on its significance. It is, in fact, an imitation of *weaving*. The first movements represent the shooting of the shuttle from side to side, and the passage of the woof over and under the threads of the warp; the last movements indicate the tightening of the threads, and bringing together of the cloth.*

There is a very similar Swedish dance, called "Weaving Woollen," in which the words sung are—

Weave the woollen and bind it together,
Let the shuttle go round!

The originally imitative character of the dance is thus well illustrated. The "Hemp-dressers' Dance," in which George III. figured, seems to have resembled this, according to the description quoted in the memoir referred to in the heading of this chapter.

No. 21.

Oats, Pease, Beans, and Barley Grows.

This round, although very familiar to all American children, seems, strangely enough, to be unknown in Great Britain; yet it is still a favorite in France, Provence, Spain, Italy, Sicily, Germany, and Sweden; it was

* An acquaintance says, that in the interior of New York State the men and girls stand in the row by sevens; an arrangement which she suggests may imitate the different colors of strands.

played by Froissart (born 1337), and Rabelais (born 1483); while the general resemblance of the song in European countries proves that in the five centuries through which we thus trace it, even the words have undergone little change. Like the first game of our collection, it is properly a dance rather of young people than of children; and a comparative examination of versions inclines us to the belief that it is of Romance descent. The lines of the French refrain,* and the general form of the dance, suggest that the song may probably have had (perhaps in remote classic time) a religious and symbolic meaning, and formed part of rustic festivities designed to promote the fertility of the fields; an object which undoubtedly formed the original purpose of the May festival. So much for conjecture; but, in any case, it is pleasant to think of the many generations of children, in so many widely separated lands, who have rejoiced in the pretty game.

The ring circles, singing, about a child in the centre—

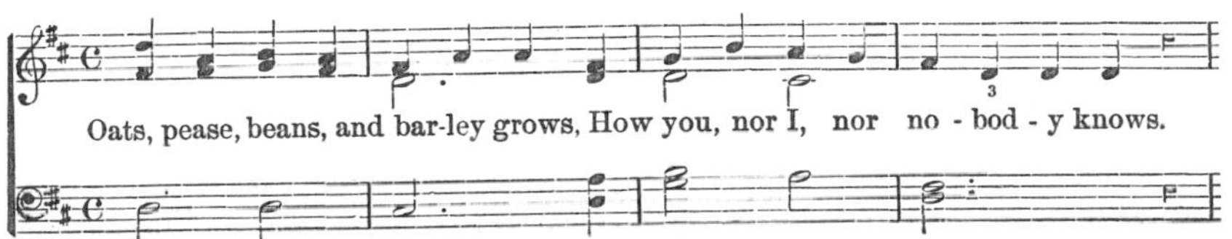

Oats, pease, beans, and barley grows,
Oats, pease, beans, and barley grows;
How you, nor I, nor nobody knows,
Oats, pease, beans, and barley grows.

The children now pause, and sing with appropriate gestures—

Thus the farmer sows his seed,
Stands erect and takes his ease,
Stamps his foot, and claps his hands,
And turns about to view his lands.

* Oats, oats, oats,
May the good God prosper you!

Waiting for a partner,
Waiting for a partner,
Open the ring and take her in,
And kiss her when you get her in.

The boy selects a girl, and the two kneel in the ring, and salute—

Now you're married, you must obey,
You must be true to all you say,
You must be kind, you must be good,
And make your husband chop the wood.

What we have said of the permanency of the words applies only to the action, the essential part, of the game. The *amatory chorus*, by which the song is made to serve the purpose of love-making, is very variable. Thus we have the quaint conclusion of the last line at greater length:

And now you're married in Hymen's band,
You must obey your wife's command;
You must obey your constant good,
And keep your wife in hickory wood—
Split the wood and carry it in, [*twice*]
And then she'll let you kiss her again.

"Splitting the wood" was a very troublesome part of the New England farmer's ménage.

More commonplace are the choruses:

You must be good, you must be true,
And do as you see others do.

Or—

And live together all your life,
And I pronounce you man and wife.

Or again—

And love each other like sister and brother,
And now kneel down and kiss each other.*

In place of "sister and brother," the malicious wit of little girls substituted "cats and dogs."†

* These choruses, which may be paralleled from Great Britain, do not in themselves belong to any particular game.

† We find the same benevolent wish, under like circumstances, in a Swedish game. Is the correspondence accident or tradition?

In the early part of the century the essential stanza went thus in New Hampshire:

> Thus my father sows his seed,
> Stands erect and takes his ease,
> Stamps his foot, and claps his hands,
> Whirls about, and thus he stands.

The Swedish quatrain is nearly the same:

> I had a father, he sowed this way,
> And when he had done, he stood this way;
> He stamped with his foot, he clapped with his hand,
> He turned about, he was so glad.

The French rhyme, by its exact correspondence, proves the great antiquity of the formula.*

The German game, as is often the case with German children's games and ballads in general, is more modernized than in the other tongues, and has become a coarse jest. It is represented how the farmer sows his oats, cuts it, binds it, carries it home, stores it, threshes it, takes it to market, sells it, spends the money in carousal, comes home drunk, and quarrels with his wife, because she has cooked him no supper! Verily, a satire from the lips of children!

Fauriel, in his history of Provençal literature, alludes to this song, which it seems he had seen danced in Provence, and considers to be derived from, and to represent, choral dances of Greek rustics. "The words of the song," he says, speaking of these ancient dances, "described an action, a succession of different situations, which the dancers reproduced by their gestures. The song was divided into many stanzas, and terminated by a refrain alike for all. The dancers acted or gesticulated only to imitate the action or situation described in each stanza; at the refrain they took each other by the hand and danced a round, with a movement more or less lively. There are everywhere popular dances derived from

> * Qui veut ouir, qui veut savoir,
> Comment on sème l'aveine?
> Mon père la sèmait ainsi,
> Puis il se reposait à demi;
> Frappe du pied, puis de la main,
> Un petit tour pour ton voisin;
> Aveine, aveine, aveine,
> Que le Bon Dieu t'amène!

these, which more or less resemble them. . . . I remember to have seen in Provence some of these dances, of which the theme seems to be very ancient—one, among the rest, imitating successively the habitual actions of a poor laborer, working in his field, sowing his wheat or oats, mowing, and so on to the end. Each of the numerous couplets of the song was sung with a slow and dragging motion, as if to imitate the fatigue and the sullen air of the poor laborer; and the refrain was of a very lively movement, the dancers then giving way to all their gayety." *

The French, Italian, and Spanish versions of this game also represent a series of actions, sowing, reaping, etc., of which our own rhyme has retained only one stanza. There is a whole class of similar rounds, which describe the labors of the farmer, vine-dresser, etc. That such a song, danced in sowing-time, and representing the progress and abundance of the crop, should be supposed to bring a blessing on the labors of the year, is quite in conformity with what we know of popular belief, ancient and modern. When a French savant asked the peasants of La Châtre why they performed the dance of "Threading the Needle" (see No. 29), the answer was, "To make the hemp grow." It is not in the least unlikely that the original of the present chant was sung, with a like object, by Italian rustics in the days of Virgil.

No. 22.

Who'll Be the Binder?

Couples circle in a ring about a single player—

It rains, it hails, it's cold stormy weather,
In comes the farmer drinking all the cider;
You be the reaping-boy and I'll be the binder;
I've lost my true love, and don't know where to find her.

Each girl then lets go of her partner's arm, and takes the arm of the one in advance, and the solitary player endeavors meanwhile to slip into the line.

The following is a variation:

It snows and it blows, and it's cold frosty weather,
Here comes the farmer drinking all his cider;
I'll be the reaper, who'll be the binder?
I've lost my true love, where shall I find her?

* Fauriel supposed the present round to be derived from Massiliot Greeks; but he was unacquainted with its diffusion in Europe.

It is played by children in New York city as a kissing-game in the ring, as follows:

In comes the farmer, drinking all the cider;
I have a true love and don't know where to find her.
Go round the ring, and see if you can find her;
If you cannot find her, go and choose another one.

We meet our game once more in North Germany. But its prettiest form is among the Fins of the Baltic coast, where it is extremely pleasing and pastoral:

Reap we the oat harvest,
Who will come and bind it?
Ah, perhaps his darling,
Treasure of his bosom.
Where have I last seen her?
Yesterday at evening,
Yesterday at morning!
When will she come hither,
With her little household,
With her gentle escort,
People of her village?
Who has not a partner,
Let him pay a forfeit!

It is a remarkable fact that, even where this simple people have borrowed the dramatic idea of an amusement from their more civilized neighbors, they have developed it with a sweetness and grace which put the latter to shame.

No. 23.

As We Go Round the Mulberry Bush.

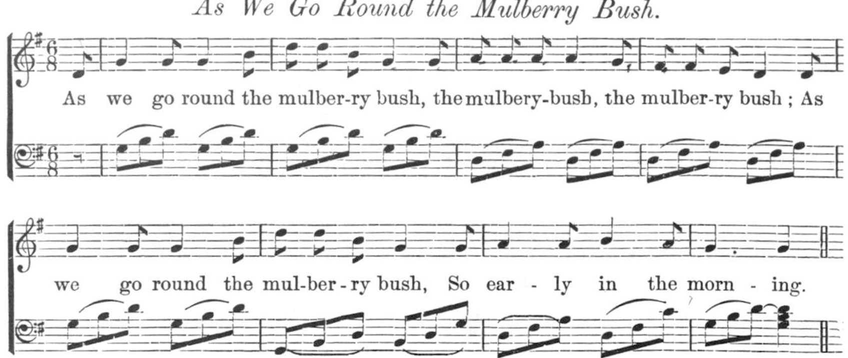

As we go round the mulberry bush,
The mulberry bush, the mulberry bush;
As we go round the mulberry bush,
So early in the morning.

This is the way we wash our clothes,
All of a Monday morning.

This is the way we iron our clothes,
All of a Tuesday morning.

This is the way we scrub our floor,
All of a Wednesday morning.

This is the way we mend our clothes,
All of a Thursday morning.

This is the way we sweep the house,
All of a Friday morning.

This is the way we bake our bread,
All of a Saturday morning.

This is the way we go to church,
All of a Sunday morning.

In Massachusetts the song goes—

> Here we go round the *barberry bush*,
> So early in the morning.

A variation makes the last line—

> All on a frosty morning.

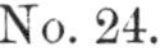

No. 24.

Do, Do, Pity my Case.

> Do, do, pity my case,
> In some lady's garden;
> My clothes to wash when I get home,
> In some lady's garden.
>
> Do, do, pity my case,
> In some lady's garden;
> My clothes to iron when I get home,
> In some lady's garden.

And so on, the performers lamenting the duty which lies upon them of scrubbing their floors, baking their bread, etc. *Louisiana.*

This pretty dance, with its idiomatic English, which comes to us from the extreme South, is obviously not modern. The chorus refers, not to the place of the labor, but to the locality of the dance: it may have been originally *in my lady's garden*. Our informant remembers the game as danced by negro children, their scanty garments flying as the ring spun about the trunk of some large tree; but (though the naive appeal to pity may seem characteristic of Southern indolence) this is evidently no negro song.

No. 25.

When I Was a Shoemaker.

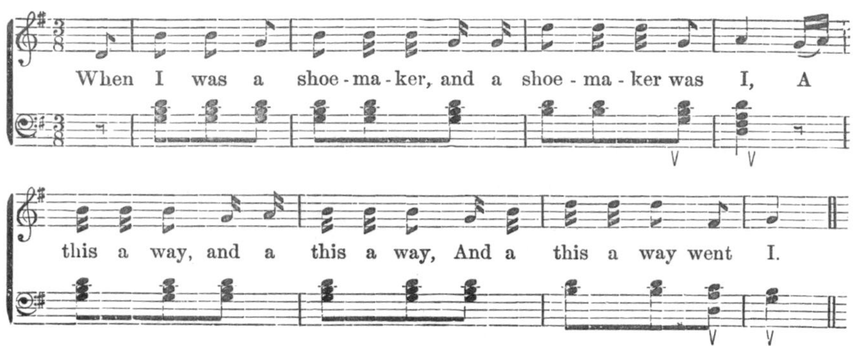

A ROUND.

When I was a shoemaker,
And a shoemaker was I,
This way,* and this way,
And this way went I.

When I was a gentleman,
And a gentleman was I,
This way, and this way,
And this way went I.

When I was a lady,
And a lady was I,
This way, and this way,
And this way went I.

So on, indefinitely. The gentleman places his hands in his waistcoat pockets, and promenades up and down; the lady gathers her skirts haughtily together; the fireman makes a sound in imitation of the horns which firemen formerly blew; the shoemaker and hair-dresser are represented by appropriate motions, etc. *New York streets.*

As with most street-games, further inquiry has shown us that the song is old in America. Not merely the substance (which is identical with our last two numbers), but also the expression, is paralleled in France and Italy, and even on the extreme limits of European Russia.

* Sung "*a this a way.*"

The well-known French name of this game, "The Bridge of Avignon,"* indicates a high antiquity. This bridge, which figures in French nursery-lore as London Bridge does in our own, was built in 1177. Bridges, in the Middle Age, were the most important structures in the land, places of festivity and solemnity, dances, trials, and executions.

No. 26.

Here We Come Gathering Nuts of May.

Two opposite rows of girls. One side advances and sings, the other side replying:

"Here we come gathering nuts of May, [*thrice*]
On a May morning early."

"Whom will you gather for nuts of May,
On a May morning early?"

"We'll gather [naming a girl] for nuts of May,
On a May morning early."

"Whom will you send to fetch her away,
On a May morning early?"

"We'll send [naming a strong girl] to pull her away,
On a May morning early."

The game is continued until all players are brought to one side.

Charlestown, W. Va.

This game is probably a recent importation from England, where it is very well known. It seems likely that the imitative dance really belongs to the season of nut-gathering,† and that the phrase, "Nuts of *May*," and the refrain, have crept in from its later use as a May-game.

* Sur le Pont d'Avignon,
Les messieurs font ça,
Et puis encore ça.

Then come "les dames," "les cordonniers," etc.

In the corresponding Russian game, a single player mimics the walk of old men, priests, or the habits of any trade or person in the company.

† Nous sommes à trois fillettes,
Pour aller cueillir noisettes,
Quand les noisettes sont cueillies,
Nous sommes mises à danser.

No. 27.

Here I Brew, and Here I Bake.

A ring of children clasp hands by clenching fingers; a single child within the circle repeats the rhyme, making appropriate gestures over successive pairs of hands; at the last words he (or she) throws himself (or herself) against what is thought the most penetrable point.

Here I brew and here I bake,
And here I make my wedding-cake,
And here I must break through.

The following is a different version:

Here I bake and here I brew,
And here I lay my wedding-shoe,
And here I must and shall break through.

If the first attempt is not successful, the player within the ring runs to attack some other point. After the ring is broken, the child on his right continues the game. In New York, a violent form of the same sport goes by the name of "Bull in the Ring."

No. 28.

Draw a Bucket of Water.

Four girls cross hands, and pull in rhythmical movement against each other while singing, one pair changing the position of their hands from above to below that of the other pair at the words, "Here we go under," etc.

Draw a bucket of water
For my lady's daughter.
  One in a rush,
  Two in a rush,
Here we go under the mulberry bush.

New York.

In Massachusetts this was a ring game:

Draw a pail of water
For my lady's daughter.
Give her a ring and a silver pin,
And pay for my lady's pop under.

At the last words the girl within the ring endeavors to pass under the hands of one of the couples.

No. 29.

Threading the Needle.

A boy and a girl, standing each on a stool, make an arch of their hands, under which an endless chain passes, until the hands are dropped, and one of the players is enclosed.

The needle's eye
That doth supply
The thread that runs so true;
Ah! many a lass
Have I let pass
Because I wanted you.

Or—

The needle's eye
You can't pass by,
The thread it runs so true;
It has caught many a seemly lass,
And now it has caught you.

Massachusetts.

In the following more complicated form of the game, in use half a century ago, both a boy and a girl were caught by the players who raised their arms:

The needle's eye
None can surpass
But those who travel through;
It hath caught many a smiling lass,
But now it hath caught you.

There's none so sweet
That is dressed so neat;*
I do intend,
Before I end,
To make this couple meet.

* "We considered this a personal compliment. I remember we used to feel very much pleased—children are so sensitive!"—*Informant.*

The pair then kissed, and the game proceeded as in "London Bridge," ending with a tug-of-war.

The name, "Threading the Needle," is still applied, in a district of central France, to a dance in which many hundred persons take part, in which from time to time the pair who form the head of the row raise their arms to allow the line to pass through, coiling and winding like a great serpent.

IV.

HUMOR AND SATIRE.

Andante.
Perrette est bien malade,
En danger de mourir.

Presto.
Son ami la va voire;
Te laira' tu mourir?

Andante.
Non, non, répondit-elle,
Je ne veux pas mourir.

Canadian Song.

No. 30.

Soldier, Soldier, Will You Marry Me?

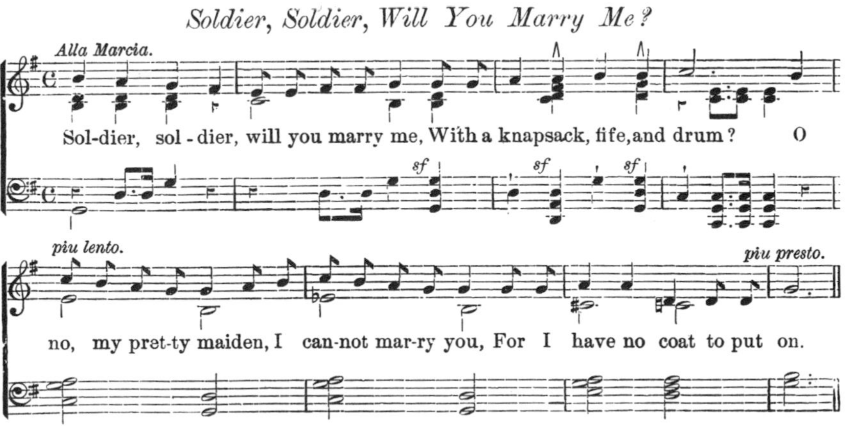

First voice.—"Soldier, soldier, will you marry me,
With a knapsack, fife, and drum?"
"Oh no, my pretty maiden, I cannot marry you,
For I have no coat to put on."

Second voice.—Then away she ran to the tailor's shop,
As fast as legs could run;
And bought him one of the very best,
And the soldier put it on.

The question is then repeated, the soldier pleading his want of shoes gloves, etc., which the confiding fair procures, until at last—

"Soldier, soldier, will you marry me,
With your knapsack, fife, and drum?"
"Oh no, my pretty maiden, I cannot marry you,
For I have—a good wife—at home!"

This piece and the following are more or less familiar as children's songs through the United States. Our version was sung by children of from five to eight years of age, and made a favorite amusement at the afternoon gatherings. When one couple had finished, another pair would begin, and so on for hours at a time. The object was to provide for the soldier the most varied wardrobe possible; while the maiden put the question with spirit, laying her hand on her heart, respecting which the prevailing opinion was that it was under the left arm.

No. 31.

Quaker Courtship.

In this piece, two children (in costume or otherwise) impersonate a Quaker paying his addresses to a young lady of the world.

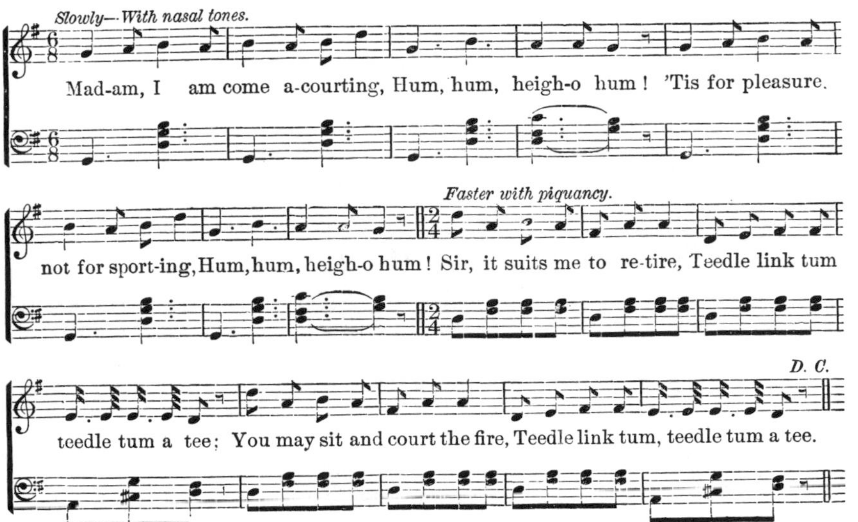

"Madam, I am come a-courting—
Hum, hum, heigho hum!
'Tis for pleasure, not for sporting—
Hum, hum, heigho hum!"

"Sir, it suits me to retire,
Teedle link tum, teedle tum a tee;
You may sit and court the fire,
Teedle link tum, teedle tum a tee."

"Madam, here's a ring worth forty shilling,
Thou may'st have it if thou art willing."

"What care I for rings or money?
I'll have a man who will call me honey."

"Madam, thou art tall and slender;
Madam, I know thy heart is tender."

"Sir, I see you are a flatterer,
And I never loved a Quaker."

"Must I give up my religion?
Must I be a Presbyterian?"

"Cheer up, cheer up, loving brother,
If you can't catch one fish, catch another."

Hartford, Conn.

No. 32.

Lazy Mary.

A mother and daughter in the centre of a ring, the daughter kneeling with closed eyes. Mother advances—

"Lazy Mary, will you get up,
Will you get up, will you get up,
Will you get up to-day?"

"What will you give me for my breakfast,
If I get up, if I get up,
If I get up to-day?"

The reply is, "A slice of bread and a cup of tea," whereon Mary answers, "No, mother, I won't get up," and responds similarly to the call to dinner; but for supper the mother offers "a nice young man with rosy cheeks," which is accepted with the words, "Yes, mother, I will get up," whereon the ring clap their hands. The round is familiar in New York streets. There is a corresponding English song, with a tragic ending.

No. 33.

Whistle, Daughter, Whistle.

"Whistle, daughter, whistle,
And I'll give you a sheep."
[*After an interval.*] "Mother, I'm asleep."

"Whistle, daughter, whistle,
And I'll give you a cow."
[*A faint attempt.*] "Mother, I don't know how."

"Whistle, daughter, whistle,
And I'll give you a man."
[*A loud and clear whistle.*] "Mother, now I can!" *New York.*

The subject of this and the preceding number has furnished endless mirth to popular poetry. The present song is ancient; for it is identical with a German, Flemish, and French round of the fifteenth or sixteenth century, in which a *nun* (or monk) is tempted to *dance* by similar offers. The spirit of the latter piece seems to be rather light-hearted ridicule than puritanic satire, and the allusion does not show that the piece is subsequent to the Reformation.

No. 34.

There were Three Jolly Welshmen.

There were three jolly Welshmen,
And I have heard them say,
That they would go a-hunting
Upon St. David's day—
Look—a—there—now!

They hunted, they hunted,
And nothing could they find,
But a woman in the road,
And her they left behind—
Look—a—there—now!

One said it was a woman,
The other said nay;
One said it was an angel
With the wings blowed away—
Look—a—there—now!

We have obtained only three verses of the song, which was a favorite with little children as they sat on the door-step of a summer's evening. Another version of the ancient jest comes to us as sung by college students:

(*Slow and mournful, in C minor.*)

And so they went along,
To see what they could see,
And soon they saw a frog
A-sitting under a tree.
(*Recit.*) So—they—did.

7

One said it was a frog,
But the other said nay—
One said it was a canary-bird
With the feathers blown away.
(*Recit.*) So—it—was.

And so they went along,
To see what they could see,
And soon they saw a barn
A-standing by a tree.

One said it was a barn,
But the other said nay,
One said it was a meeting-house
With the steeple blown away.

And so they went along,
To see what they could see,
And soon they saw an owl,
A-sitting on a tree.

One said it was an owl,
But the other said nay,
One said it was the Evil One!
And they all ran away.

No. 35.

A Hallowe'en Rhyme.

A ROUND.

Oh, dear doctor, don't you cry!
Your true love will come by-and-by.

If she comes all dressed in green,
That's a sign she's to be seen.

If she comes all dressed in white,
That's a sign she'll cry all night.

If she comes all dressed in gray,
That's a sign that she's away.

If she comes all dressed in blue,
That's a sign she'll marry you.

New York.

A variation:

Oh, Miss Betsy, don't you cry!
For your true love will come *by'm-bye;*
When he comes he'll dress in blue—
Then he'll bring you something new.

Massachusetts.

These corrupt rhymes are only interesting as illustrating the permanence of Hallowe'en customs, even in America. The Scotch rhyme of Chambers goes—

This knot, this knot, this knot I knit,
To see the thing I ne'er saw yet—
To see my love in his array,
And what he walks in every day;
And what his occupation be,
This night I in my sleep may see.
And if my love be clad in green,
His love for me is well seen;
And if my love be clad in gray,
His love for me is far away;
But if my love be clad in blue,
His love for me is very true.

After repeating these words, the girl puts her knotted garter beneath her pillow, and sleeps on it, when her future husband will appear to her in a dream.

No. 36.

The Doctor's Prescription.

A ROUND.

Oh, dear doctor, can you tell,
What will make poor —— well?
She is sick and like to die,
And that will make poor —— cry.

A kiss was the prescription.

We insert this silly little round, chiefly because, according to Madame Celnart, a French equivalent was in favor, not with infants, but ladies and gentlemen in polite society, only half a century since. Our authority says: "The master or the mistress of this round is called *doctor*. This doctor takes the arm of the person seated on his right, regards him or her with an eye of compassion, feels his pulse, and then gives his order, which everybody repeats, singing, 'Give me your arm that I may cure you, for you seem to me to look ill.'* Then, designating by a glance some person of the other sex, he says, 'Embrace monsieur (or madame) to cure you; it is an excellent remedy.' All the persons in the ring are submitted to this treatment, which the physician knows how to render piquant by the choice of the panacea which he recommends to his patient; when everybody is cured, the doctor passes over his science and dignity to the last person who has tested the efficacy of his prescription, and in his turn falls sick, to make trial of the pleasing remedy."

The general theme of our vulgarized round is more agreeably expressed in the quaint and ancient Canadian song which we have cited as the motto of the present chapter.

No. 37.

Old Grimes.

Old Grimes is dead and in his grave laid,
In his grave, in his grave, in his grave laid—
O aye O!

There grew up an apple-tree over his head—
The apples were ripe and ready to fall—
Then came an old woman a-picking them up—
Old Grimes got up and gave her a kick—
And made her go hobbledy, hobbledy, hip—
The bridles and saddles they hang on the shelf—
And if you want any more you must sing it yourself—
O aye O!

New York streets.

* Donne-moi ton bras que je te guérisse,
Car tu m'as l'air malade,
Loula,
Car tu m'as l'air malade!

A friend informs us that he has often heard the words of this unintelligible round sung as a "shanty," or song used by sailors at their work, with the chorus, *yeo heave-ho!* In Cambridge, Mass., the name of the deceased was "Old Cromwell." We have also a version of half a century since, beginning,

> Jemmy and Nancy went up to Whitehall,
> Jemmy fell sick among them all.

No. 38.

The Baptist Game.

Such is the peculiar title of this amusement in Virginia, where it is said to be enjoyed by pious people who will not dance. There is a row of couples, with an odd player at the head. At the sudden close of the song occurs a grand rush and change of partners.

Come, all ye young men, in your evil ways,
And sow your wild oats in your youthful days;
You shall be happy,
You shall be happy,
When you grow old.

The night is far spent, and the day's coming on,
So give us your arm, and we'll jog along,
You shall be happy,
You shall be happy,
When you grow old.

Albemarle Co., Va.

This game, with verbal identity (save the title), was a few years since an amusement of well-bred girls in New York city. It has also been familiar in Massachusetts, with the exception of one line—

Come all ye *old maids* in your sinful ways!

No. 39.

Trials, Troubles, and Tribulations.

All participating are blindfolded, and, joining hands, march forward, singing—

Here we go through the Jewish nation,
Trials, troubles, and tribulation.

The fun consists in bringing up against a door, or in causing a general downfall by tripping over some obstacle. *New York.*

No. 40.

Happy is the Miller.

An odd number of players, of whom the one not paired stands in the centre of the ring. The others march in couples, each consisting of a girl and a boy, till the sudden end of the song, when each boy grasps the girl in front of him.

Happy is the miller, who lives by himself,
All the bread and cheese he piles upon the shelf,
One hand in the hopper, and the other in the bag,
The wheel turns around, and he cries out, Grab!

Western New York.

Another version:

Happy is the miller that lives in the mill;
While the mill goes round, he works with a will;
One hand in the hopper, and one in the bag,
The mill goes around, and he cries out, Grab!

Cincinnati.

The miller, whose pay used to be taken in a proportion of corn ground, was a common object of popular satire.

In Germany the mill-wheel, as it slowly revolves, is said to exclaim—

There is—a thief—in the mill!

Then, moving more quickly—

Who is he? who is he? who is he?

And at last answers very fast, and without pausing—

The miller! the miller! the miller!

"Round and Round, the Mill Goes Round," is mentioned as an English dance at the end of the seventeenth century. A song of "The Happy Miller" is printed in "Pills to Purge Melancholy" (1707), of which the first verse is—

How happy is the mortal that lives by his mill!
That depends on his own, not on Fortune's wheel;
By the sleight of his hand, and the strength of his back,
How merrily his mill goes, clack, clack, clack!

This song was doubtless founded on the popular game; but the modern children's sport has preserved the idea, if not the elegance, of the old dance better than the printed words of a hundred and seventy years since. A variation of the same game is still familiar in Canada and Sweden.*

No. 41.

The Miller of Gosport.

That the prejudice against the honesty of the miller was not confined to the Old World will appear from the following ballad:

There was an old miller in Gosport did dwell:
He had three sons whom he loved full well;
He called them to him, one—by—one,
Saying, "My—life—is—al—most—done!"†

He called to him his eldest son,
Saying, "My life is almost done,

* The Canadian words are, "J'entends le moulin, tique, tique, tique." Probably the old English dance ended, "How merrily the mill goes, clack, clack, clack!" after which, as now in Canada, partners were changed, and the odd player in the centre had an opportunity to secure a place, or to find a mate.

† The pauses lengthen as the patient grows weaker.

And if I to you the mill shall make,
Pray, say what toll you mean to take?"

"Father," says he, "my name is Dick,
And aout of each bushel I'll take one peck—
Of every bushel—that—I—grind,
I'll take one peck to ease my mind."

"Thou foolish son," the old man said,
"Thou hasn't but one half larnt thy trade!
The mill to you I'll never give,
For by such toll no man can thrive."

He called to him his second son,
Saying, "My life is almost done,
And if I to you the mill shall make,
Pray, say what toll you mean to take?"

"Father," says he, "my name is Ralph,
And aout of each bushel I'll take one half—
Of every bushel that I grind,
I'll take one half to ease my mind."

"Thou foolish son," the old man said,
"Thou hasn't but one half larnt thy trade;
The mill to you I'll never give,
For by such toll no man can thrive."

He called to him his youngest son,
Saying, "My life is almost done;
And if I to you the mill shall make,
Pray, say what toll you mean to take?"

"Father," says he, "I *am* your boy,
And in taking of toll shall be all my joy;
That an honest living I ne'er may lack,
I'll take the whole, and steal the sack."

"Thou *art* my son," the old man said;
"Thou'st larnt thy good—old—fayther's trade;
The mill to you I do—betide"—
And—so—he—closed—his eyes—and—died.

Another version finds its way to us from the West, and ends with an uncomplimentary opinion as to the habitation of the miller in the other world.

V.

FLOWER ORACLES, ETC.

A spire of grass hath made me gay;
It saith, I shall find mercy mild.
I measured in the selfsame way
I have seen practised by a child.
Come look and listen if she really does:
She does, does not, she does, does not, she does.
Each time I try, the end so augureth.
That comforts me—'tis right that we have faith.

Walther von der Vogelweide [A.D. 1170–1230].

No. 42.

Flower Oracles.

PLUCKING one by one the petals of the ox-eye daisy (*Leucanthemum vulgare*), children ask:

Rich man, poor man, beggar-man, thief,
Doctor, lawyer, Indian chief.*

Girls then take a second flower, and, getting some one else to name it, proceed, in order to determine where they are to live:

Big house, little house, pigsty, barn.

And in like manner use a third to discover in what dress they are to be married:

Silk, satin, calico, rags.

Finally, they consult a fourth, to find out what the bridal equipage is to be:

Coach, wagon, wheelbarrow, chaise.

* Played also on buttons. A friend informs us that, as a child, he had his buttons altered, in order that the oracle might return an agreeable response.

Another version gives for the second line of the first formula:

Doctor, lawyer, merchant, chief.

In Switzerland, girls in like manner say, as they pick off the flower-leaves of the common daisy (*Bellis perennis*):

Be single, marry, or go into the cloister?

And boys—

Rich, poor, moderate?

The marguerite (*Doronicum bellidiastrum*) is asked in the same country:

Heaven, hell, purgatory, paradise?

And in Styria is called "Love's Measure," because it determines the return of affection according to the well-known formula, "He loves me, he loves me not," for which a French equivalent is:

Je t'aime, un peu, beaucoup,
Tendrement, pas du tout.

But in Switzerland again the questions for the marguerite exactly match ours:

Nobleman, beggar-man, farmer, soldier, student,
Emperor, king, gentleman.

The verse is similar in Italy. It is curious to see the precise correspondence of English and Continental forms.

Mediæval writers do not mention this use of flower-petals, but frequently allude to the custom of drawing spires of grass, to secure the longer (or shorter, as might be agreed). Thus lads might draw grasses, for the purpose of deciding to which of the two a maiden might belong as a partner. This was so usual a way of deciding a controversy that it was even recognized in law, where the parties to a suit drew straws from a thatch or sheaf. Children still resort to a like arbitrament, where one holds the straws in the hand, and the other draws, the shorter straw winning. To our surprise, we find that girls in Massachusetts still keep up the mediæval usage; they draw stalks of grass in the field, and match them, to decide who shall begin a game—be "it." *

* In Cambridge, Mass.

We have seen that the formula "Loves me, loves me not," was used in the Middle Age with grasses. In Italy the oracle is consulted by means of the branch of a tree. A twig is taken having alternate leaves, and they are detached one by one, the consulter always turning the head as the words of the oracle are spoken. The formulas for this purpose closely resemble our own: thus, "This year, another year, soon, never," which is exactly identical with the English "This year, next year, some time, never;" or, "He loves me, longs for me, desires me, wishes me well, wishes me ill, does not care;" or, as in the Swiss form given, "Paradise, Purgatory, *Caldron*" (that is, Inferno).

No. 43.

Use of Flowers in Games.

Flowers are gathered and loved by children as they have always been, and are used by them in all sorts of imaginative exercises of their own invention, as, for instance, by girls in their imitative housekeeping; but there is singularly little employment of them in any definite games. Formerly it was otherwise; but the deep sympathy which blooming youth once felt and expressed for the bloom of the year seems to have almost disappeared.

In the Middle Age, as in classic antiquity, flowers were much in use for dances. Great attention was paid to the significance of particular blooms. "What flowers will you give me for a garland? What flowers are proper for adornment?" are mentioned as names of sports. It was a practice for the lover to approach his mistress with a flower or fruit which he offered for her acceptance. If the girl accepted the gift, the youth led her out, and the dance began. Another ancient practice was to throw to a girl some bloom, at the same time pronouncing a couplet which rhymed with the name of the flower. The ball, too, with which youths and maids played, was sometimes made of flowers.

Almost the only relic of ancient usage of this sort, with us, is the employment little girls make of dandelions, with which (in some parts of the country) they make long garlands, cutting off the heads and stringing them together.

This use of the dandelion is very old, from which it derives one of its many German names, the *chain-flower* or *ring-flower*. On account of its early bloom and golden hue it is especially the flower of spring, and seems to have had a religious and symbolic meaning. In Switzerland these garlands are used in the dance, the children holding a long wreath of the flowers so as to form a circle within the ring; and whoever breaks the chain pays forfeit. The plant is said to be of healing virtue, gives happiness to the lover, and, if plucked on particular days, will heal troubles of the eye. It has these qualities on account of its brightness, which causes it to be associated with the victorious power of light.

There are other ways of using this flower. A dandelion in seed is held to the lips; if the seeds can all be blown off in three attempts, it is a sign of successful love, of marriage within the year; or, with little girls, that "my mother wants me."

Little girls also split the stalks of the flower, and, dipping them in cold water, produce "curls," with which they adorn themselves. This usage, too, is German.

We may speak of the trifling lore of one or two other flowers. A buttercup is held against one child's chin by another, and a bright reflection is supposed (prosaically enough) to indicate a fondness for butter!

It was formerly said in New England that the heart's-ease (*Viola tricolor*) represented a "step-mother sitting on two chairs." The petals being turned up, the step-mother is seen to have two chairs, her children one each, and her step-children only one between them.

That this flower represents an unkind step-mother is stated in a Low-German rhyme of the fifteenth century; and step-mother is also an English name for the heart's-ease. There is another reason for the title besides that we have given. In Switzerland the flower is considered a type of malice, because the older the flower is the more yellow and "jealous" it becomes. Thus we have another striking example of the original similarity of English and German usage.

Boys in the spring are fond of blowing on the fresh blades of grass, with which they can make a loud but harsh trumpeting. This practice, in Germany, is mentioned at the beginning of the thirteenth century.

It is the custom still for boys to make whistles in the spring from the loosened bark of the willow; but they do not guess that this was originally a superstitious rite, the pipe cut from a tree which grows in the water being supposed to have the power of causing rain. The Swiss children, though unconsciously, still invoke the water-spirit as they separate the bark from the wood:

Franz, Franz,
Lend me your pipe.

No. 44.

Counting Apple-seeds.

The following rhyme, used in New England at the beginning of the present century, remains unchanged in a single word, except the omission of the last three lines.

Apples formerly were an essential part of every entertainment in the country; in the winter season, a dish of such always stood on the side-board. As the hours went by, a foaming dish of eggnog would be brought in, always with a red-hot poker inserted, for the purpose of keeping up the proper temperature. It was then that the apple, having been properly named, with a fillip of the finger was divided, to decide the fate of the person concerned according to its number of seeds.

One, I love,
Two, I love,
Three, I love, I say,
Four, I love with all my heart,
And five, I cast away;
Six, he loves,
Seven, she loves,
Eight, they both love;
Nine, he comes,
Ten, he tarries,
Eleven, he courts,
Twelve, he marries;
Thirteen wishes,
Fourteen kisses,
All the rest little witches.

No. 45.

Rose in the Garden.

We insert here, on account of the allusions to nature which they contain, several pieces which might also have found a place elsewhere in our collection; the present, for instance, being eminently a "love-game."

A single player stands in the centre of the ring, which circles and sings:

There's a rose in the garden for you, fair man,
There's a rose in the garden for you, fair maid;
There's a rose in the garden, pluck it if you can,
Be sure you don't choose a false-hearted one.

The youth or girl in the centre chooses a partner, and the ring sings:

It's a bargain, it's a bargain, for you, fair man,
It's a bargain, it's a bargain, for you, fair maid.

Now follows a fragment of romance, which in our version is unhappily corrupt:

You promised to marry me six months ago,
I hold you to your bargain, *you old rogue you.*"

After a kiss, the first player takes his or her place in the ring, and the partner selected is left to continue the game.

Deerfield, Mass. (about 1810).

To the same game, perhaps, belongs the following fragment:

Here stands a red rose in the ring—
Promised to marry a long time ago.

The comparison of a youth or maid to a rose is not uncommon in dances. We have a pretty French example in the Canadian round cited below;* and another English instance in our No. 62.

* Dans ma main droite je tiens rosier,
Qui fleurira, qui fleurira,
Qui fleurira au mois de Mai.
Entrez en danse, joli rosier,
Et embrassez qui vous plaira.—*Canadian Round.*

No. 46.

There was a Tree Stood in the Ground.

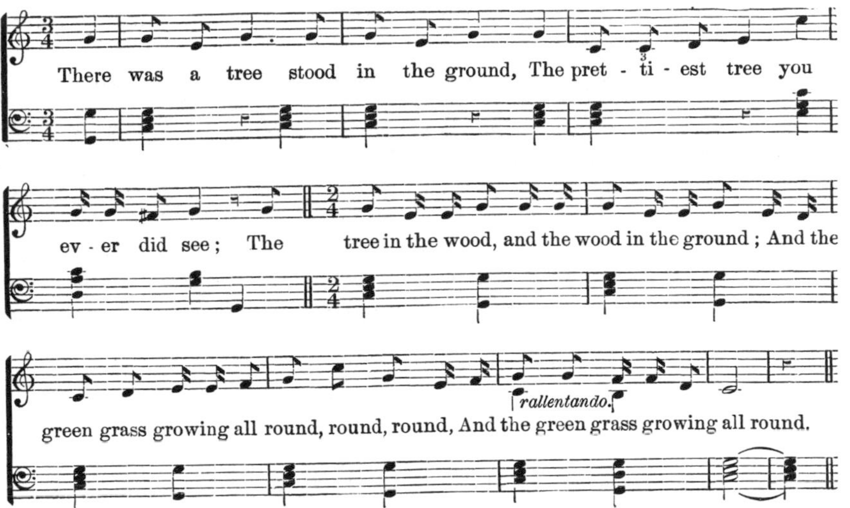

There was a tree stood in the ground,
The prettiest tree you ever did see;
The tree in the wood, and the wood in the ground;
And the green grass growing all round, round, round,
And the green grass growing all round.

And on this tree there was a limb,
The prettiest limb you ever did see;
The limb on the tree, and the tree in the wood,
The tree in the wood, and the wood in the ground,
And the green grass growing all round, round, round,
And the green grass growing all round.

And on this limb there was a bough,
The prettiest bough you ever did see;
The bough on the limb, and the limb on the tree, etc.

And on this bough there was a twig,
The prettiest twig you ever did see;
The twig on the bough, and the bough on the limb, etc.

And on this twig there was a nest,
The prettiest nest you ever did see;
The nest on the twig, and the twig on the bough, etc.

And in this nest there were some eggs,*
The prettiest eggs you ever did see;
The eggs in the nest, and the nest on the twig, etc.

And in the eggs there was a bird,
The prettiest bird you ever did see;
The bird in the eggs, and the eggs in the nest, etc.

And on the bird there was a wing,
The prettiest wing you ever did see;
The wing on the bird, and the bird in the eggs, etc.

And on the wing there was a feather,
The prettiest feather you ever did see;
The feather on the wing, and the wing on the bird, etc.

And on the feather there was some down,
The prettiest down you ever did see;
The down on the feather, and the feather on the wing,
The feather on the wing, and the wing on the bird,
The wing on the bird, and the bird in the eggs,
The bird in the eggs, and the eggs in the nest,
The eggs in the nest, and the nest on the twig,
The nest on the twig, and the twig on the bough,
The twig on the bough, and the bough on the limb,
The bough on the limb, and the limb on the tree,
The limb on the tree, and the tree in the wood,
The tree in the wood, and the wood in the ground,
And the green grass growing all round, round, round,
And the green grass growing all round.

Savannah, Georgia.

This song is not known in the North, and it is equally unrecorded in English nursery-lore, but is very familiar in France (as well as Germany, Denmark, etc.). We are inclined to look on it as an adaptation from

* So recited.

the French, made by the children of *émigrés*, like the curious game which makes our next number.*

No. 47.

Green!

In parts of Georgia and South Carolina, as soon as a group of girls are fairly out of the house for a morning's play, one suddenly points the finger at a companion with the exclamation, "Green!" The child so accosted must then produce some fragment of verdure, the leaf of a tree, a blade of grass, etc., from the apparel, or else pay forfeit to the first after the manner of "philopœna." It is rarely, therefore, that a child will go abroad without a bit of "green," the practice almost amounting to a superstition. The object of each is to make the rest believe that the required piece of verdure has been forgotten, and yet to keep it at hand. Sometimes it is drawn from the shoe, or carried in the brooch, or in the garter. Nurses find in the pockets, or in the lining of garments, all man-

* A French version:

Au dedans Paris,
Vous ne savez ce qu'il y a?

Il y a-t-un bois,
C'est le plus beau bois
Parmi tous les bois;
Le bois est dans Paris.
Ah! le joli bois,
Madame;
Ah! le joli bois!

* * * * *

Il y a-t-une plume,
C'est la plus belle plume
De toutes les plumes;
La plume est sur l'oiseau,
L'oiseau est dans l'œuf,
L'œuf est dans le nid,
Le nid est sur la feuille,
La feuille est sur la branche,
L'arbre est dans le bois.
Ah! le joli bois,
Madame;
Ah! le joli bois!

ner of fragments which have served this purpose. This curious practice is not known elsewhere in America; but it is mentioned by Rabelais, under the name by which it is still played in parts of Central France, "Je vous prends sans vert"—"I catch you without green." The game, however, is not merely a children's sport, and is played differently from our description. At Châtillon-sur-Inde it is during Lent, and only after the singing of the *Angelus*, that "green" is played. If any lady accost you and shows you her bough, you must immediately exhibit yours. If you have not such a one, or if your green is of a shade less rich than your adversary's, you lose a point; in case of doubt, the matter is referred to an umpire. The game was much in vogue from the thirteenth to the fourteenth century, and is described as a May-game. "During the first days of May, every one took care to carry on his person a little green bough, and those who were not so provided were liable to hear themselves addressed, *I catch you without green*, and to receive, at the same instant, a pail of water on the head. This amusement, however, was in use only among the members of certain societies, who took the name of *Sans-vert*. Those who belonged to these had a right to visit each other at any hour of the day, and administer the bath whenever they found each other unprovided. In addition, the members so surprised were condemned to a pecuniary fine, and the income of these fines was devoted to merry repasts which, at certain seasons of the year, united all the comrades of the *Sans-vert*." *

The practice has given to the French language a proverb: *to take any one without green*, to take him unawares.

Our child's game was doubtless imported by Huguenot immigrants, who established themselves in the states referred to two centuries since, where they long preserved their language and customs, and from whom many well-known families are descended.

* The custom has been supposed to be derived from the ancient Roman usage of gathering *green* on the calends of May, with which to decorate the house.

VI.

BIRD AND BEAST.

"My brother, the hare, . . . my sisters, the doves." . . .
St. Francis of Assisi.

No. 48.

My Household.

The names of animals being distributed among children, one, in the centre of the ring, sings the words; at the proper point the child who represents the animal must imitate its cry; and as at each verse the animals who have already figured join in, the game becomes rather noisy.

I had a little rooster, and my rooster pleased me,
I fed my rooster beneath that tree;
My rooster went—Cookery-cooery!
Other folks feed their rooster, I feed my rooster too.

I had a little lamb, and my lamb pleased me,
I fed my lamb beneath that tree;
My lamb went—Ma—a—a!
Other folks feed their lamb, I feed my lamb too.

And so on with the names of other beasts. *Georgia.*

In another version, it is under the "green bay-tree" (*Magnolia glauca*), that the animals are stabled.

This is another of the games which have been widely distributed through Europe, and date back to a remote past. At present, with us it is a child's jest, the noisy imitation of animal cries; but, as in all such cases, sense preceded sound. Comparing German versions, we see that our game is properly a song, the idea of which consists in the enumeration by significant and comical names of the members and possessions of a family. "When I was a poor woman, I went over the Rhine: my goose was called

Wag-tail, my maid *So he said*, my pig *Lard-pot*, my flea *Hop-i'-straw*," etc. A more courtly version gives us a pleasing pilgrim's song: "Whence come you?—From sunset. Whither will you?—To sunrise. To what country?—Home. Where is it?—A hundred miles away. What is your name?—The world names me *Leap a-field*, my sword is *Honor worth*, my wife *Pastime*, her maid *Lie-a-bed*, my child *Rush-about*," etc.

Thus we see the ancient earnestness appearing behind the modern mirth. It is likely that the origin of the song would take us back to those lists of mythical titles which were regarded as conveying real knowledge of the relations of things, at a time when a large part of learning consisted in the knowledge of the significant names which were given to objects.

No. 49.

Frog-pond.

A party of children, who represent frogs by a hopping motion. At the word "kough," they imitate the croaking of the frog.

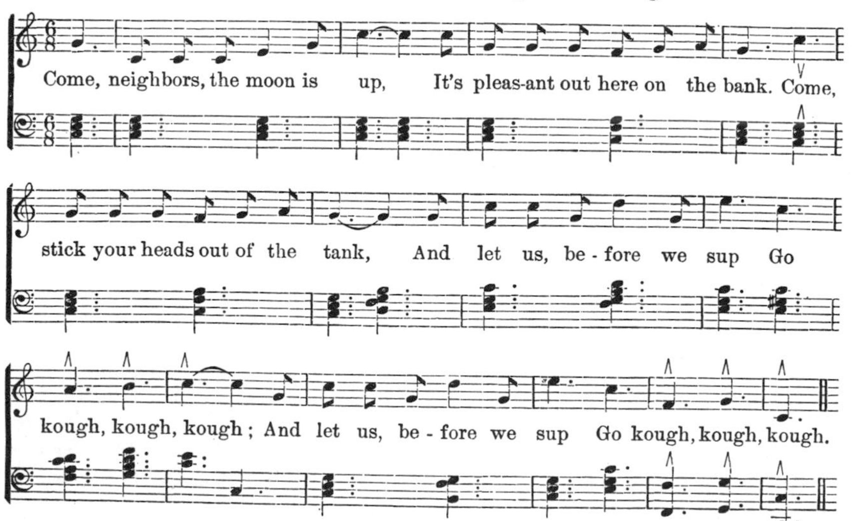

Come, neighbors, the moon is up,
It's pleasant out here on the bank.
Come, stick your heads out of the tank,

And let us, before we sup,
  Go kough, kough, kough.
And let us, before we sup,
  Go kough, kough, kough.

Enter child in character of duck—

Hush, yonder is the waddling duck,
He's coming, I don't mean to stay.
We'd better by half hop our way,
If we don't he will gobble us up,
  With a kough, kough, kough.
If we don't he will gobble us up,
  With a kough, kough, kough.

Every frog hops to his separate den, while pursued by the duck, the game after the duck's advent being extremely animated. *Georgia.*

No. 50.

Bloody Tom.

Within the ring is the shepherd; the wolf approaches from without. A dialogue ensues:

"Who comes here?"
"Bloody Tom."
"What do you want?"
"My sheep."
"Take the worst, and leave the best,
And never come back to trouble the rest."

Salem, Mass.

A New Hampshire version makes the game represent a fox, who carries off chickens, thus:

"Who comes here this dark night?"
"Who but bloody Tom!—Which you druther be, picked or scalded?"

The Esthonian Fins have a characteristic children's game, based on the same idea, which may be quoted, to show how much imagination and spirit enter into the sports of a simple people. A watchman on duty at the sheepfold announces his office in a soliloquy:

Thus I guard my mother's lambkins,
Guard the flocks of my good mother,
Here before God's holy temple,
Here behind Maria's cloister,
Near the halls of our Creator.
At the house the mother, knitting,
Shapes the stockings of blue woollen,
Woollen stockings seamed with scarlet,
Jackets of the snow-white worsted.
I build hedges, stakes I sharpen,
Mould the brazen gratings strongly,
That the thieves come in and steal not,
Take not from the flock its sheep-dog,
Nor the wolf steal in and plunder,
Seize my mother's tender lambkins,
Rob the young lambs of my father.

A girl entices away the shepherd, while a boy as wolf carries off part of the herd, and another as dog barks. The mother of the family hastens up, beats the traitor, and the herdsmen go with staves to seek the lost lamb. The garland it wore is found and identified. With shouts of, "Lamb, lamb," it is found at last, caressed, and its bruises examined.

No. 51.

Blue-birds and Yellow-birds.

A ring of girls with their hands clasped and lifted. A girl, called (according to the color of her dress) blue-bird, black-bird, yellow-bird, etc., enters, and passes into the ring under an arch formed by a pair of lifted hands, singing to any suitable tune:

Here comes a blue-bird through the window,
Here comes a blue-bird through the window,
Here comes a blue-bird through the window,
High diddle dum day!

She seizes a child, and waltzes off with her, singing:

Take a little dance and a hop-i'-the-corner,*
Take a little dance and a hop-i'-the-corner,
Take a little dance and a hop-i'-the-corner,
High diddle dum day!

After the dance the chosen partner leads, named, as before, according to the color of her costume. The child, as she enters, must imitate by her raised arms the flight of a bird, making a very pretty dance.

Cincinnati.

No. 52.

Ducks Fly.

A girl, speaking the words "Ducks fly," raises her hand to imitate the flight of the bird; so on with robins, eagles, etc., while all the rest must imitate her example; but she finally says "Cats fly," or some similar expression, when any child who is incautious enough to raise the hand (or thumb) must pay forfeit. *New York.*

Trifling as the catch is, it has been popular in Europe. In some countries, instead of birds who fly, the question is of beasts who have or do not have horns.

* Pronounced *hop-sie-corner.*

VII.

HUMAN LIFE.

Lilies are white, rosemary's green;
When you are king, I will be queen.

Roses are red, lavender's blue;
If you will have me, I will have you.
Gammer Gurton's Garland.

No. 53.

King and Queen.

This game is now a mere jest. A row of chairs is so arranged as to leave a vacant space, which is concealed by shawls or other coverings, and represents a throne. The courtiers having taken their places, the newly elected monarch is ceremoniously seated by the side of his consort, and the fun consists in witnessing his downfall.

By Strutt's description, it appears that in the beginning of the century this was in use as a species of "hazing" in English girls' schools:

"In some great boarding-schools for the fair sex it is customary, upon the introduction of a novice, for the scholars to receive her with much pretended solemnity, and decorate a throne in which she is to be installed, in order to hear a set speech, addressed to her by one of the young ladies in the name of the rest. The throne is wide enough for three persons to sit conveniently, and is made with two stools, having a tub nearly filled with water between them, and the whole is covered with a counterpane or blanket, ornamented with ribands and other trifling fineries, and drawn very tightly over the two stools, upon each of which a lady is seated to keep the blanket from giving way when the new scholar takes her place; and these are called her maids of honor. The speech consists of high-flown compliments calculated to flatter the vanity of the stranger; and as soon as it is concluded, the maids of honor rising suddenly together, the counterpane of course gives way, and poor miss is unexpectedly immerged in the water."

In Austria the same game is called "conferring knighthood." All present are dressed as knights, in paper helmets, great mustachios, sticks for lances, wooden swords, etc. Two, who represent the oldest knights, are seated on the two stools, between which is a vacant space, while the rest form a half-circle about the *Grand Master*, who wears a mask and wig, and holds a great roll of paper. Meanwhile the candidate, in a separate room, is prepared by two knights for the ceremony; these instruct him in his behavior, until the embassy arrives to lead him before the Grand Master. The latter delivers a solemn address, and from the document in his hands reads the rule of the order—silence, courage, truth, etc. Then follows the vow, the delivery of the knightly costume, and the solemn bestowal of the stroke which dubs the victim a knight. He is finally invited to take his seat in the circle, with the result described in our own jest.

The name, "King and Queen," recalls a game as old as history, that of electing a king, who proceeded to confer offices of state, and assign duties. Herodotus tells us how the child Cyrus showed his royal birth by the severity with which he punished his disobedient subjects. In Switzerland, the children still choose, by "counting out," a king and an executioner. The king proceeds to impose tasks. Geiler of Kaisersberg, in a sermon, A.D. 1507, gives the formula then in use in the game: "Sir king, I wish to serve you." "And what is your service?" "What you command me, I would execute." "I bid you do an honor to the king." For this game, as still played in Switzerland, a queen is also chosen; after a time, the king exclaims, "I make a journey," when the whole company, in couples, follow him through the chambers of the house or streets of the town on his royal progress. The old English game of "Questions and Commands" seems to have been the same. A writer in the *Gentlemen's Magazine*, February, 1738, gives its formula: "King I am," says one boy; another answers, "I am your man." Then his majesty demands what service will he do him; to which the obsequious courtier replies, "The best, and worst, and all I can."

No. 54.

Follow Your Leader.

In this game, the leader having been chosen by "speaking first," or "counting out," the rest must do whatever he does. It is usually played out-of-doors, and the children "follow their leader" in a row, across roads, fences, and ditches, jumping from heights, and creeping under barriers.* We are told that the game is played in a peculiarly reckless fashion in the South, where the leader will sometimes go under a horse's legs or between the wheels of a wagon, whereupon the driver, knowing what to expect, will stop for the rest.

No doubt this sport, now a mere exhibition of daring, has an ancient origin and history. Perhaps it was a development of the *king game*, already referred to.

The technical word for challenge among children in America is "stump." One boy "stumps" another to do a thing. Whence derived?

No. 55.

Truth.

The game of "Truth," as played in Massachusetts, is described by Miss Alcott in her "Little Women," chapter xii. The players are there said to pile up their hands, choose a number, and draw out in turn, and the person who draws his or her hand from the pile at the number selected has to answer truly any questions put by the rest.

We have heard of a party of young people who met regularly to play this game, but have been assured that it proved prolific of quarrels.

No. 56.

Initiation.

We have seen that the imitation of the ceremony of knighthood is still a form of childish amusement in Europe. Here follows a jesting New England formula for such a purpose, though not a game of children, but belonging to an older age:

* A friend recollects how he "followed his leader" over the roofs of houses in Boston.

"You must promise to obey three rules: first, never to do to-day what you can put off till to-morrow; secondly, never to eat brown bread when you can get white; thirdly, never to kiss the maid when you can kiss the mistress, unless the maid is prettier than the mistress."

These vows having been taken, it is then said, "Now I dub you knight of the whistle." Meantime a whistle having been attached to the back of the candidate, the fun consists in his attempts to discover the person who blew it.

No. 57.

Judge and Jury.

A child is chosen to be judge, two others for jurors (or, to speak with our little informant, *juries*), who sit at his right and left hand.

Each child must ask the permission of the judge before taking any step. A platter is brought in, and a child, rising, asks the judge, "May I go into the middle of the room?" "May I turn the platter?" "On which side shall it fall?"

If the platter falls on the wrong side, forfeit must be paid.

Cambridge, Mass.

The nursery, we see, does not understand republicanism. The fairy tale has never got beyond the period in which the monarch orders the wicked witch to immediate execution.

In the ancient world, however, where the courts were a place of resort, and law was not a specialized profession, the case was different. Maximus of Tyre tells us that the children had their laws and tribunals; condemnation extended to the forfeiture of toys. Cato the Younger, according to Plutarch, had his detestation of tyranny first awakened by the punishment inflicted on a playmate by such a tribunal. One of the younger boys had been sentenced to imprisonment; the doom was duly carried into effect, but Cato, moved by his cries, rescued him.

In a German game there is a king, a judge, an executioner, an accuser, and a thief. The parts are assigned by drawing lots, but the accuser does not know the name of the thief, and, if he makes an error, has to undergo the penalty in his stead. The judge finally addresses the king, inquiring if his majesty approves of his decision; and the king replies, "Yes, your sentence entitles you to my favor;" or, "No, your sentence entitles you to so many blows." Thus we see how modern child's play respects the dignity of the king as the fountain of law.

In a Swiss sport the thief flies, and is chased over stock and stone until caught, when he is made to kneel down, his cap pushed over his brows, and his head immediately struck off with the edge of a board. So is preserved the memory of the severity of ancient criminal law.

No. 58.

Three Jolly Sailors.

Here comes a set of jolly sailor-boys,
  Who lately came on shore;
They spend their time in drinking of the wine,
  As they have done before.
As we go round, and around and around,
  As we go round once more.

New York streets.

At the second verse, the little girls by whom this round is danced turn so as to follow each other in an endless chain, each grasping the skirts of the child in front, while they move faster and faster to the lively tune.

Some of our readers may think this song not a very creditable specimen of modern invention; but it is no doubt a relic of antiquity. A similar round, given in "Deuteromelia," 1609 (as cited by Chappell), begins:

We be three poor mariners, newly come from the seas;
We spend our lives in jeopardy, while others live at ease.

The children of the poorer class, therefore, who still keep up in the streets of our cities the present ring-dance, are only maintaining the customs which belonged to courtiers and noble ladies in the time of Shakespeare.

No. 59.

Marching to Quebec.

This piece of doggerel may be of revolutionary origin, as it can be traced to near the beginning of the present century. It is unusual for political or military events to be alluded to in children's games.

As we were marching to Quebec,
  The drums were loudly beating;
The Americans have won the day,
  The British are retreating.
    March! march! march! march!

So the game was played in Philadelphia in the childhood of a lady born at the end of the last century. In Massachusetts and Maine it continued to be popular until within a few years, as follows:

We were marching to Quebec,
  The drums were loudly beating;
America has gained the day,
  The British are retreating.

The war is o'er, and they are turned back,
  For evermore departed;
So open the ring, and take one in,
  For they are broken-hearted.

Oh, you're the one that I love best,
  I praise you high and dearly;
My heart you'll get, my hand I'll give,
  The kiss is most sincerely.

Worcester, Mass.

That the population of Dutch extraction in New York had no deep sympathy with the patriotic sentiments of revolutionary times seems to be indicated in a satirical stanza, which has come to us from an informant who learned it in youth of her aged grandmother, and which appears also to have been originally a dance-song. We hope that errors in spelling American Dutch may be forgiven:

Loope, Junger, de roier kome—
Spann de wagen voor de Paarde!

That is,

> Run, lads, the king's men are coming;
> Harness the wagons before the horses!

in jesting allusion to the speed with which the patriots were supposed to make off. The refrain is in part unintelligible to us, but seems to belong to a dance.

No. 60.

Sudden Departure.

A visitor approaches the ring from without, and pleads:

> It snows and it blows, and it cuts off my nose,
> So pray, little girl, let me in;
> I'll light my pipe, and warm my toes,
> And then I'll be gone again.

He is admitted into the circle, and proceeds to perform the designated actions. Having "lighted his pipe and warmed his toes," he suddenly attempts to make his exit from the ring (all the members of which have clasped hands in expectation of his onset), throwing himself with that object against a pair of linked arms.

No. 61.

Scorn.

Such was, and perhaps still is, the name of an amusement of a not very agreeable nature, familiar at children's parties in New England. A girl was seated on a chair in the middle of the room, and one child after another was led to her throne. She would turn away with an expression of contempt, until some one approached that pleased her, who, after a kiss, took her place.

"Derision" is the name of a game mentioned by Froissart as an amusement of his childhood. It is not at all unlikely that the present sport represents the old French pastime.

Speaking of representations of the passions, we may say that we have heard of a game formerly played in New York, called "Hatred and Revenge;" but have not succeeded in obtaining it.

VIII.

THE PLEASURES OF MOTION.

He asked a shepherd who stood near:
"Why do these lads make merry here,
Why is their round so gay?"
"They dance about a violet sweet, a lad hath found to-day."
The drum, the harp, and fife, resounded round their play,
All were of heart elate,
Each dancing with his mate.
I, Nithart, led the row,
Once and again, around the violet to and fro.

Minnesinger, 13th century.

No. 62.

Ring Around the Rosie.

This little round, universally familiar in America, meets us again in Germany and Provence. After the transit of various languages, and thousands of miles, the song retains the same essential characteristics.

Ring a ring a rosie,
A bottle full of posie,
All the girls in our town,
Ring for little Josie.

New Bedford, Mass. (about 1790).

Another version:

Round the ring of roses,
Pots full of posies,

The one who stoops last
Shall tell whom she loves best.

At the end of the words the children suddenly stoop, and the last to get down undergoes some penalty, or has to take the place of the child in the centre, who represents the "rosie" (rose-tree; French, *rosier*).

Vulgarized forms of the round are common:

Ring around the rosie,
Squat among the posies.

Ring around the roses,
Pocket full of posies,
One, two, three—squat!

And finally it is deformed past recognition:

A ring, a ring, a ransy,
Buttermilk and tansy,
Flower here and flower there,
And all—squat!

This last corruption was in use some forty years since in Connecticut.

No. 63.

Go Round and Round the Valley.

A ring of dancers with clasped hands. A girl circles about the outside of the rest, who join in singing—

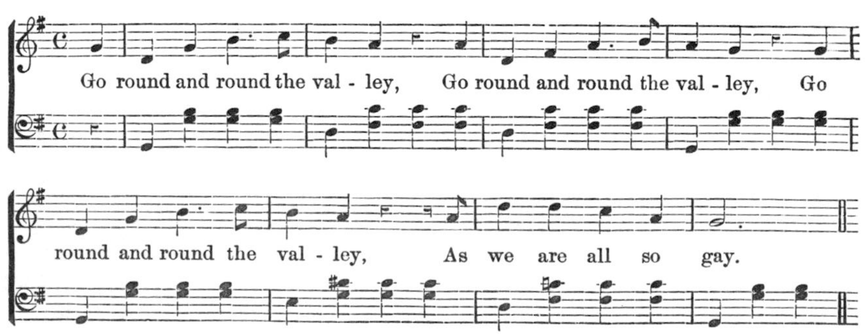

Go round and round the valley,
As we are all so gay.

The players now let go hands, and she winds in and out of the circle, singing—

Go in and out of the windows,
As we are all so gay.

She now stands facing one of the children, who sing—

Go back, and face your lover,
As we are all so gay.

Taking the hand of one of the children, she salutes her—

Such love have I to show you,
As we are all so gay.

The child selected then takes her place. *New York streets.*

No. 64.

The Farmer in the Dell.

A single child stands in the centre of the ring, which sings:

The farmer in the dell,
The farmer in the dell,
Heigh ho! for Rowley O!
The farmer in the dell.

The first child chooses and places beside himself a second, then a third, and so on, while the rest sing to the same tune:

The farmer takes the wife—
The wife takes the child—
The child takes the nurse—
The nurse takes the dog—
The dog takes the cat—
The cat takes the rat—
The rat takes the cheese—
The cheese stands alone.

The "cheese" is "clapped out," and must begin again as the "farmer."

New York streets.

No. 65.

The Game of Rivers.

A girl is chosen to be the *Ocean*. The rest represent *rivers*. The rivers, by very devious courses (around school-desks, etc.), flow into the Ocean. Not unfrequently in their course to the sea, the rivers encounter somewhat violently. *New York.*

No. 66.

Quaker, How is Thee?

"Quaker, Quaker, how is thee?"
"Very well, I thank thee."
"How's thy neighbor, next to thee?"
"I don't know, but I'll go see."

The question is accompanied by a rapid movement of the right hand. The second child in the ring inquires in the same manner of the third; and so all round. Then the same question is asked with a like gesture of the left hand, and, after this has gone round, with both hands, left foot, right foot, both feet, and finally by uniting all the motions at once. "A nice long game," as our little informant said.

New York, Philadelphia, etc.

No. 67.

Darby Jig.

This absurd little rhyme was formerly used to accompany an animated dance, in which the arms were placed behind the waist, and the hands rested on the hips, with alternate motion.

Darby, darby, jig, jig, jig,
I've been to bed with a big, big wig!
I went to France to learn to dance—
Darby, darby, jig, jig, jig!

Philadelphia; Massachusetts.

No. 68.

Right Elbow In.

Put your right elbow in,
Put your right elbow out,
Shake yourselves a little,
And turn yourselves about.

Put your left elbow in,
Put your left elbow out,
Shake yourselves a little,
And turn yourselves about.

Then followed *right ear* and *left ear*, *right foot* and *left foot*, etc. The words we give were in use some sixty years since, when the game was danced deliberately and decorously, as old fashion was, with slow rhythmical motion. Now it has been turned into a romp, under various names (in Boston, "Ugly Mug"). The English name is "Hinkumbooby."

No. 69.

My Master Sent Me.

"My master sent me to you, sir."
"For what, sir?"
"To do with one as I do, sir."

The person who gives orders beats time with one foot, then both feet, one hand and both feet, two hands and both feet, etc. The game, like the preceding, is performed with a dancing motion. *New York.*

No. 70.

Humpty Dumpty.

This game is for girls only. All present sit in a circle, then each girl gathers her skirts tightly, so as to enclose her feet. The leader begins some rhyme; all join in, and at a word previously agreed on, keeping the skirt tightly grasped, throw themselves over backward. The object now is to recover the former position without letting go the skirt.

New York.

No. 71.

Pease Porridge Hot.

This familiar little rhyme is accompanied by two players with alternate striking of the hands together and against the knees, in a way easier to practise than to describe. School-girls often use it to warm their hands on cold winter mornings.

Pease porridge hot,
  Pease porridge cold,
Pease porridge in the pot,
  Nine days old.

No. 72.

Rhymes for a Race.

Up the street, down the street,
Here's the way we go.
Forty horses standing in a row;
[Dolly] on the white one,
[Harry] on the black one,
Riding to Harrisburg *five* miles away.

Philadelphia.

We suppose the above formula to be a rhyme for starting in a race. The common schoolboy verse—

> One to make ready,
> Two to prepare,
> Three to *go slambang*,
> Right—down—there,

appears to be a parody of the older English rhyme,

> One to make ready,
> And two to prepare,
> Good luck to the rider,
> And away goes the mare.

No. 73.

Twine the Garland.

We find mentioned in the "Girls' Own Book," Boston, 1856, a dance of girls which has the characteristics of an old game. Girls take hold of hands, one standing still; the rest twist about her until they form a knot. They then untwist in the same manner, singing, "Twine the garland, girls!" and, "Untwine the garland, girls!"

No. 74.

Hopping-dance.

This name was formerly given in New England to a dance similar to that known in Scotland as *Curcuddie.* The hands were clasped under the knees, and the children slowly and solemnly described squares and triangles on the floor.

We may add here an unnamed amusement for school-girls, which consists in joining hands behind the back (giving the right hand to the left hand of a partner), and then turning, while retaining the hold, so as to stand facing each other. This movement is then repeated until the couple whirl about with considerable rapidity.

IX.

MIRTH AND JEST.

—fulle stuffed a male
Of disportes and newe pleyes.
Chaucer's Dreme.

No. 75.

Club Fist.

A CHILD lays on a table his clenched fist, with the thumb elevated; another grasps the raised thumb with his own fist, and so on until a pile of fists is built up. A player, who remains apart from the group, then addresses the child whose hand is at the top:

"What's that?"
"A pear."
"Take it off or I'll knock it off."

The same conversation is repeated with the next child, and so on; the fist being withdrawn as speedily as possible, to escape a rap from the questioner. When only one is left, the following dialogue ensues:

"What have you got there?"
"Bread and cheese."
"Where's my share?"
"Cat's got it."
"Where's the cat?"
"In the woods."
"Where's the woods?"
"Fire burned it."
"Where's the fire?"
"Water quenched it."
"Where's the water?"
"Ox drank it."

"Where's the ox?"
"Butcher killed it."
"Where's the butcher?"
"Rope hung him."
"Where's the rope?"
"Rat gnawed it."
"Where's the rat?"
"Cat caught it."
"Where's the cat?"

"Behind the church-door. The first who laughs, or grins, or shows the teeth has three pinches and three knocks."

Then follows a general scattering; for some child is sure to laugh, and if he does not do so of his own accord, his neighbors will certainly tweak him, poke him, or otherwise excite his risibility. *Georgia.*

In Pennsylvania the conversation ends:

"Where's the butcher?"
"He's behind the door cracking nuts, and whoever speaks first I'll slap his fingers,
Because I am the keeper of the keys,
And I do whatever I please."

This dialogue, based on a well-known nursery tale, has maintained itself with remarkable persistence, and even verbal identity, in several European languages. We meet it in Germany and Denmark, as well as England.

No. 76.

Robin's Alive.

This celebrated game was formerly much played in New England during the winter evenings. A stick was lighted, and passed from hand to hand. It was an object to transfer it as quickly as possible; but each player, before handing it to his neighbor, must repeat the rhyme—

The bird is alive, and alive like to be,
If it dies in my hand you may back-saddle me.

Or else, "Robin's alive," etc.

The "back-saddling" consisted in depositing the person, in whose hand the light went out, upon the back on the floor, and afterwards piling upon him (or her) chairs and other furniture.

Another formula is given in the "Girls' Own Book:"

"Robin's alive, and alive he shall be; if he dies in my hand, my mouth shall be bridled, my back shall be saddled, and I be sent home to the king's Whitehall."

When the light expired it was said: "Robin is dead, and dead he shall be; he has died in your hand, and your mouth shall be bridled, your back shall be saddled, to send you home to the king's Whitehall."

This game is played all over Europe with similar formulas; but we are not aware that the "back-saddling" feature has been practised out of England and America. The person in whose possession the light is extinguished usually pays forfeit.

It has been suggested, with plausibility, that the sport is connected with an ancient rite: namely, the races of torch-bearers, which formed part of certain festal ceremonies, and in which the courier in whose hands the torch went out was a loser. Such contests are repeatedly alluded to by classic writers; but their exact conduct is involved in some obscurity. In such a race, at Athens, the torch was kindled on the altar of Prometheus, and handed to the runner, whose duty it was to pass it, while still alight, to a second, and so on. This ceremony has suggested a celebrated line to Lucretius, who compares the flying ages to "runners who pass from one to another the torch of life."

No. 77.

Laughter Games.

There is a whole class of games of which the object is to excite to laughter by means of some ridiculous action.

Such games are sometimes played with a lighted candle. The players approach each other from opposite sides of the room, and sustain a dialogue in solemn tones, while they must keep a grave countenance on penalty of paying forfeit. For example:

"The king of Turkey is dead." "What did he die of?" "Doing so" (some ridiculous gesture).

A more characteristic version (in Nantucket, Mass.) had it: "The royal

Russian princess, Husty Fusty, is defunct." To which it was necessary to answer soberly—"I'm very sorry to hear it; even the cats bewail her loss."

A game which was formerly popular with children in Massachusetts was to lean a staff in the corner, while a player was seated in the centre of the ring. Another child now entered, took up the staff, approached and addressed the one sitting, and a rhymed dialogue ensued:

> "My father sent me here with a staff,
> To speak to you, and not to laugh."
> "Methinks you smile." "Methinks I don't.
> I smooth my face with ease and grace,
> And set my staff in its proper place."

If the staff-bearer laughed, he or she must take the chair; otherwise the next player continued the game.

A third amusement is for girls to excite one another to laugh by gently pinching in succession the ears, nose, lips, etc., while making use of some ridiculous expression.

This usage is alluded to more than three centuries ago by Rabelais.

In a Swiss game, this performance is complicated by a jest. Each child pinches his neighbor's ear; but by agreement the players blacken their fingers, keeping two of the party in ignorance. Each of the two victims imagines it to be the other who is the object of the uproarious mirth of the company.

No. 78.

Bachelor's Kitchen.

The children sit in a row, with the exception of one, who goes in succession to each child, and asks him what he will give to the bachelor's kitchen. Each answers what he pleases, as a saucepan, a mousetrap, etc. When all have replied, the questioner returns to the first child, and puts all sorts of questions, which must be answered by the article which he before gave to the kitchen, and by no other word. For instance, he asks, "What do you wear on your head?" "Mousetrap." The object is to make the answerer laugh, and he is asked a number of questions, until he either laughs or is given up as a hard subject. The questioner then passes to the next child, and so on through the whole row. Those who laugh, or add any other word to their answer, must pay a forfeit, which is redeemed in the same way as in other games. *Cambridge, Mass.*

No. 79.

The Church and the Steeple.

Little girls, with appropriate motions of the closed fist, or of the inverted hand with raised fingers, say,

Here is the church,
Here is the steeple,
Here is the parson,
And all the people.

An Italian finger-game well exhibits the different mental state of children in the two countries. The words are: "This is the Inferno, and this the Paradiso." The fingers of the two hands, crossed within, represent the disturbed world of wretchedness; the back of the hands, turned, where all is calm, typify Paradise.

No. 80.

What Color?

A tumbler of water and a thimble are required. One child is sent out of the room, and to each of the others a different color is allotted. The first is then expected to name the color of some child. If she succeeds in her guess, a thimbleful of water is thrown in her face. The guessing is continued till this takes place, when the thrower becomes the guesser for the next turn. *Cincinnati.*

No. 81.

Beetle and Wedge.

There are games in which the guesser has only *Scogan's choice** between two sorts of disaster.

* *Scogan's choice* is equivalent to *Hobson's choice;* both are heroes of old jest-books.

Thus, a party of boys pitch on two who are unacquainted with the game, and ask them if they would not like to play "Beetle and Wedge." "The fun is to be the Beetle and the Wedge," they explain. The victims consenting, the Beetle is then driven against the Wedge, back to back, with a force that "sends him flying." This amusement belongs to Connecticut.

In Philadelphia a boy is asked whether he prefers *mustard* or *pepper;* in either case receiving corresponding personal inflictions. So in the English game of "Trades" a boy is made to guess the trade of the questioner, and is *hammered, planed*, or *rasped*, accordingly.

No. 82.

Present and Advise.

All the children, except two, are seated in a row. One of these whispers in the ear of each child, "I present you with this." The second, in like manner, adds, "I advise you what to do with it."

Another old whispering-game, belonging, like the preceding, to New York, is called "Sentiment." Each child tells his neighbor on the right the name of a person, and repeats to the one on the left a verse of poetry, usually of a sentimental character. The name and verse are then to be repeated together as in the former game.

No. 83.

Genteel Lady.

"I, genteel lady, always genteel, come from the genteel lady, always genteel, beg leave to inform you that my ship has just come in from China laden with apricots."

The next player has to repeat, adding some object beginning with *b*, such as biscuit; the next player one beginning with *c*, and so down the alphabet. If any one hesitates, or makes a mistake, a lighted "lamp-lighter" (New England, *spill*) is stuck in her hair, and she is the "one-horned," instead of the "genteel" lady; and for two mistakes the two-horned" lady, and so on. This juxtaposition of curls and "lamp-lighters" is by no means always safe. *Georgia.*

Of this game we observe that, like several amusements familiar in this State, it is of French origin.*

No. 84.

Beast, Bird, or Fish.

A member of the party throws to another a knotted handkerchief, saying one of the above words, and counting up to ten. The catcher must answer in the given time the name of some animal of the kind required, not already cited by some other player.

Whoever fails to reply while the counting is going on, is out of the game. After the names of commoner animals are exhausted, the game becomes a test of quickness and memory.

No. 85.

Wheel of Fortune.

A picture of a wheel is drawn upon the slate, and a number written between each of its spokes. The eyes being then closed, the child whose turn it is raises a pencil in the air, twirling it, and saying,

Tit for tat,
Butter for fat,
If you kill my dog I'll kill your cat.

At the last word the pencil is brought down; if the point of the pencil falls on a space, the number there written is scored; if on a line, or outside the circle, or on a number previously secured (and erased by a line), the turn is forfeited. The game is continued until a certain number has been scored by the winning player. *Georgia.*

* The game is called "Le Chevalier Gentil," and proceeds thus: "Bon jour, chevalier gentil, toujours gentil; moi chevalier gentil, toujours gentil, je viens de la part du chevalier gentil, toujours gentil (so designating the left-hand neighbor) vous dire qu'il y a un aigle à bec d'or, à pattes d'argent," etc. A player who misses receives "un petit cornet de papier," and is known as "chevalier cornu, biscornu," etc., or "damoiselle cornette à tant de cornes."

No. 86.

Catches.

"I went up one pair of stairs."
"Just like me."
"There was a monkey."
"Just like me."
"I one'd it."
"I two'd it," etc.
"I ate [eight] it."

This (to children) exquisitely witty dialogue has its German counterpart.—"I went into the wood." "So did I." "I took an axe." "So did I." "I made a trough." "So did I." "Seven pigs ate of it." "So did I." *

Equally well known is the jest, "I am a gold lock," "I am a gold key," etc.—ending "I am a monk-lock," "I am a mon-key."

We may mention also a familiar catch, "Say my cat, my cat, and not my dog." "My dog" must not be spoken.

Of a different character are the following jests:

The lights being extinguished, a knife is passed round the circle of players, and the following conversation ensues, each phrase being continued from left to right of the ring:

"What's this?"
"A dagger."
"Where did you get it?"
"Stole it."
"What was done with it?"

All of the company who understand the jest shriek aloud, which accomplishes the object of terrifying the rest.

Somewhat similar (in New York) is the following:

"Neighbor, I've got a hatchet to sell."
"Did you buy it?"
"No."

* A French catch: "J'ai monté un escalier." "Comme moi." "Je suis entré dans la chambre." "Comme moi." "J'ai vu une petite boîte." "Comme moi." "Je l'ai ouverte." "Comme moi." "Il y avait une grosse bête." "Comme moi."

"Did you steal it?"
"Sh—"

In the following conversation, one sentence at a time is repeated in a whisper to the left-hand neighbor, and so passed round the circle, the fun consisting in the imitation of crowing at the end.

"Hath she feathers?" "Feathers she hath." "Doth she crow?" "Crow she doth." "How doth she crow?" (An imitation of crowing follows.)

No. 87.

Intery Mintery.

An evening amusement formerly common in Massachusetts. All present laid their hands with fingers resting on the knees. The speaker then told off the words of the rhyme, one for each finger. The rhyme being thus recited, that finger to which the last syllable fell must be quickly withdrawn, on penalty of being sharply rapped by the hand of the leader. After all had been counted out but one person, he or she was liable to the same risk for every word of the rhyme—the result of which situation is alluded to by the epithet "black finger."

Intery mintery cutery corn,
Apple-seed and apple-thorn,
Wire, briar, limber lock,
Twelve geese in a flock;
Sit and sing by a spring,
O-u-t spells out, and in again.
Over yonder steep hills,
Where my father he dwells,
He has jewels, he has rings,
And very many pretty things.
Strike Jack, lick Tom,
Blow the bellows,
Black finger—out-of-the-game.

No. 88.

Redeeming Forfeits.

The girl who is to assign the penalty by which the forfeit must be redeemed lays her head on the lap of another who sits on a chair, while a third, standing behind, holds the article over her head and asks:

> "Here is a forfeit, a very fine forfeit; what shall be done to redeem it?"
> "Is it fine or superfine?" (*i. e.*, does it belong to a gentleman or to a lady).

The sentence is then declared.

Another formula, used in the Middle and Southern States, is:

> "Heavy, heavy, what hangs over you?"

The German usage is nearly the same, the question being "Lord judge, what is your sentence, what shall he do whose pledge I have in my hand?"

The following are examples of old penalties, which usually involved kissing, with infinite variety of method:

To go to Rome. To kiss every girl in the room.
Flat-irons. The lad and lass lay their hands on the wall and kiss.
Measuring yards of tape, and cutting it off. To kiss with the arms extended.
"*I'm in the well.*" "How many fathoms deep?" (Any number is answered.) "Whom will you have to take you out?" (Some one of the company is named.) Each fathom represents a kiss.

No. 89.

Old Mother Tipsy-toe.

This is a very popular game with girls in various parts of the United States.

The children sit in a row, with the exception of the mother, who comes up and asks each child in turn, "How did you tear your dress?" After hearing their various excuses, she again traverses the row, indicating the part of the dress to be mended, and saying:

> I give you so much work to do,
> Use thimble, thread, and needle too;

If you don't get it done before I come back,
I'll give you a slap across your back.

She slaps her children on the shoulder and goes out, forbidding them to follow her. As soon as her back is turned, they all jump up and run after her, shouting, "Old mother Tipsy-toe,"* or, as in a variation from New York:

Old mother Tippety-toe, old mother Tippety-toe,
I'll follow my mother wherever she go.

The mother now goes into a shop, and orders various articles, the children repeating after her whatever she says. For instance, the mother says, "I want two pounds of butter." "I want two pounds of butter," shout the children in chorus. Finally she says, "And I want a stick to whip my children with," upon which she turns to leave the shop, while the children rush before her, and scramble back to their seats before their mother comes home. The latter then goes to each child in turn, saying, "Let me see how well you have mended your dress." The children all hold the hem of their dresses as firmly as they can, with their hands somewhat apart. The mother strikes with her hand the part of the dress that is between their hands; and if they let it go, she scolds and beats them for their bad mending. *Cambridge, Mass.*

In another way of playing, which makes the game one of chase, "Old mammy Tipsy-toe" addresses her children:

I give you this much work to do,
  Use thread and needle, thimble too;
If you don't have it done
  By the time that I come home,
You'll be beaten black and blue
  With my old shoe.

She then makes preparations to depart:

I'm going to Lady Washington's,
  To get a cup of tea,
And five loaves of gingerbread,
  So don't you follow me.

The children, of course, pursue her with shouts of defiance, upon which

* Or, as played by the children from whom this version was obtained, *Old mother Cripsy-crops.* The name "Tipsy-toe" is derived from the limping gait supposed to belong to witches. See No. 154, C.

she turns and chases them, while they rush to their places. She comes back, and demands of the children:

"Have you been out to-day?" "No." "You have. Where have you been?" "To grandmother's." "What did you get?" "A slice of cake." "Where is my share?" "In the bandbox." "But I might break my neck getting it." "I wish you would." On this, she chases the children, who fly and scatter. Any child she catches is out of the game, which is continued until all are captured. *Philadelphia.*

No. 90.

Who Stole the Cardinal's Hat?

The children being seated in a circle, a child, who does not take part in the game, whispers to each of the rest a name representing some color, as "Red-cap," "Blue-cap," "Yellow-cap," etc. Two players are excepted, one of whom is called "My man John," and one represents the cardinal. The latter now leaves the room, first placing in the hands of "John" a little billet of wood, bidding him take care of the Cardinal's hat, which at the same time he declares to be of some particular color, as green. "John" conceals this somewhere in the room. The child who went out then enters, armed with a cane, and demands the Cardinal's hat. "John" affects to have forgotten all about it, and asks, "What color was it? green?" and so on until he guesses the color. Being thus reminded, he declares that some one of the group, as, for example, "Red-cap," has stolen it. "Red-cap" is now asked by the questioner, "Red-cap, did you steal the Cardinal's hat?" He also must pass on the charge, saying, "No, it was White-cap" (or any other color). If he omits to do so, or names a color not included among the players, he must pay forfeit. Meanwhile the questioner becomes indignant at the numerous denials, and proceeds to extort confession by torture, rapping with his cane the fingers of those whom he addresses. If he succeeds in obliging any child to confess, the latter must pay forfeit. At last "My man John" owns the theft, produces the hat, and the game is begun again, until a sufficient number of forfeits have been collected. *Saratoga, New York.*

This game is also played in Switzerland. The name of a color having been given to each child, a ball is stealthily passed about the circle. The

"Abbot of St. Gall" enters, and exclaims, "The Abbot of St. Gall has lost his night-cap; they say White stole it." The player whose color is named, if he has the ball, must pass it behind his back to another, saying, "Not White, Red has it." Whoever is caught in passing the ball, or names a color not in the game, or fails to answer when his name is called, must pay forfeit, or have his face marked with burned cork. It will be seen that the Swiss game corresponds to the American, except that in the latter the ball is concealed instead of being passed round; but we think it likely that the memory of our informant (a child) may have been at fault in this respect.

The *Gentleman's Magazine*, February, 1738, mentions a game called "The Parson hath lost his Fuddling Cap." *The Spectator*, No. 268, also refers to this sport: "I desire to know in your next if the merry game of 'The Parson has lost his Cloak," is not mightily in vogue amongst the fine ladies this Christmas, because I see they wear hoods of all colours, which I suppose is for that purpose." From this last extract it appears that the names "Red-cap," etc., are a reminiscence of the variously colored hoods once employed in the game.

X.

GUESSING-GAMES.

"As boys, when they play at 'how many,' hold out their hands in such a way that, having few, they pretend to have many, and having many, they make believe to have few."—XENOPHON, *Treatise on the Duties of a Cavalry Officer.*

No. 91.

Odd or Even.

A SMALL number of beans or other counters are held in the hand, and the question is, Odd or Even? If the guess is even, and the true number odd, it is said "Give me one to make it odd," and *vice versâ*. The game is continued until all the counters belong to one or other of the two players.

This amusement was familiar in ancient Greece and Rome, as it is in modern Europe. In the classic game the player gained or lost as many as he held in his hand.

No. 92.

Hul Gul.

This game is played by three, four, or more, who stand in a circle. A child then addresses his left-hand neighbor, and the dialogue is:

"Hul Gul."
"Hands full."
"Parcel how many?"

The second player then guesses the number, two guesses being sometimes allowed. If, for example, the guess is five, and the real number seven, the first responds, "Give me two to make it seven," and so on until all the counters have been gained by one player. The number allowed to be taken is often limited, by agreement, to six or ten.

The counters are beans, grains of corn, marbles, nuts, and, in the South, *chinquapins.**

A childish trick is to expand the hand as if unable to hold the number of counters, when in fact they are but one or two. Oddly enough, this same device is alluded to by Xenophon as in use in his day in the game of "How many?"—the classic equivalent of our game, in which the question was, "How many have I in the hand?" just as we say, "Parcel how many?" So, in these sports, the interval of two thousand years vanishes.

No. 93.

How many Fingers?

A child hides his head on another's lap, and guesses the number of fingers raised. We find a rhyme for this given in the "Girls' Own Book."

> "Mingledy, mingledy, clap, clap, clap,
> How many fingers do I hold up?"
> "Three."
> "Three you said, and two it was," etc.

Another form of this game consists in schoolboys mounting on each other's back and raising fingers, of which the number is to be guessed. The English formula for this purpose is given by Tylor thus, "Buck, buck, how many horns do I hold up?" We are not aware that the practice continues to exist in this country.

In the famous finger-game of "Morra," the sum of the fingers raised by the two players is counted. The game is played with such rapidity, and the calling is so rapid, that conjecture plays a larger part in the game than eyesight. "Morra" has been a favorite for nearly four thousand years, for it is represented on early Egyptian monuments, where the players are depicted as using the right hand, and scoring with the left, very much as is done in the south of Europe at the present day.

It is very likely, however, that the nursery usage we are now concerned

* "Chinquapin (*Castanea primula*), an ovoid, pointed, sweet nut, half the size of a common chestnut."

with is as old. Petronius Arbiter, in the time of Nero, describes Trimalchio as so playing with a boy. The latter, "mounting as on horseback, smote his shoulders with the open hand, and laughing said, "Bucca, bucca, how many?" *

We will not undertake to decide whether the reported coincidence of the Latin and English formulas is a genuine example of transmission. The game, however, and the question, "How many?" have certainly endured for two thousand years, and very likely existed as long before the days of Petronius, or from a time as remote as that to which can be traced the more complicated game of "Morra."

No. 94.

Right or Left.

A common way of deciding a dispute, selecting players, or determining who shall begin a game, is to take a pebble or other object in the closed fist, and make a comrade guess in which hand it is contained.

The old-fashioned way of holding the hands, both in England and Germany, was to place one fist on top of the other; and a like usage formerly prevailed in New England, though we have not met with the English rhyme:

Handy-dandy riddledy ro,
Which will you have, high or low?

No. 95.

Under which Finger?

A child takes a bean in the hand, closes it, and asks a companion to guess under which finger it lies; if the latter fails, he must pay a bean.

* Bucca, bucca, quot sunt hic?"

No. 96.

Comes, it Comes.

A simple guessing-game, familiar to children in New England. One child of the party says to another, "It comes, it comes." The player addressed replies, "What do you come by?" The first replies by naming the initial letter of some object in the room; if, for instance, it is the table he has in mind, he says, "I come by T." The rest must now guess what thing, beginning with this letter, is meant.

No. 97.

Hold Fast My Gold Ring.

The children sit in a circle, with hands closed; one takes the ring, and goes around with it, tapping the closed fists of the players as if inserting the ring, and saying:

Biddy, biddy, hold fast my gold ring,
Till I go to London, and come back again.

Each child, in turn, is then required to guess who has the ring, and, if successful, takes the leader's place; if unsuccessful, he pays forfeit.

Georgia.

This is known in Massachusetts as,

Button, button, who's got the button?

Another form of the question is, "Fox, fox, who's got the box?"
In England the game goes,

My lady's lost her diamond ring,
I pitch on you to find it.

No. 98.

My Lady Queen Anne.

A ball is concealed with some one of the children who form the circle. A girl is placed in the centre, and a dialogue ensues; the ring singing:

"My lady Queen Anne,
She sits in the sun,
As fair as a lily,
As brown as a bun.
The king sends you three letters, and bids you read one."

The girl answers:

"I cannot read one unless I read all,
So pray, Mr. [or Miss] ——, deliver the ball."

If the person named has the ball, he or she takes her place; if not, she continues as before. In England, a rhyme is given for the latter case:

"The ball is mine, and none of thine,
So you, proud queen, may sit on your throne,
While we, your messengers, go and come."

No. 99.

The Wandering Dollar.

A coin is passed about the circle, and the central player is to guess who has it. The dollar is held in the palm, then passed about the ring by each player alternately clapping his hands together, and then extending his arms so as to touch the hands of his neighbor. For this purpose the right hand should be held downward, and the left turned upward, as the arms are extended. The coin is to be *palmed* from hand to hand, and the rhythmical motions being accompanied with song (to almost any tune) make a very pretty game, but one which requires much practice to master. The verse sung is,

Dollar, dollar, how you wander,
From the one unto the other!

Is it fair, is it fair,
To leave Miss [Anna] so long without a chair?

Cincinnati.

The game is a modern translation from the German, presumably by the children themselves.

No. 100.

Thimble in Sight.

Among games of search may be mentioned the present, in which, the greater part of the company being sent out of the room, a thimble must be placed so as to escape notice, and yet in such a position as to be visible when the attention is once directed to it. As each of the party discovers the thimble, he indicates his success by saying "Rorum torum corum," or some such formula, and then takes his seat.

In other games, in which some small object is hidden, there are various ways of assisting the seeker when at fault; thus, it is said you *freeze*, you are *cold*, you are *warm*, you *burn*, according as the object is approached; or the search is directed by *magical music*, which grows louder as the person comes nearer to his object. These usages belong also to other countries. More original is a practice, common in Massachusetts, according to which the height of the concealed object above the floor of the room is indicated by the words "So high water," addressed by one of the company to the person who has been sent out, as he enters and begins his search.

XI.

GAMES OF CHASE.

The spring clade all in gladness
  Doth laugh at winter's sadness,
And to the bag-pipes round,
  The maids tread out their ground.

Fy, then, why are we musing,
  Youth's sweet delight refusing?
Say, dainty nymph, and speak,
  Shall we play Barley Break?

Old Song.

No. 101.

How many Miles to Babylon?

A PARTY of young people stand at each end of a space, such as a portico, a field, etc., and a single player is stationed in the middle. The former address the latter:

"Marlow, marlow, marlow bright,
How many miles to Babylon?"
"Threescore and ten."
"Can I get there by candlelight?"
"Yes, if your legs are as long as light,
But take care of the old gray witch by the road-side."

The players at the ends of the field then run from side to side, and must be caught by the central player, whom they then assist to catch the rest. *Georgia.*

This sport, which has been universally familiar in America, is a form of the old English game of "Barley Break," and probably the "marlow bright" of our version is a corruption of that name.

The Scotch variety given by Chambers has a very chivalric turn, which may give an idea of the song which must have accompanied the game in the time of Queen Elizabeth:

> "King and queen of Cantelon,
> How many miles to Babylon?"
> "Eight and eight, and other eight."
> "Will I get there by candlelight?"
> "If your horse be good and your spurs be bright."
> "How many men have ye?"
> "Mae nor ye daur come and see."

The poets of the Elizabethan age fully describe the game of "Barley Break," and seem to think it the most delightful of youthful amusements. They represent Diana and her nymphs as amusing themselves with this sport.

It appears from Sidney's description that the game was played by three couples, each of a youth and a maid, one couple standing at each end of the area, and the third remaining in the centre. The mating was determined by lot, and the last pair mated were obliged to take the central position, and saluted each other by a kiss. This pair were required to pursue with joined hands, while the others were at liberty to separate. Any maid caught replaced the maid, and any youth the youth, of the central couple. Notwithstanding the courtly nature of the sport, that its fundamental idea is the same as that of our game appears by the name of the central space, as Sidney gives it in the "Arcadia:"

> Then couples three be streight allotted there,
> They of both ends the middle two do flie,
> The two that in mid-place Hell called were,
> Must strive with waiting foot and watching eye
> To catch of them, and them to Hell to bear,
> That they, as well as they, Hell may supplie.

A New England variation introduces blindfolding, thus adapting the game to a chamber. Two children are made to kneel on stools, their eyes bandaged, and the rest must run between. The dialogue is:

> "How many miles to Barbary-cross?"
> "Fourscore."
> "Are there any bears in the way?"
> "Yes, a great many; take care they don't catch you!"

No. 102.

Hawk and Chickens.

A hen with her brood. A child represents the "Old Buzzard," about whom the rest circle. The hen addresses the latter:

"Chickany, chickany, crany, crow.
Down in the gutter
To get the hog's supper—
What o'clock is it, old buzzard?"

The Buzzard, meanwhile, is busied in building up a fire with sticks, and abruptly names any hour, when the question and answer are repeated for each child of the ring, until twelve o'clock, thus—

"Half-past ten."
"What o'clock is it, old buzzard?"
"Half-past eleven."
"What o'clock is it, old buzzard?"
"Twelve o'clock."

The ring now halts, and the dialogue proceeds:

"Old buzzard, old buzzard, what are you doing?"
"Picking up sticks."
"What do you want the sticks for?"
"To build a fire."
"What are you building a fire for?"
"To broil a chicken."
"Where are you going to get the chicken?"
"Out of your flock."

The Buzzard gives chase and captures a child. He brings him back, lays him down, and proceeds to dress him for dinner. All the rest stand round in admiring silence. The Buzzard asks,

"Will you be picked or scraped?"

According to the choice he proceeds as if picking the feathers of a bird or scaling a fish, and continues, with appropriate action,

"Will you be pickled or salted?"
"Will you be roasted or stewed?"

He drags the victim into one or another corner of the room, according to the reply, and the game proceeds as before.* *New England.*

In the Southern States a witch takes the place of the bird of prey, and the rhyme is,

"Chickamy, chickamy, crany, crow,
I went to the well to wash my toe,
And when I came back my chicken was gone;
What o'clock, old witch?"

The witch names any hour, and questions and answers are repeated as before, up to twelve:

"What are you doing, old witch?"
"I am making a fire to cook a chicken."
"Where are you going to get it?"
"Out of your coop."
"I've got the lock."
"I've got the key."
"Well, we'll see who will have it."

The witch tries to get past the hen, and seize the last of the line; the mother, spreading out her arms, bars the passage. The witch cries,

"I must have a chick."
"You sha'n't have a chick."

Each child caught drops out, and as the line grows shorter the struggle becomes desperate. *Georgia.*

This latter way of playing is the older form of the game, and is also familiar, though without words, in the North, where it is known as "Fox and Chickens."

This game is one of the most widely diffused, and the dialogue is marvellously identical, from Russia to Italy.

In Schleswig-Holstein the conversation runs thus:

"Hawk, what are you lighting?"
"A fire."

* The first lines, "Chickany," etc., are from one old version, the rest from another. In the first the bird of prey was called the "Blind Buzzard," and the game ended as Blind-man's Buff.

"What is the fire for?"
"To make ashes."
"What are the ashes for?"
"To sharpen a knife."
"What is the knife for?"
"To cut off chickens' heads."
"What have the chickens done?"
"Gone into my master's corn."

In our own country, among the Pennsylvania Germans, or, to use their own agreeable idiom, "De Pennsylfaunisch Deitsch," this game enjoys the distinction of being almost the only child's game which is accompanied by words, and is played as follows:

A boy who is digging in the earth is accosted by a second, who carries a handful of sticks, the longest of which represents the needle:

"Woy, woy, was grawbst?"
"Meine Moder hat eine silberne Nodel verloren."
"Is sie des?"
"Ne."
"Is sie des?"
"Ne."
"Is sie des?"
"Yaw."*

The stooping child now rises and pursues the rest.

A similar dialogue is used for a game of chase in New York:

"Old mother, what are you looking for?"
"A needle."
"What do you want a needle for?"
"To sew my bag with."
"What do you want your bag for?"
"To keep my steel in."
"What do you want your steel for?"
"To sharpen my knife to cut off your head."

In the same spirit, the Venetian game has:

"Sister, what are you looking for?"
"A knife to kill you with."

* That is: "Hawk, hawk, what are you digging for?" "My mother has lost a silver needle." "Is it this?" "No." "Is it this?" "No." "Is it this?" "Yes."

Whereupon she pursues the questioners. In this version we find also the inquiry about the hour, the putting of the pot on the fire, the searching for the knife, and final scattering.

The Fins on the Baltic coast, too, have the game in the form of a long song, beginning,

> Close together! see the hawk yon!
> Close together! see his talons?

Which exactly corresponds to the Scotch,

> Keep in, keep in, wherever ye be—
> The greedy gled is seeking ye!

No. 103.

Tag.

In this game a child, usually selected by "counting out," pursues his comrades till he has caught one who must replace him. There is generally some asylum of refuge, where the pursued are safe.

The original form of this game seems to have been "Iron Tag," or "Tag on Iron," once universal in the United States, and still here and there played. In Germany and Italy, also, this is the usual form of the sport. In this game the pursued party is safe whenever touching iron in any shape, as the ring of a post, horse-shoe, etc.* A writer in the *Gentleman's Magazine*, February, 1738, speaking of this amusement, says that "the lad saves himself by the touching of cold iron," and that "in later times this play has been altered amongst children of quality, by touching of gold instead of iron." In like manner, owing to the occasional scarcity of iron objects, *wood-tag* and *stone-tag* have been varieties of the sport in America.

This form of the game exhibits its original meaning. As in several other games of chase, the pursuer represents an evil spirit, from whose attack, according to ancient superstition, iron was a protection. Hence the challenge, in Silesia and Switzerland, is, "Father, I have no iron, hit me."† The chaser, it seems, was conceived as the aged but powerful

* "So-and-so had a nail driven into his shoe, and insisted that he could not be touched while standing on iron."—*A Bostonian informant.*

† The French name in Berry is *Tu l'as;* elsewhere *La caye;* in Limousin, *Cabé,* which may have been derived from *hoc habe.*

dwarf, of malignant character. Thus we get a vivid idea of the extent to which such representations once affected the lives even of children, and see that an amusement which is now a mere pleasurable muscular exercise followed the direction imposed by belief.

There are numerous varieties of this game. In *cross-tag*, the pursuer must follow whoever comes between him and the pursued. In *squat-tag*, the fugitive is safe while in that position, or is allowed a given number of "squats," during which he cannot be touched. A peculiar variety (in Philadelphia) is "Tag, tag, tell a body." In this game every child is forbidden to tell who is "it," on penalty of replacing him. Sometimes the name of the pursuer is kept secret until revealed by his actions, or the child who has been tagged deceives the rest by keeping up his speed. On the other hand, the catcher is sometimes bound to turn his cap inside out, whence the game is called *turn-cap*.

"Pickadill" is a kind of tag played in Massachusetts during the winter. A large circle is made in the snow, with quartering paths; if there are many players, two circles are made. There is one tagger, and the centre is the place of safety.

"London Loo" is a particular species of the game (in Philadelphia) in which the following formula is used:

"1, 2, 3, 4, 5, 6, 7, 8, 9, 10—London!"
"Loo!"
"I'll try to catch one of you.'

No. 104.

Den.

This is an out-of-doors game. Each boy represents a wild beast, and has a separate tree, which represents his "den." Any player who leaves his den is liable to be tagged by any who has started out at a later moment. The best runner usually ventures first, a second pursues him, and so on, until all may be out at once. If a player can tag any one whom he has a right to capture, he takes him home to his own den, and the latter must help him to take the rest. The pursuer cannot be tagged while bringing home his prisoner. *Cambridge, Mass.*

No. 105.

*I Spy.**

This game is world-old and world-wide. To judge by the description of Pollux (in the second century), it was then played exactly as American children play it to-day. "One of the party places himself in the middle of his comrades, and closes his eyes, unless some other covers them for him. The players run away and scatter. Then the pursuer opens his eyes and proceeds to look for them. It is each player's object to reach that one's† ground before him."

An ancient painting represents this game. Cupids are playing together. One of these, with his face turned away, has his hands before his eyes, and appears to be counting. Another is running to a place of concealment, while a third peeps from behind the door.

Children, with us, usually count a hundred before beginning the search; but there is an abbreviated method, not accounted fair—

Ten, ten, and double ten,
Forty-five and fifteen.

The "home" is usually a tree. When the seeker catches sight of any of the players, he (or she) runs to the tree, and touches it thrice, saying, "One, two, three, for ——" (naming the child). On the other hand, if the latter can reach the tree first, he touches it, saying, "One, two, three, for myself."‡

In a variety of the game, a stick is set up against a tree. One of the players seizes it, and throws it as far as possible. The children hide, while the one who happens to be "it" gets and replaces the stick, after which he proceeds to look for the rest. Those whom he discovers he captures as above described, until all are taken. If any of the hiders can reach the tree and throw down the stick, all prisoners are released, and the seeker must begin over again. A similar game, in New York, is called "Yards off."

"Hide and Seek" differs only in this, that there is no home to be touched, but the game is ended when the concealment is discovered. When the players are hidden they announce it by "whooping."

* Pronounced *Hie* Spy.

† He who is "it."

‡ The identical words in Switzerland—"eis, zwei, drü für mich;" or, "eis, zwei, drü für den oder den."

No. 106.

Sheep and Wolf.

This is a very ancient hiding-game. A wolf is chosen by "counting out" or otherwise, who conceals himself, and then indicates that he is ready by howling.

The rest of the party, who are supposed to be sheep, walk round the corner in a casual way, until one calls out, "I spy a wolf," whereupon all immediately take to their heels. Whoever is caught by the wolf before reaching home must take his place for the next turn. This game is nearly identical in most European countries. *New York.*

No. 107.

Blank and Ladder.

A boy is selected by the following peculiar counting rhyme:

In came a little man with a white hat;
  If you want a pretty girl, pray take that;
Take your choice of one, two, or three,
  If you want a pretty girl, pray take she.

Lad after lad being successively excluded, the last remaining is "it," and has to hide himself, when he calls out,

Blank and ladder!

The searcher may summon the fugitive to indicate his whereabouts:

Halloo if you're far off, whistle if you're nigh.

Salem, Mass.

In Portland, Me., the shout of the concealed party is, "Blank, blank, Cornelia!" and in the western part of the State of New York, "Blanca-lilo!"

The searcher, on discovering one of the hidden players, calls "Hi spy!" and tries to touch the latter before he can reach goal, the rule being that

Elbow and knee
Always go free.

No. 108.

Blind-man's Buff.

A blindfolded player is led into the centre of a room, taken by the shoulders, and turned about three times, after which he must catch somebody to replace him.

For this initiation there is in the Middle States a rhyme:

> "How many horses have you in your father's stable?"
> "Three; black, white, and gray."
> "Turn about, and turn about, and catch whom you may." *

The English name, "Hoodman-blind," is derived from the manner of blindfolding formerly in use. When caps were worn which could be drawn at will over the face, the caps, reversed so as to cover the countenance, formed the mask.

This game belongs to all ages and most countries, and is known by many different names, frequently taken from animals, for example: "Blind Cow" in Germany; "Blind Goat" in Sweden; "Blind Mouse" in South Germany and Servia; "Blind Hen" in Spain; "Blind Fly," or "Blind Cat," in Italy. To the English name, "Blind-man's Buff," correspond the Polish "Blind Old Man," and the Norwegian "Blind Thief." In these titles a mythologic allusion is probably contained, which is quite clear in the Scotch "Belly-blind," † the latter name representing a malicious demon. Thus again appears the conception of a supernatural adversary so common in games of pursuit.

A familiar variation makes this a ring-game. The blindfolded person stands in the centre, with a staff, while the ring circles about him. When he strikes the floor three times, the ring must pause. The person in whose direction he points must grasp the staff, and utter some sound, disguising the voice as much as possible. The first must then guess the name from the sound. In New York this form of the game is called "Peggy in the Ring," and the request is "to squeak."

* The formula of German children in New York, translated, runs: "Blind cow, we lead thee." "Where?" "To the stable." "What to do there?" "To eat soup." "I have no spoon." "Go get one." The "blind cow" then seeks her "spoon."

† Professor F. J. Child has shown that *Billie Blin*, which occurs in English ballads, is originally a name of Odin, expressing the *gracious* side (German *billig*) of the blind deity. But it seems to have passed into a bad use, as a murderous dwarf or fairy.

In Cincinnati the game is also played in a dark room, without bandaging the eyes, and is then called "Devil in the Dark."

Another variety, also commonly played without blindfolding, goes by the name of "Still Pond," or "Still Palm." The child who is "it," counting up to ten, says,

Still proving,
No moving.

All now keep their places. The catcher must guess by the touch the name of his captive.

The game of which we write is described by Pollux, as played seventeen hundred years since in various forms, all of which are still familiar: "The game of 'Muinda,' when any one, closing his eyes, cries, 'Look out!' and whomsoever he catches he makes him close his eyes instead; or when, keeping his eyes shut, he seeks after the children who have hidden until he catches them; or else he closes his eyes while the others touch him, and if anybody gives a clue himself, he speaks out and guesses till he gets it right."

When a bandage was used, the game was called the "Brazen Fly" (we may suppose a gaudy species of insect, from the zigzag motion, as boys run when chasing butterflies), and is thus described by the same author: "The eyes of a boy having been bound with a bandage, he goes round, saying, 'I shall chase the *brazen fly*;' but the others, answering, 'You will chase him but not catch him,' hit him with whips of papyrus, till he catches one of them." These papyrus whips were the equivalent of our knotted handkerchiefs.

No. 109.

Witch in the Jar.

One of the children is selected for a witch, and each of the others chooses some tree or post for a goal. The witch then marks out on the ground with a stick as many circles as there are players, which she calls "jars." The children run out from their homes, and are pursued by the witch. Whenever she catches one, she puts him in one of her jars, from which he cannot escape unless some one else chooses to free him by touching. Once freed, he cannot be recaught until he has reached his home, and ventures out once more. The freer, however, can be caught, and as the witch keeps guard over her prisoners, it is a dangerous task for a player to attempt to set his companions free. When all are caught, a new witch is chosen.

No. 110.

Prisoner's Base.

This game is also called "Prisoner's Bars;" but the first name, mentioned in "Cymbeline," seems the older, from which the latter has arisen by misunderstanding.

The game, which is also popular in Europe, is originally an imitation of warfare. The two armies stand facing each other, and have their *bases* each on a line parallel with that of the adversary. But in the United States the game has been changed, so that the two parties stand on the same line, and the bases are placed diagonally opposite at a distance of some thirty yards, so that each base is nearer to the enemy's forces than to those of the side to which it belongs. The game is opened by a challenge given by one leader to the other; each player can tag any one of the opponents who has quitted his line before he has left his own. Any player tagged must go to his base. Any player who can reach his base in safety may release a prisoner.

As it often happens that a half-dozen runners may be pursuing a single fugitive, who is cut off from his friends, the chase may be prolonged far from the point of departure, through streets of the town or fields of the country.

No. 111.

Defence of the Castle.

After the battle of Dunbar, Oliver Cromwell sent Colonel Fenwick with two regiments to reduce Hume Castle. The governor, Cockburn, when ordered to surrender, replied by quoting the following lines, which must have belonged to a boys' game of his day:

I, William of the Wastle,
Am now in my castle,
And a' the dogs in the town
Winna gae me gang down.

The rhyme, with small change, is still familiar in Scotland, and the game well known in Pennsylvania, where the defiance runs, less chivalrously,

Hally, hally, hastle,
Come into my new castle!

Or, with a change of usage,

Hally, hally, hastle,
Get off of my new castle!

In the first case the defender maintains his post against assailants; in the latter, he endeavors to capture one of a group who have established themselves in his castle, represented usually by a cellar-door.

No. 112.

Lil Lil.

This game is played in an open field. A boy stands in the centre of the field, and the other players at the sides. With the cry "Lil lil!" they run across. The tagger must touch a runner three times on the back, and whoever is so caught must assist him. There is a rhyme for this game—

Lil, lil,
Over the hill,
Wash my lady's dishes,
Hang them on the bushes, etc.

"Lil lil!" is also a cry (in Boston) of children "coasting," when the track is to be cleared.

No. 113.

Charley Barley.

Charley, barley, buck and rye,
What's the way the Frenchmen fly?
Some fly east, and some fly west,
And some fly over the cuckoo's nest.

Portland, Me.

We have not obtained information as to the manner in which this game was played, but it is evidently identical with the Scotch rhyme:

Hickety, bickety, pease, scone,
Where shall this poor Scotchman gang?
Will he gang east, or will he gang west,
Or will he gang to the craw's nest?

In the Scotch game, a boy, whose eyes are bandaged, rests his head against a wall, while the rest come up and lay their hands upon his back. He sends them to different places, according to the rhyme, and calls out, "Hickety, bickety!" till they have returned, when the last in must take his place. The "crow's nest" is close beside the blindfolded boy, and is a coveted position.

This game is also played in Switzerland. Each of the children receives the name of some animal, as Goat, Wolf, Snake, Frog, etc. To the swifter and more dangerous beasts are assigned the more distant positions. The keeper then shouts out that supper is ready, whereupon all rush home, each animal uttering his own peculiar cry. The last in is punished.

No. 114.

Milking-pails.

All the players join hands in a row, except one, who stands facing them at a distance of a few feet. The row slowly advances towards the solitary child, and then retreats, singing,

"Will you buy me a pair of milking-pails,
  Oh, mother! Oh, mother?
Will you buy me a pair of milking-pails,
  Oh, gentle mother of mine?"

The mother, advancing and retreating in her turn, sings,

"Where is the money to come from,
  Oh, daughter! Oh, daughter?
Where is the money to come from,
  Oh, gentle daughter of mine?"

The dialogue then continues to the same air,

"Where shall your father sleep?"
"Sleep in the servant's bed."
"Where shall the servant sleep?"
"Sleep in the stable."
"Where shall the pigs sleep?"
"In the wash-tub."
"Where shall we wash the clothes?"
"Wash them in the river."
"What if they should swim away?"
"You can jump in and go after them."

On this the indignant mother chases her daughters, and whoever is first caught must take the mother's place.

This game does not appear to be established in America, though we have heard of it as played in West Virginia. Our present version is from children lately arrived from England, where it seems to be a favorite.

No. 115.

Stealing Grapes.

A circle of children with arms raised. Enter keeper of garden:

"What are you doing in my vineyard?"
"Stealing grapes."
"What will you do if the black man comes?"
"Rush through if I can."

New York.

This game is probably a recent translation from the German. It is also played in Italy in a more humorous form. The thief exclaims, as he picks each, "A delicious grape!" The guardian demands,

"What did you pick that grape for?"
"Because it's first-rate."
"What would you do if I took a stick and chased you?"
"Pick a bunch and run."

Which he accordingly does.

No. 116.

Stealing Sticks.

A company of players divide, each having the same number of sticks, which they deposit on each side of a line; whoever crosses the line may seize a stick, but if caught is confined in a prison, marked out for the purpose.

This is the game of "Scots and English," and may be classed among sports originating in border warfare.

No. 117.

Hunt the Squirrel.

A ring of players is formed, about the outside of which circles a child who carries a knotted kandkerchief, with which he finally taps another on the shoulder, and starts to run round the ring. The child touched must pick up the handkerchief, and run in the opposite direction from the first. The two players, when they meet, must courtesy three times. The toucher endeavors to secure the other's place in the ring, failing which, he must begin again. As he goes about the circle, he recites the words:

Hunt the squirrel through the wood,
I lost him, I found him;
I have a little dog at home,
He won't bite you,
He won't bite you,
And he *will* bite you.

Cambridge, Mass.

In Philadelphia, a corresponding rhyme begins:

I carried water in my glove,
I sent a letter to my love.

A variation from New York:

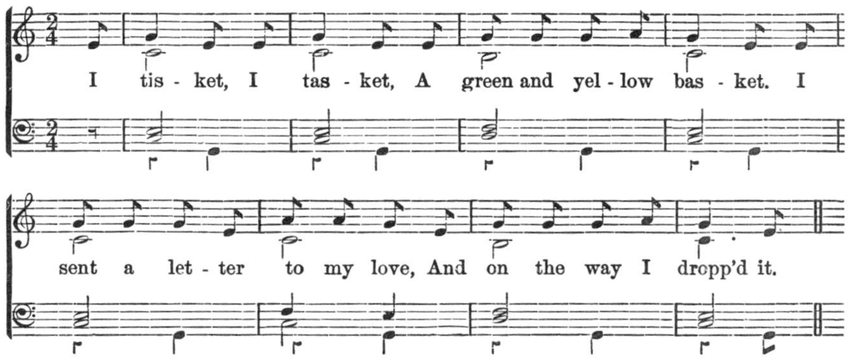

The name of the game in England is "Drop-glove."

Another and apparently older way of playing "Hunt the Squirrel" is a game in which the child touched follows the toucher until he has caught him, pursuing him both in and out of the ring, being obliged to enter and leave the circle at the same point as the latter.

A kissing-game, in which the player who makes the circuit taps another on the shoulder, and then takes flight, while the person touched is entitled to a kiss if he can capture the fugitive before the latter has made the tour of the circle and gained the vacant place, is a favorite among the "Pennsylvania Dutch," under the name of "Hen-slauch" (Hand-slag), that is, striking with the hand. The game is there called "Ring," and has inspired certain verses of Harbach, the nearest approach to a poet which that unimaginative race has produced.*

In a similar game, formerly played in Massachusetts, the leader of the game touches one of the party on the shoulder, and asks, "Have you seen my sheep?" The first replies, "How was it dressed?" The toucher now describes the costume of some player, who, as soon as he recognizes the description of himself, must take flight, and endeavor to regain his place in safety.

* See his "Schulhaus an dem Krik."

XII.

CERTAIN GAMES OF VERY LITTLE GIRLS.

Dans mon cœur il n'y a pas d'amour,
Mais il y en aura quelque jour.

French Round.

No. 118.

Sail the Ship.

Two little girls, clinching fingers, and bracing their feet against each other, whirl rapidly round, a movement which they call "Sailing the ship."

No. 119.

Three Around.

Three little girls join hands and swing about, being the simplest form of motion without song, to which they give the name of "Three Around."

No. 120.

Iron Gates.

Two little girls clasp hands tightly, singing,

Iron gates,
Never break,

While a third throws herself against them, and endeavors to break through.

No. 121.

Charley Over the Water.

Children sing, as they dance with clasped hands about one who stands in the centre of the ring:

Charley over the water,
Charley over the sea,
Charley catch a black-bird,
Can't catch *me!*

At the last word all stoop, and if the child in the centre can catch any other before assuming that position, the latter must replace him.

Almost any summer evening, in certain streets of New York, children may be seen playing this round, which they sing on one note, with a shriek to conclude.

No. 122.

Frog in the Sea.

Frog in the sea,
Can't catch me?

Played like the preceding. *Philadelphia.*

No. 123.

Defiance.

A mother and children:

"Mother, can I pick a rose?"
"Yes, my dearest daughter, if you don't tear your clothes,
But remember, to-morrow is your sister's wedding-day."

The children now retire to a safe distance, and sing:

"I picked a rose.
I tore my clothes!"
"Come home!"
"I don't hear you."
"I'll send your father after you."
"I don't hear you."
"I'll send your brother after you."
"I don't hear you."
"I'll send the dog after you."
"I don't hear you."
"I'll send myself after you."
"Sen' 'em along!"

A chase follows, and the child caught must replace the mother.

The dialogue (which belongs to Georgia) is also extended by the mother's threatening to send the *cow*, or the *trees*, after the children.

This game is differently played by little girls in Philadelphia, thus:

"Oh, mother, mother, may I go out to play?"
"No, no, no, it's a very cold day."
"Yes, yes, yes, it's a very warm day,
So take three steps, and away, away, away."
"Where's your manners?"
"I haven't any."

The indignant mother now pursues the disobedient children.

No. 124.

My Lady's Wardrobe.

The children sit in a ring, and are named according to the articles of a lady's wardrobe. The child in the centre of the circle of players names some article, as, "My lady wants her brush, brush, brush." She who has received that name must answer before the third utterance or pay forfeit. The speaker naturally pronounces the word as fast as possible.

No. 125.

Housekeeping.

(A ROUND.)

Kittie put the kettle on,
Kettle on, kettle on,
Kittie put the kettle on,
We'll all have tea.

To this familiar little round, girls five or six years of age, in New York, sometimes prefix a fragment of some ballad—

Here stands a red rose in the ring—
Promised to marry a long time ago.

No. 126.

A March.

March, march, two by two,
Dressed in yellow, pink, and blue.

Philadelphia.

No. 127.

Rhymes for Tickling.

1. Tickle'e, tickle'e on the knee;
If you laugh, you don't love me.

Philadelphia.

2. If you're a little lady, as I take you for to be,
You will neither laugh nor smile when I tickle your knee.

Georgia.

3. Old maid, old maid, you'll surely be,
If you laugh or you smile while I tickle your knee.

Massachusetts.

XIII.

BALL, AND SIMILAR SPORTS.

I call, I call; who doe ye call?
  The maids to catch this cowslip ball;
But since these cowslips fading be,
  Troth, leave the flowers, and maids take me.
Yet, if but neither you will doe,
  Speak but the word, and I'll take you.

Herrick.

No. 128.

The "Times" of Sports.

In an account of boys' sports, it would not be proper to omit some allusion to the custom of having a certain "time" of the year devoted to each amusement. These "times" succeeded each other almost as regularly as the flowers of summer, the children dropping one and taking up another every year at the same season. This succession, which the children themselves could hardly explain beforehand, but remembered when the occasion came, has impressed itself on observers as almost a matter of instinct. There was, however, a considerable degree of variation in the succession of sports in different parts of the country, and as the practice, though by no means obsolete, is now less strictly observed than formerly, we cannot give any very exact details on this head. It seems, however, that this succession was only partly dependent on the climate, and in part inherited from the mother country.

Thus, in all the states from Maine to Georgia, the first "time" was *marble-time.* In New England, the snow had hardly disappeared, when boys began to make the necessary holes in the ground, kneeling for that purpose on the night-frozen soil, from which the moisture was just oozing out, to the great detriment of their pantaloons. A friend, indeed, asserts that this was the *object* of the choice of seasons. But at the same time boys in Georgia (and, indeed, in England and Germany) were playing the same game.

The subsequent succession of sports in New York is indicated by the adage, "Top-time's gone, kite-time's come, and April Fool's day will soon be here."

In Georgia the succession was, kites, tops, and hoops. In that region the season for popguns is when the *China-berries** ripen. It is a provision of Providence, a clear case of design, thinks a friend, that just at that season the elder pith is ripe enough to be pushed out, and so leave the stalks empty to form the barrel of the weapon.

Ball is especially a holiday game. In Boston, *Fast-day* (the first Thursday of April) was particularly devoted to this sport. In England, the playing of ball at Easter-tide seems to have been a custom of the festival, inherited probably from pre-Christian ages. Foot-ball was a regular amusement on the afternoon of a New England Thanksgiving.

The invariable succession of children's sports has been also remarked in other countries. A Swiss writer says, "The principal games of boys belong to the first third of the year, return always in a like order, and replace each other after an equal interval, as if it were in the natural course of events, and without the individual child being able to say who had given the sign and made the beginning."

We may remark that another American usage has been remarked in other countries. In the last generation the boys of different towns, or of different quarters of the same town, waged regular and constant war. In Boston, for example, there was a well-defined line, beyond which no "North-ender" dared be seen. Any luckless lad obliged to go into the hostile district took good care to keep his eyes open, to dodge cautiously about the corners, and to be ready for instant flight in case of detection. So in France and Switzerland, where this warfare is a sort of game, a relic, no doubt, of the ancient separatism, which made every community in a measure an independent state. The chief weapons are stones, as they were formerly in the United States. In the old town of Marblehead boys were accustomed to "rock" any stranger, and no unknown driver dared to enter its limits with a vehicle.

* "Do you like best to stay at father's or grandma's?" "There's the most berries at grandma's—I'll rather be there." *Georgia Boy.*

No. 129.

Camping the Ball.

In the vocabulary of a Massachusetts schoolboy, to "camp" a foot-ball is to kick it, while held between the hands, from one side of the field to the other. In England, country-folk speak of the "camp-game" of ball, of the "camping-ground." In this amusement there are lines which mark the rear limit of the respective sides, while the ball is placed in the middle, and the object of either party is to drive it, with foot or hand, over the enemy's line. Similar, in the United States, is the old-fashioned game of foot-ball, in which, to use the expression of the play-ground, two captains "choose up" sides, selecting alternately from those present, and first play is determined by lot.

This description of football, or the English "camp-game," will answer very well for a translation of the account which Pollux, writing in Greek in the second century, gave of the "common ball," or "ball battle," * of his day. Almost exactly the same was the ancient Norse game, except that the resemblance to warfare was closer; the players were matched by age, and played against each other in the order of choice. The balls were heavy, sometimes made of horn, so that we read of men killed and wounded in the encounter. In like manner, up to a very recent time, in Lower Germany, villages contended against each other, hurling wooden balls loaded with lead, man against man. Thus the game was really "kemping" (*Kemp*, a warrior, champion), and the field a kemping-ground.

It was natural that, while the men contended, the boys also should have their mimic sports, in all respects similar; and we read in a Saga how the seven-year-old Egil slew with an axe his antagonist Grim, who had very properly knocked him down for breaking a bat over Grim's head. In those days such feats were held to presage an honorable career.

The Persians and Turks still practise a different sort of game, which is played on horseback, the riders using a racket to strike with. Five or six horsemen circle about, and strike the ball at each other; if it drops on the ground, a slave picks it up. The ball is heavy, covered with hard leather, and capable of doing serious harm. This game is, in fact, an imitation of warfare, a modification of casting the "jered," or javelin. The

* Sphaeromachia.

"Arabian Nights" recite how, while the Caliph Haroun Al-Raschid was playing, a spy aimed a ball at him from behind, with the intent of assassination.

The Byzantine court adopted from the East the playing on horseback and the racket, but introduced these into a game resembling the ancient "ball-battle." The historian Cinnamus describes the Emperor Manuel, in the twelfth century, as fond of this species of polo.

From Eastern custom we get our tennis, while most of our games with bat and ball seem to have come down to us from the ancient North.

The history of the change from actual to imitative warfare, from the latter to a harmless and courtly amusement or to a rustic pastime, from this last again in our own days to a scientific sport, may supply material for serious reflection.

No. 130.

Hand-ball.

No doubt our Saxon ancestors had, besides the half-military exercise referred to, other sports with the ball, better adapted to girls and children, though no description of such has come down to us. We know, however, that the Roman games with the ball were essentially the same as our own. Girls still strike, as then, balls with the palm of the hand to keep up their bouncing, or fling them against the wall to drive them back on the return, or pass the ball from hand to hand in the ring or row. Boys in those days, standing on the corners of a triangle, sent back the ball on the fly or the bounce, giving with one hand and taking with the other, much as they do to-day. The ball itself was very much the same in the time of the early empire as now, soft or hard, plain or covered with painted or embroidered cloth, a large hollow balloon, or a small light sphere. Children's balls were made with a rattle inside, and divided into gaudy divisions like the lobes of an orange, then as at present.

The oldest mention of a girls' game of ball is in the "Odyssey." It is a grand washing-day in the palace of Alcinous, and Nausicaa, daughter of the house, is to preside over the operation. So the "shining" but soiled raiment is brought out of a storeroom, loaded on a mule-wagon, with food, wine, and dainties, not forgetting a flask of oil for use after the bath. When the clothes have been scoured in pits along the river-side, and spread out to dry on the rocks by the shore, the maidens bathe, anoint themselves, and lunch. Afterwards the ball is brought out; the game is accompanied with song, in which the princess leads, and far excels the rest. The party is on the point of returning, the mules have been harnessed, and the clothes folded, when Nausicaa has a fancy for a romp; she throws the ball at one of her damsels, but misses her aim, and the ball falls into the eddying river, while the maidens shriek out loudly.

Misson (about 1700) mentions "the throwing at one another of tennis-balls by girls" in England, as a practice of a particular season of the year.

The German poets of the Middle Ages abound in allusions to the game, which is described with the same fresh poetical feeling that inspires the whole period. It was the first sport of summer. "When I saw the girls on the street throwing the ball, then came to our ears the song of the birds," says Walter von der Vogelweide. A common way of playing was for youths and maids to contend for the ball, which the possessor then threw to the one he or she "loved the best." A minnesinger pleasantly depicts the eager girls calling to some skilful and favorite lad, as he is about to throw, holding out their hands,

"Thou art mine, cousin—throw it here, this way!"

No. 131.

Stool-Ball.

William Bradford, the second Governor of Massachusetts, records, under date of the second Christmas-day of the colony: "The day called Christmas-Day, ye Govr caled them out to worke (as was used), but ye most of this new company excused themselves, and said it wente against their consciences to work on y^t^ day. So ye Govr tould them that if they made it mater of conscience, he would spare them till they were better informed. So he led away ye rest, and left them; but when they came home at noone from their worke, he found them in ye streete at play openly, some pitching ye bar, and some at stoole-ball and such like sports. So he went to them, and took away their implements, and tould them that it was against his conscience, that they should play and others work. If they would make ye keeping of it mater of devotion, let them keep their houses, but there should be no gameing or revelling in y[e] streets. Since which time nothing hath been attempted that way, at least openly."

Stool-ball was so named from the setting-up of a stool to be bowled at. The ball was struck with the hand by the player at the stool. If the ball struck the stool, the players changed places. In another form of the game, which seems to be that referred to here, there were several stools, men at each, and a bowler outside. When the ball was hit (with the hand) the players must change places, and the bowler was at liberty to hit with the ball any player while between the stools, and so put him out.

Bradford, as a Puritan, had perhaps some reason for his aversion to hand-ball on holidays, seeing that it appears to be connected with ancient religious usage. "Stool-ball" was especially an Easter-game, played by ladies for small stakes, particularly a *tansy* or Easter-cake;* thus we have the name in a pretty rhyme of the seventeenth century—

At stool-ball, Lucia, let us play,
For sugar, cakes, or wine;
Or for a tansey let us pay,
The loss be mine or thine.
If thou, my dear, a winner be,
At trundling of the ball,
The wager thou shalt have, and me,
And my misfortunes all.

According to a curious extract from a manuscript given by Ducange, of the diocese of Auxerre, it was an ancient custom to play in the church, on Easter Monday, a solemn game of ball, while singing anthems proper to the season.

"The ball having been received from a proselyte, the dean, or another in his stead, he and the rest wearing the *almutia*, sang the antiphonal which begins, "*Victimæ Paschali laudes*," then seizing the ball with his left hand, he led the dance, the others, taking hold of hands, variously inflecting the chorus, while the ball was delivered or thrown by the dean to one or more of the choristers alternately, so as to weave a garland, as it were. The game and motions were conducted according to the numbers of the prose. The dancing having been finished, the chorus after the dance hastened to the banquet."

* Made, according to Johnson, with the leaves of newly sprung herbs.

This dance was not merely a local custom, but practised in other towns. At Vienne it was conducted by the archbishop in his palace.

No doubt we have here a survival of the ancient games of the spring festival, in a day when mirth and the exhibition of physical prowess were considered acceptable to deity, and elevated into religious exercises.

No. 132.

Call-Ball.

This game (commonly called Callie-ball, or Ballie-callie), was formerly a common sport of school-boys in New England. The ball was thrown against a house, and at the same time a name called. The lad named must strike back the ball on its rebound.

We are not well informed as to the sequence, but the game in Austria, where it is well known, goes on as follows: If the player, whose name is called, drops the ball, he must pick it up as quickly as possible, while the rest scatter. He then calls "Stand!" upon which the players halt, and he flings it at whom he pleases. If he misses his aim, he must place himself in a bent position with his hands against a wall, until every player has taken a shot at him.

The delightful lines of Herrick, cited as the motto of the present chapter, show us youths and maids playing at "call-ball;" but the game here appears to consist simply in calling out the name of the person of the opposite sex who is to catch the ball, as in the mediæval sport referred to in No. 130.

No. 133.

Haley-Over.

The players are divided into equal parties, who take position on different sides of a building, out of sight of each other. A lad then throws the ball over the roof of the house, to any height or in any direction he pleases. It is the object of the opposite side to catch the ball on its descent; and if any player succeed in doing so, he immediately darts round the corner, and attempts to hit with the ball some player of the other side, who scatter in all directions. To this end, he may either throw the ball from a distance, or chase any antagonist till he has come up with him, and has an easier mark. If he succeed in hitting a boy, the latter must follow the former back to his own side, to which he henceforward belongs. The game is continued until all players have been brought over to one side. The party from which the ball has been thrown have no means of knowing whether it has been caught or not, until its return, and must be prepared to see an adversary suddenly appear, ball in hand, and ready to throw. Hence the excitement of the game, which belongs to Connecticut.

No. 134.

School-Ball.

In this amusement of New England school-girls, the ball is tossed by the *teacher* to the head of the class, and, after being returned by the latter, sent to the next of the row, and so on. If any girl misses, she must go to the foot, and if the *teacher* misses, the *first scholar* takes her place.

No. 135.

Wicket.

This exercise is an old-fashioned game resembling cricket. A peculiar, long, shovel-shaped bat is used, flat, straight on one side and spoon-shaped on the other. The ball is bowled at the wicket, which is defended by the player. When the ball is struck, a run must be made to the base of the bowler, and return.

No. 136.

Hockey.

This sport is also called *Shinny.* The ball is struck on the ground with a bent stick, the object being to drive it over the enemy's line. The game is much played on the ice, as has been the case from the oldest times in the North; for this is doubtless a descendant of the games with bat and ball described in Icelandic Sagas. The name of "Bat and Ball," also given to this sport, indicates that in many districts this was the usual way of playing ball with the bat.

No. 137.

Roll-Ball.

A row of holes large enough to contain the ball is made, one for each boy. The player to whom is allotted the last hole takes the ball, stands off, and rolls it in such a way as to stop in one of the holes. The boy into whose place the ball has rolled seizes it, while the rest scatter, and throws it at some one of the group; if he succeeds in hitting him, a stone is placed in the hole of that boy; if not, the thrower must put a stone in his own. The rolling of the ball is then repeated. When five stones (called *babies**) are lodged in any hole, that boy is out of the game.

This New England game is exactly paralleled in Switzerland and Austria.

No. 138.

Hat-Ball.

This is the same game as the preceding, played (among the Pennsylvania Germans) with *hats* instead of *holes*. The ball is tossed into the hat of the player who is to begin. The first to get five stones in his hat loses, and must undergo the punishment of being "paddled," passing under the legs of the row of players for that purpose.

No. 139.

Corner-Ball.

This is also an old game kept up by the Pennsylvania Germans—Pennsylvania Dutch,† as they are commonly called. Four players stand on the four angles of a square, and the four adversaries in the centre.

* The identical name in Austria, "Kinder."

† They are descendants of emigrants from the Upper Rhine, and speak a dialect resembling that of the Palatinate, but mixed with English words.

The ball is passed from one to another of the players in the corners, and finally thrown at the central players. For this purpose the following rhyme (which our readers may translate if they can) is used by the boy who aims the ball at the players in the centre. These last, if they can catch the ball, may fling it back.

Bŏla we Sols,
Butar we Schmŏls,
Pĕf'r gat uf,
War fongt schmeist druf.

If the player in the corner hits a central player, the latter is out, and *vice versâ.*

The last player of the losing party has to stand with his head against a wall till every antagonist has flung the ball at him.

No. 140.

Base-ball.

It is only within a few years that Base-ball has become the "national sport" of America. The present scientific game, which we naturally do not intend to describe, was known in Massachusetts, twenty years ago, as the "New York game." A ruder form of Base-ball has been played in some Massachusetts towns for a century; while in other parts of New England no game with the ball was formerly known except "Hockey." There was great local variety in these sports.

We may refer to some features of the old-fashioned game which possess interest. The first duty, in games with the bat, is "to choose up." The two best players, or any two selected, toss the bat from one to another; the tosser places his right hand above the hand of the catcher, who in turn follows with his own left, and so on.* He who can get the last hold has first choice; but the hold must be proved by ability to whirl the bat three times round the head, and throw it. Another test of a suf-

* The like method in Austria, where the general idea of the game, and many particulars, are the same. There are, however, only two bases. The same way, even to the ability to throw the bat with two fingers, which is the test of a doubtful hold, is used in Switzerland to determine choice of sides in the game answering to No. 139. These coincidences seem to point to a remote antiquity of usage.

ficient grasp is for a player to hammer with a second bat on the hand which is uppermost. In this last case, therefore, the grasp must be low enough for the wood of the bat to be struck by the blow.

In this game there were three "bases" besides the "home" base, at about the same distance as at present; but the number of players was indeterminate. The pitcher threw the ball, and the catcher stood close behind the striker. When the batsman struck the ball, a run must be made; and the ball was not, as at present, thrown *to* the base, but *at* the runner, usually with all the force possible. If he was hit, he was out, and each member of the side had to be put out separately. There were, moreover, ways in which a side could recover its lost players. When all were out but one, who was on one of the bases, the pitcher and catcher, approaching to within some thirty feet, tossed the ball to and fro, and the runner must "steal" his next base, while the two former watched his movements, ready to throw to the nearest fielder of their side, who in turn would hurl the ball at the remaining player. If under these circumstances he could reach home untouched, he might "put in" any player of his side.

As there was never any umpire in these games, the field for controversy was unlimited. One way, as we recollect, of settling disputes was as follows: All proceeding to the spot of the doubtful catch, the best player on one side hurled the ball with all his force upwards; if it was caught by the designated player of the other party, the point was given in the latter's favor, and *vice versâ.*

We need only mention the game of "Old Cat," in which there are two goals—the striker's and the pitcher's—and the run is made from the former to the latter and return. The game is then named from the number of batters, "One Old Cat," or "Two Old Cat."

No. 141.

Marbles.

We do not intend to describe the various games of marbles, which might probably fill a small volume. Of these there are two principal types. One consists in striking the marbles out of a ring, by shooting from a line, or *taw,* drawn as a limit; the other, in making the tour of a series of holes made for the purpose. Whoever first gets back to the starting-point, or taw, wins.

The first of these games may be descended from a sport of Roman children, mentioned by Ovid, and still in existence, in which nuts are rolled down an inclined plane, with the object of striking the nut of the adversary. The second seems to be the childish reduction of a game with the ball, similar to "Golf."

Extensive is the lore of marbles. When a lad wishes to change his position, so that, while preserving the same distance from his mark, he may have a more favorable position, he exclaims, "Roundings." If, however, his antagonist is quick enough, he will cry "Fen [defend] roundings." The game, when played to win the marbles of the opponent, is said to be "in earnest." If any accident happens, and the opponent's play is to be checked, a Georgia lad will say "King's excuse." That this is an ancient phrase is shown by the corruption of the same cry in Pennsylvania, "King's scruse." Under certain circumstances a boy who puts down a second marble is said to "dub" (double) a marble, or to play "dubs."*

No. 142.

Cat.

The "cat" is a little billet of wood, about four inches long, and pointed at the ends, which is to be struck with a light stick. A player stands at a little distance, and endeavors to throw this missile into a hole or circle previously made. Another stands over the circle, and defends it with his stick. If the cat falls in the circle, the batter is out. If, on the other hand, it falls out of the circle, he has the right of making a stroke. Placing the cat within the circle, he hits it on one end with his bat; and, as it bounds upwards, endeavors to strike it as far away as possible. If the cat is caught, he is out; otherwise, he is entitled to score a number, proportioned to the distance which the cat has been struck, estimated in jumps or foot-lengths. This score, however, is subject to a peculiar negotiation. The pitcher offers the batter a certain number of

* "Fen burnings!" "Roundings!" "Dubs!" "Knuckle down tight where you lay!" "Burnings" signifies breathing on a marble, and thereby getting certain advantages. The lads whom we quote never used the word marbles, but *mibs.* "Let's play mibs."

points—as, for example, five. If this is not accepted, he raises his bid to eight, ten, or as high as he thinks proper; but if his final offer is refused, the pitcher measures the distance (in jumps or lengths of the foot), and if he can accomplish it in a less number than that offered, the striker or his side lose that number of points; otherwise, the number measured is scored. The game is an agreed number of hundreds. This game is now played in Hindostan, as well as in Italy and Germany.

No. 143.

Cherry-pits.

Cherry-pits are referred to as used in boys' games as early as A.D. 1522, and are still so used in the streets of New York.

The pits are thrown over the palm by the boy whose turn it is to play; they must fall so far apart that the finger can be passed between them. Then the player with a fillip of the thumb makes his pit strike the enemy's, and wins both. If he misses, the next takes his place.

This game, like the rest, has its regular season, at which all the boys in the neighborhood may be seen playing it.*

No. 144.

Buttons.

Buttons are in extensive use in the sports of German children, with whom they form a sort of coinage, each sort having a stipulated exchangeable value. Traces of similar usage exist in the United States.

A common New York game consists in throwing buttons. A line is drawn, and a hole made about twelve feet off. The players toss their buttons, and whoever comes nearest the hole has the first shot. He endeavors to drive the buttons of the rest into the hole, striking them with the extended thumb by a movement of the whole hand, which is kept flat and stiff. When he misses the next takes his turn, and so on. Whoever drives the adversary's button into the hole wins it.

* "Cherry-pits are in now; buttons won't be in for a fortnight."—*New York boy.*

Another game, for two players, is called "Spans." The buttons are cast against the wall, and if a player's button falls within a span of the adversary's, he may aim at it and win it by striking as before.

No. 145.

Hop-Scotch.

A figure of about twelve feet in length, similar to that represented in the diagram, is described on the ground, and selection made of a small flat stone, having sharp edges. From a line drawn at a distance of a few paces, a stone is tossed into No. 1, after which the boy or girl hops on one foot into No. 1, and kicks out the stone, which is then thrown into No. 2. The player now hops into No. 1, and jumps into No. 2, in such a way that one foot is in the division 2, and one foot in 1. The stone is kicked into 1, and then out, and so on. In passing through divisions 1 and 2, 4 and 5, 8 and 9, a straddle must be made, one foot being placed in each; in the others a hop only must be taken. A failure to throw the stone into the right place, or to kick it into the right division, or leaving it on any line, or touching the raised foot, or stepping on a line, puts out, and the next takes his or her turn.

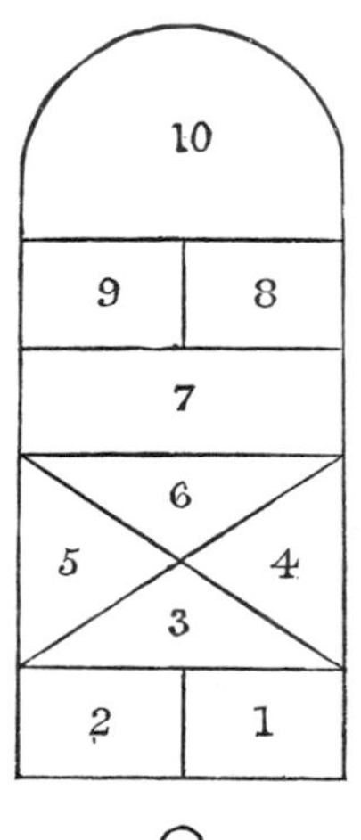

In other localities, no straddling step is taken, but the player, in certain divisions, is allowed to place the stone on his foot, and so expel it from the figure at a single kick; the compartments also vary in number and arrangement.

This is one of the universal games, common from England to Hindostan. Everywhere the game consists in describing on the soil an oblong figure with several divisions, and in tossing a flat stone or potsherd into them, and then kicking it out with a hopping motion; the arrangement of the divisions differs. From the shape of the last compartment, the game is called in Italy "The Bell," and in Austria "The Temple." In Italy the three last divisions are the *Inferno*, *Purgatorio*, and *Paradiso*. In New York the last is called *Pot*.

No. 146.

Duck on a Rock.

We will suppose a party of boys to be debating what game to play. "What shall we play?" "Duck on a Rock," suggests one. The idea is instantly taken up. "My one duck," cries some boy. "My duck," shouts a second, seizing a stone. The last to "speak" gets no duck, and has to guard the "drake." The drake is a good-sized stone, which is placed on an elevated position, or boulder, if such be at hand. The "ducks" are stones about the size of the fist. The object is to knock the drake off the rock. After each player has thrown his duck, and missed, he must recover it. The guardian stands by the "rock," but cannot tag a player until the latter has touched his own duck, when he must replace the keeper. Meanwhile, if the drake is knocked off the rock, the keeper must replace it before he can tag any one, and this is therefore the signal for a rush to recover the thrown ducks. The game is not without a spice of danger from these missiles.

No. 147.

Mumblety-peg.

In this game of boys and girls, a knife is cast to the earth, on a piece of turf, with the point downwards, and must remain sticking there; there are several successive positions of throwing, as follows: (1) the knife is held in the palm, first of the right and afterwards of the left hand, point outward, and thrown so as to revolve towards the player; (2) it is rested successively on the right and left fist, with the point uppermost, and thrown sideways; (3) the knife is pressed with the point resting on each finger and thumb of both hands in succession, and cast outwards; after this it is held by the point, and *flipped* (4) from the breast, nose, and each eye; (5) from each ear, crossing arms, and taking hold of the opposite ear with the free hand; (6) over the head backwards. If the knife does not "stick," the next player takes his turn; the first to conclude the series wins. The winner is allowed to drive a peg into the ground with three blows of the knife, which the other must extract with his teeth, whence the name, "Mumblety-peg." Another title is "Stick-knife."

No. 148.

Five-stones.

Such was the title of the common game in a New England town (Salem, Mass.).* The same amusement, under the same name, was popular in Greece more than two thousand years ago, being mentioned as a girls' game by Aristophanes. It is thus described by Pollux: "The game of 'five-stones;' little stones, pebbles, or bones are thrown up, so as to catch them on the back of the turned hand, or if not all are caught, the rest must be picked up with the fingers, while the others remain on the hand."

A pleasing painting in the Museum of Naples represents goddesses playing at "Five-stones." Aglaë is looking on; three of her bones lie on the ground, one is pressed by her thumb, the fifth is hidden by her garments. Hileæra has just thrown; she has caught three, the other two are falling to the ground. Niobe, Latona, and Phœbe are standing behind.

One of the movements of the Spanish game is still exactly the same as that described by the Greek writers of the second century. The game in America, as played in the childhood of the writer, also began with catching the stones on the back of the hand, at first one only out of the five tossed up, then two, three, four, and, finally, the whole five.

The game now consists of an indefinite number of figures, of which the names and arrangements vary in different localities. In all those described below, a single stone is tossed up, to be caught in the palm, and while this is in the air the others must be taken into the hand, or certain motions made.

Ones, twos, threes, fours.—The stones are rolled on the table or floor, either directly from the right hand, or over the back of the left hand resting on the table. A single stone being selected and tossed in the air, as above mentioned, the rest must be picked up; in the first figure one at a time, in the second by groups of two, in the third by three and one, and finally the whole four together. In case of an error, the next takes his turn.

* Communicated by the late Mr. George Nichols, of Cambridge, Mass., formerly of Salem. The common name, *Jack-stones*, seems to be a corruption for *Chuck-stones*, small stones which can be chucked or thrown. "Chuckie-stanes," in Scotland, means small pebbles. "Checkstones, small pebbles with which children play."—*Dialect of Craven.*

Jumping the Ditch.—The four stones remaining, after one has been chosen, are placed in a line; the first and third of the row are then to be caught up together, and afterwards the second and fourth.

Knock at the Door, Strike the Match, Wash the Clothes, etc.—A selected stone being thrown up, motions corresponding to the title are to be made on the floor while it is in the air.

Set the Table.—Four stones are placed in a heap, as if to represent a pile of plates. One of these is taken from the heap, in the usual manner. It is then held between the thumb and palm of the right hand, and, with a second toss of the chosen stone, is deposited on the floor at the corner of an imaginary square. The square having been completed by four stones, motions are made to indicate the arrangement of the glasses, etc. *Clear the Table* is the reverse movement, in which the stones are again brought to the centre.

The Well.—The left hand is laid on the table with the thumb and index finger joined. Into the opening so formed the four stones are pushed, by a fillip of the finger. The hand is then removed from the table, and the stones must be caught up together as they lie. The figures vary, according as the thumb and index are made to form an arch or circle, are laid on the table or floor horizontally, or in an upright position, or, finally, as the hand is raised above the table in the form of a cup. These varieties receive the names of *Peas in the Pod, Doves in the Cot*, etc.

Horses in the Stall.—The left hand is laid on the table with the fingers extended, and four stones placed in front of the openings, representing stalls. A stone being thrown up as usual, the four others are filliped into the openings, and afterwards must be picked up together from the positions in which they lie. In *Horses out of the Stall* the stones are brought out from between the fingers, and then caught up.

Other movements are *Feeding the Elephant, Spinning the Wheel, Going up the Ladder*, etc., to the number of thirty or more. Failing to catch the stone thrown up, or not succeeding in the required motion, or touching a stone unnecessarily, constitute errors, in which case it is often required to go back to the very beginning of the game.

Instead of pebbles, little double tripods of iron, probably representing the more ancient *bones*, are generally in use; and the fifth stone, or "jack," is often replaced by a ball or marble, the latter being allowed to bound before it is caught. This usage seems to be of German origin. Sometimes marbles are used, the "jack" being of a different color from the rest, and school-girls take pride in the beauty of the agates they employ for this purpose.

About Boston a similar game is much played under the name of "Ota-dama," or "Japanese jacks." Seven little silk bags are filled with rice, one, of a different color from the rest, being called the "jack." The game consists of four parts. In the first figure, the silk bags being placed on the floor, the "jack" is thrown up, and the other six picked up one by one, being so deposited as to keep them together in groups of twos, so that two at a time may be caught up, which is the next thing to be done. Then come groups of three, four and two, and five and one, next the six together, the bags, after being caught, being so dropped as to prepare for the following movements. The next motion is "tattoo," which consists in throwing up the "jack" and catching it on the back of the hand, then throwing it up again from the back of the hand and catching it in the fingers, without turning over the palm.

The second figure contains "second ones," "second twos," "second threes," "second fours," "second fives," "second sixes." These are the same as in the first figure, except that in each case the bags caught, instead of being merely dropped from the hand, as before, are tossed up together with the "jack," which last must be caught again before falling. In the second and third figures "tattoo" follows every movement.

The third figure begins with "third sixes," in which, the six bags being caught up and held tightly, the "jack" is again tossed, the six slapped on the floor, and the "jack" caught on the back of the hand. The second motion is "fourth sixes," which resembles second sixes, except that the "jack" is now caught on the back of the hand. Next comes "touch." The six bags are caught up, thrown with the "jack" into the air, and the floor is touched with the middle finger, before catching the "jack." After this follows "fours and threes," in which, the six bags having been caught up, the palm is turned uppermost with the seven bags (including the "jack"), and it is required to throw off first four at a time, and afterwards the other three. "Pack up" is the next motion. The six bags are caught up, compactly arranged in the palm of the hand, and must be thrown up and caught on the back of the hand. Two chances are allowed. The bags dropped the first time may be tried by themselves. Then "third ones," which is the same as "second ones," except that, the bags being placed in a row with the "jack" at the left, the "jack" is constantly exchanged for each bag that is caught up. "Tattoo" follows each of these movements.

The fourth and last figure is done with the left hand. The palm is turned towards the floor, upon which all the bags lie in a row, the "jack" at the right; a bag is then picked up by the thumb and forefinger, keeping the other fingers extended, and is tossed on the back of the hand. It must remain there while the second bag is picked up, and is tossed off the hand when the second is tossed on. This motion is repeated with the other five, ending with the "jack," and the game is finished with "tattoo."

The game is played by two or more. In case of an error, the next plays; but an error in the last figure requires the player to go back to the beginning of the game. The "jack" is often made square and somewhat flat, while the other bags are drawn up at two ends, and have a rounder shape. It is necessary that they should be soft and flexible.

This game is of Japanese origin, "Tedama"*—that is, "Hand-balls"—being its proper name. As the specimen given shows, it closely resembles the ancient game of "Five-stones." We are informed, on Japanese authority, that stones are habitually used by boys in playing, and that the number of these varies. There can be no doubt that the two forms of this amusement are branches of the same root; and we thus have an example of a game which, having preserved its essential characteristics for thousands of years, has fairly circumnavigated the globe, so that the two currents of tradition, westward and eastward, from Europe and Asia, have met in America.

* O-tédama (pronounce as in Italian) is, we learn, compounded of *O*, the, *te*, hand, and *tama*, balls. It is played with song, which consists in chanting the titles of the several movements; thus, in the first figure, (1) O Hito, (2) O Fu, (3) O Mi, (4) O Yo, (5) O Itzu, (6) O Mu. The second figure, in which begins *Tonkiri* ("tattoo"), is called Zakara (a meaningless word); and the chant is, (1) O Hito Zakara, (2) O Fu Zakara, (3) O Mi Zakara, etc. These numbers are children's numeration, of which there are two sorts; the present series continues, (7) Nana, (8) Ya, (9) Kono, (10) To. We have varying forms from a friend in Hartford, Conn., where the song has been borrowed from Japanese students. Probably provincial usages in Japan differ. We give the above terms (not the game, which is current in the United States), as written by a Japanese gentleman. It is noteworthy that this childish system has no connection with the regular table.

XIV.

RHYMES FOR COUNTING OUT.

Petite fille de Paris,
Prête-moi tes souliers gris,
Pour aller en Paradis.
Nous irons un à un,
Dans le chemin des Saints;
Deux à deux,
Sur le chemin des cieux.

French Counting Rhyme.

No. 149.

Counting Rhymes.

THERE are various ways in which children decide who shall begin in a game, or, as the phrase is, be "it."* When this position is an advantage, it is often determined by the simple process of "speaking first." So far as can be determined when all are shouting at once, the first speaker is then entitled to the best place. Otherwise it is the practice to draw straws, the shortest gaining; to "toss up" a coin, "heads or tails;" or to choose between the two hands, one of which holds a pebble.

The most interesting way of decision, however, is by employing the rhymes for "counting out." A child tells off with his finger one word of the rhyme for each of the group, and he on whom the last word falls is "out."† This process of exclusion is continued until one only is left, who has the usually unpleasant duty of leading in the sport. All European nations possess such rhymes, and apply them in a like manner. These have the common peculiarity of having very little sense, being

* The French expression is the same, *l'être* or *en être*. The Germans do not use an equivalent, but say to be *in*, to be *out; sein daran, sein daraus.*

† An old way of arranging this is for each of the group to put a finger inside a hat, in order that the words may be told off on the fingers.

often mere jargons of unmeaning sounds. This does not prevent them from being very ancient. People of advanced years often wonder to find their grandchildren using the same formulas, without the change of a word. The identity between American and English usage establishes the currency of some such for three centuries, since they must have been in common use at the time of the settlement of this country. We may be tolerably sure that Shakespeare and Sidney directed their childish sports by the very same rhymes which are still employed for the purpose. Furthermore, German and other languages, while they rarely exhibit the identical phrases, present us with types which resemble our own, and obviously have a common origin. Such a relation implies a very great antiquity; and it becomes a matter of no little curiosity to determine the origin of a practice which must have been consecrated by the childish usage of all the great names of modern history.

This origin is by no means clear; but we may make remarks which will at least clear away misconceptions. We begin with that class of formulas which we have marked from 1 to 13 inclusive.

Respecting these rhymes, we observe, in the first place, that they are meaningless. We might suppose that they were originally otherwise; for example, we might presume that the first of the formulas given below had once been an imitation or parody of some list of saints, or of some charm or prayer. A wider view, however, shows that the rhymes are in fact a mere jargon of sound, and that such significance, where it appears to exist, has been interpreted into the lines. We observe further, that, in despite of the antiquity of some of these formulas, their liability to variation is so great that phrases totally different in sound and apparent sense may at any time be developed out of them.

These variations are effected chiefly in two ways—rhyme and alliteration. A change in the termination of a sound has often involved the introduction of a whole line to correspond; and in this manner a fragment of nursery song may be inserted which totally alters the character of the verse. Again, the desire for a quaint alliterative effect has similarly changed the initial letters of the words of the formulas, according as the whim of the moment suggested.

From the fact that neither rhyme nor alliteration is any guide to the relations of these formulas, but seem arbitrarily introduced, we might conclude that the original type had neither one nor the other of these characteristics. This view is confirmed by European forms in which they appear as mere lists of unconnected words, possessing some equality of tone. Rhythm is a more permanent quality in them than termination or initial. From these considerations it appears likely that the original form of the rhymes of which we speak was that of a comparatively brief list of dissyllabic or trisyllabic words.

Now, when we observe that the first word of all the rhymes of this class is obviously a form of the number *one;* that the second word appears to be *two*, or a euphonic modification of *two*, and that numbers are perpetually introducing themselves into the series, it is natural to suppose that these formulas may have arisen from simple numeration.

This supposition is made more probable by a related and very curious system of counting up to twenty (of which examples will be found below), first brought into notice by Mr. Alexander J. Ellis, vice-president of the Philological Society of Great Britain, and called by him the "Anglo-Cymric Score." Dr. J. Hammond Trumbull, of Hartford, Conn., noticing the correspondence of Mr. Ellis's score with numerals attributed to a tribe of Indians in Maine (the Wawenocs), was led to make inquiries, which have resulted in showing that the method of counting in question was really employed by Indians in dealing with the colonists, having been remembered in Rhode Island, Connecticut, Massachusetts, New Hampshire, and Ohio (where it passed for genuine Indian numeration), and in this way handed down to the present generation as a curiosity. Mr. Ellis has found this score to be still in use in parts of England—principally in Cumberland, Westmoreland, and Yorkshire, where it is employed by shepherds to count their sheep, by old women to enumerate the stitches of their knitting, by boys and girls for "counting out," or by nurses to amuse children. It is, therefore, apparent that this singular method of numeration must have been tolerably familiar in the mother-country in the seventeenth century, since the Indians evidently learned it from the early settlers of New England. It appears, indeed, that not only the score itself, but also its chief variations, must have been established at that time. Mr. Ellis, however, who has shown that the basis of these formulas is Welsh, is disposed "to regard them as a comparatively recent importation" into England. Be that as it may, we see that the elements of change we have described, alliteration and rhyme, have been busy with the series. While the score has preserved its identity as a list of numerals, the successive pairs of numbers have been altered beyond all recognition, and with perfect arbitrariness.

It is plain that our counting rhymes cannot have been formed from the "Anglo-Cymric score," since the latter is only in use in parts of England, while the former are common to many European nations. Nothing, however, prevents the supposition that they owe their origin to a similar root. All that can be said is, that no modern language is responsible for the practice, which can hardly be supposed to have originated within the last thousand years.

Turning now to other types of formulas for counting, we see that any game-rhyme or nursery verse may do duty for such. Of lines used solely for this purpose, we find forms which have analogies on the continent of Europe. Some of the childish verses so used, like the French rhyme we have set at the head of our chapter, contain allusions which stamp them as ancient. On the other hand, it seems that, in our own country, little American inventions of the sort, recommended by some attractive quaintness, have gained currency, unwritten as of course they are, from Canada to the Gulf.

It appears, from foreign usage, that it was formerly common for each game to have its own especial formula for "counting out," a practice of which we have an example in No. 107.

(1.) Onery, uery, hickory, Ann,
Fillison, follason, Nicholas John,
Queevy, quavy, Virgin Mary,
Singalum, sangalum, buck.
—*Philadelphia.*

(2.) Onery, uery, ickory, Ann,
Filisy, folasy, Nicholas John,
Queevy, quavy, Irish Mary,
Stingalum, stangalum, buck.*
—*New England.*

(3.) Onery, uery, ickory, Ann,
Fillison, follason, Nicholas John,
Queevy, quavy, English navy,

* English *onery, twoery,* etc. The forms we give date back to about 1820, before the publication of the "Nursery Rhymes of England." There are numerous small variations. "*Virgin* Mary" we have from informants in the Middle States; "*Irish* Mary" was the common New England phrase.

Stinkalum, stankalum, John Buck.
B-u-c-k spells buck.
—*Cincinnati* (1880).

(4.) Onery, uery, ickory, a,
Hallibone, crackabone, ninery-lay,
Whisko, bango, poker my stick,
Mejoliky one leg!
—*Scituate, Mass.* (about 1800).

(5.) Onery, uery, hickory, able,
Hallowbone, crackabone, Timothy, ladle,
* * * * *
—*Salem, Mass.**

(6.) One's all, zuzall, titterall, tann,
Bobtailed vinegar, little Paul ran,
Harum scarum, merchant marum,
Nigger, turnpike, toll-house, out.
—*Salem, Mass.*†

(7.) One-amy, uery, hickory, seven,
Hallibone, crackabone, ten and eleven,
Peep—O, it must be done,
Twiggle, twaggle, twenty-one.
—*Georgia.*‡

(8.) Onery, uery, ickery, see,
Huckabone, crackabone, tillibonee;
Ram pang, muski dan,
Striddledum, straddledum, twenty-one.§
—*Connecticut.*

* This rhyme was used only by *girls.* Boys employed No. 2, and would have been laughed at for counting like girls.

† Used by *boys* in the western part of the town, where were the toll-house and negro settlement.

‡ English rhymes :

Oneery, twoery, ziccary, zan,
Hollowbone, crackabone, ninery, ten—etc.

§ This class of formulas (Nos. 1 to 8) appear to be mere variations of the same type, a fact which does not prevent individual forms from exhibiting a wonderful permanence. We consider as identical a class of German formulas, very wide-spread and variable, thus :

(9.) Eny, meny, mony, my,
Tusca, leina, bona, stry,
Kay bell, broken well,
We, wo, wack.*
—*Massachusetts.*

(10.) Eny, meny, mony, mine,
Hasdy, pasky, daily, ine,
Agy, dagy, walk.
—*Connecticut.*

(11.) Eny, meny, mony, mite,
Butter, lather, bony strike,
Hair cut, froth neck,
Halico balico,
We, wo, wack.
—*Philadelphia.*

(*a.*) Unichi, dunichi, tipel-te! Tibel, tabel, domine.
(*b.*) Eckati peckati zuchati me, Avi schavi domine.
(*c.*) Aeniga mäniga tumpel-ti, Tifel, tafel numine.
(*d.*) Anigl panigl subtrahi! Tivi tavi, domini.
(*e.*) Endeli bändeli deffendé, Gloria tibi domine.

A rhyme quoted by Mr. Ellis from the *Millhill Magazine* (a school paper), and credited to America, is similar:

(*f.*) Eeney, meeny, tipty te, Teena, Dinah, Domine.

The following formulas from Transylvania are of a simpler type; the first is said to imitate the *Gipsy*, the second the *Magyar*, speech:

(*g.*) Unemi, dunemi, tronemi, ronemi, donemi,
ronza, konza, jewla, dewla, tschok!

(*h.*) Aketum, täketum, tinum, tanum, ärsak, märsak, etc.

We take the latter type to be a nearer approach to the original form. All sorts of intermediate stages can be observed from between these lists and the more complicated examples; but we find no signs of numbers above ten, as in the "Anglo-Cymric score." The Russian and Finnish tongues present similar rhymed lists, while many Italian rhymes are of like origin, though disguised and extended.

* In North Germany:

Ene tene mone mei, Paster Lone bone, strei,
Ene fune herke berke, Wer? wie? wo? was?

As this is but one case of identity out of many hundreds, we suppose the rhyme borrowed from the English. There are many German rhymes beginning "Ene mene mu," or similarly; but the variation of the first sounds is endless: ene dene, ene tene, ene mene, ente twente, entele mentele, ane tane, unig tunig, oringa loringa, etc.; by association or rhyme, any nursery song may be introduced, or the first words may be dropped.

(12.) Ena, mena, mona, my,
Panalona, bona, stry,
Ee wee, fowl's neck,
Hallibone, crackabone, ten and eleven,
O-u-t spells out.

(13.) Intery, mintery, cutery corn,
Apple-seed and apple-thorn,
Wire, briar, limber lock,
Five mice in a flock;
Catch him Jack,
Hold him Tom,
Blow the bellows,
Old man out.
—*Massachusetts.*

(14.) Ikkamy, dukkamy, alligar, mole,
Dick slew alligar slum,
Hukka pukka, Peter's gum,
Francis.
—*Massachusetts.*

(15)	1. ane.	6. sother.	11. een dick.	16. een bumfrey.
	2. tane.	7. lother.	12. teen dick.	17. teen bumfrey.
	3. tother.	8. co.	13. tother dick.	18. tother bumfrey.
	4. feather.	9. deffrey.	14. feather dick.	19. feather bumfrey.
	5. fip.	10. dick.	15. bumfrey.	20. gig it.

(16)	1. een.	6. sother.	11. een dick.	16. een bumpit.
	2. teen.	7. lother.	12. teen dick.	17. teen bumpit.
	3. tuther.	8. porter.	13. tuther dick.	18. tuther bumpit.
	4. futher.	9. dubber.	14. futher dick.	19. futher bumpit.
	5. fip.	10. dick.	15. bumpit.	20. gig it.*

* These examples of the "Anglo-Cymric score" (see page 196) were obtained, No. 15 from Mrs. Ellis Allen of West Newton, now ninety years of age, who was born at Scituate, Mass., where she learned the formula; and No. 16 of her daughter, who learned it from an Indian woman, *Mary Wolsomog*, of Natick. Though mother and daughter, neither had ever heard the other's version of the score. To illustrate the relation of this score with Welsh numerals, we add two examples from Mr. Ellis's paper ("reprinted for private circulation from the Transactions of the Philological Society for 1877–8–9," pp. 316–372), selected from his fifty-three versions; the first is from England, the second from Ireland:

(17.) Stick, stock, stone dead,
Set him up,
Set him down,
Set him in the old man's crown.
—*Philadelphia.*

(18.) Apples and oranges, two for a penny,
Takes a good scholar to count as many;
O-u-t, out goes she.
—*Philadelphia.*

(19.) a, b, c, d, e, f, g,
h, i, j, k, l, m, n, o, p,
q, r, s, t,
u are out.
—*Cincinnati.*

(20.) 1, 2, 3, 4,
Mary at the kitchen-door,
5, 6, 7, 8,
Mary at the garden-gate.
—*Massachusetts* (1820).

1. aina.	6. ithy.	11. ain-a-dig.	16. ain-a-bumfit.
2. peina.	7. mithy.	12. pein-a-dig.	17. pein-a-bumfit.
3. para.	8. owera.	13. par-a-dig.	18. par-a-bumfit.
4. peddera.	9. lowera.	14. pedder-a-dig.	19. pedder-a-bumfit.
5. pimp.	10. dig.	15. bumfit.	20. giggy.

1. eina.	6. chester.	11. eina dickera.	16. eina pumpi.
2. mina.	7. nester.	12. mina dickera.	17. mina pumpi.
3. pera.	8. nera.	13. pera dickera.	18. pera pumpi.
4. peppera.	9. dickera.	14. peppera dickera.	19. peppera pumpi.
5. pinn.	10. nin.	15. pumpi.	20. ticket.

The modern Welsh numerals, as given by Mr. Ellis :

1. un.	6. chwech.	11. un ar deg.	16. un ar bymtheg.
2. dau.	7. saith.	12. deuddeg.	17. dau ar bymtheg.
3. tri.	8. wyth.	13. tri ar deg.	18. tri ar bymtheg.
4. pedwar.	9. nau.	14. pedwar ar deg.	19. pedwar ar bymtheg.
5. pump.	10. deg.	15. pymtheg.	20. ugain.

The numbers 4, 5, 15, and combinations 1+15, 2+15, 3+15, 4+15, seem to make the connection unmistakable ; but 2, 3, 6, 7, 8, 9 appear to have been arbitrarily affected by rhyme and alliteration.

(21.) 1, 2, 3, 4,
Lily at the kitchen-door,
Eating grapes off the plate,
5, 6, 7, 8.
—*Philadelphia* (1880).

(22.) 1, 2, 3, 4, 5, 6, 7, 8,
Mary sat at the garden-gate,
Eating plums off a plate,
1, 2, 3, 4, 5, 6, 7, 8.

(23.) 1, 2, 3, 4, 5, 6, 7,
All good children go to heaven.
—*Massachusetts to Pennsylvania.*

(24.) 1, 2, 3, 4, 5, 6, 7, 8,
All bad children have to wait.
—*Massachusetts.*

(25.) Monkey, monkey, bottle of beer,
How many monkeys are there here?
1, 2, 3,
You are he (she).
—*Massachusetts to Georgia.*

(26.) Linnet, linnet,
Come this minute,
Here's a house with something in it;
This was built for me, I know.
—*Philadelphia.*

(27.) School's up, school's down,
School's all around the town.

(28.) Three potatoes in a pot,
Take one out and leave it hot.
—*Philadelphia.*

(29.) Mittie Mattie had a hen,
She laid eggs for gentlemen,
Sometimes nine and sometimes ten.
—*Georgia.*

(30.) William a Trimbletoe,
He's a good fisherman,
Catch his hands, put them in pens,
Some fly East, some fly West,
Some fly over the cuckoo's nest—
O-u-t spells out and be gone.
—*Georgia.*

(31.) Red, white, and blue,
All out but you.
—*Philadelphia.*

(32.) Engine No. 9,
Out goes she.
—*Philadelphia.*

(33.) As I went up the apple-tree,
All the apples fell on me;
Bake a pudding, bake a pie,
Did you ever tell a lie?
Yes, you did, you know you did,
You broke your mother's teapot-lid—
L-i-d, that spells lid.
—*Cincinnati.*

(34.) Little man, driving cattle,
Don't you hear his money rattle?
One, two, three,
Out goes he (she).
—*Massachusetts.*

(35.) Monday's child is fair of face,
Tuesday's child is full of grace,
Wednesday's child is sour and sad,
Thursday's child is merry and glad,
Friday's child is full of sin,
Saturday's child is pure within;
The child that is born on the Sabbath day,
To heaven its steps shall tend alway.*
—*Georgia.*

* This verse is used as a counting rhyme by children in the state mentioned.

XV.

MYTHOLOGY.

In the olde dayes of the Kyng Arthour,
Of which that Britouns speken gret honour,
Al was this land fulfilled of fayrye.

The Wife of Baths Tale.

No. 150.

London Bridge.

No game has been more popular with children than this, and any summer evening, in the poorer quarters of the cities, it may still be seen how six years instructs three years in the proper way of conducting it. Two players, by their uplifted hands, form an arch, representing the bridge, under which passes the train of children, each clinging to the garments of the predecessor, and hurrying to get safely by. The last of the train is caught by the lowered arms of the guardians of the bridge, and asked, "Will you have a diamond necklace or a gold pin?" "a rose or a cabbage?" or some equivalent question. The keepers have already privately agreed which of the two each of these objects shall represent, and, according to the prisoner's choice, he is placed behind one or the other. When all are caught, the game ends with a "Tug of War," the two sides pulling against each other; and the child who lets go, and breaks the line, is pointed at and derided. The words of the rhyme sung while the row passes under the bridge are now reduced to two lines,

London Bridge is falling down,
My fair lady!

Readers may wonder why this well-known game should be classed as *mythological;* but such a character appears in the European versions. Thus, in Suabia, the two keepers of the "Golden Bridge" are called respectively the "Devil" and the "Angel," and the object is to decide who shall be devils and who angels. In France the game is known as "Heaven and Hell." The children who have made a good choice, after the selection is finished, pursue the devils, making the sign of horns with fingers extended from the forehead. In Italy, the name of the sport is "Open the Gates." The gates are those of the Inferno and of Paradise; *St. Peter* is the keeper of one, *St. Paul* of the other. The children choose between *wine* and *water;* but when the destiny of the last child is decided, the two girls who represent the keepers of the bridge break their arch of lifted hands and move in different directions, followed by their subjects, "while the cries and shrieks of the players condemned to the Inferno contrast with the pathetic songs and sweet cadences of those destined to the happiness of Paradise."

The game is mentioned by Rabelais (about A.D. 1533) under the name of the "Fallen Bridge."

In German versions, the keepers are called "Devil and Angel," "King and Emperor," or "Sun and Moon." In this latter form the game has been one of the few kept up by the Germans of Pennsylvania, who call it the "Bridge of Holland."*

Connected with this game in Massachusetts is a curious piece of local lore. A lady† recollects that, in the first years of the century, a pedler came to her father's house in Plymouth, Mass., and, in default of three cents change, left a "chap-book" or pamphlet of that value, called "Mother Goose's Melodies." In this pamphlet (the first authentic mention of a publication of that title) the song was included, in the familiar words; but, instead of *London* bridge, *Charlestown* bridge was substituted in the rhyme. In that form only the verses were familiar to herself and her companions.

Charlestown Bridge, over Charles River, connected Boston with Cambridge and other suburban towns, before that time only accessible by ferry or a long detour. The bridge was "dedicated" July 17, 1786; and was, in the eyes of the rustic population of Massachusetts, quite as important a structure as the London erection of the thirteenth century. The project was undertaken after a long incubation of sixty years, and not without many apprehensions lest the vast masses of ice rushing down the river in winter should sweep it away. The cost was fifteen thousand pounds. At the celebration, a salute of thirteen guns was fired from Fort Hill,

* Die Holländisch' Brück'.

† Mrs. R. W. Emerson, of Concord, Mass.

"almost every person of respectable character in private and public life walked in the procession," and eight hundred persons sat down to dinner. No wonder that its fame superseded, locally at least, that of the celebrated structure which was so long the wonder of London, and so sacred in nursery lore. We may thus form an idea of the importance of bridges in earlier times—which importance, and the superstitions consequent, were the root of our game—and also of the tendency of each town to localize its traditions, even those of the nursery.

With the exception of the name, the words of the song, in the chap-book referred to, were identical with those of the familiar English version. We learn from another informant that these same words (this time, however, under the proper title of London Bridge) were often used as a dance-song at children's parties about the beginning of the century. The dancers sat in a circle, a boy next a girl; as each verse was sung, the lad whose turn it was led out his partner and promenaded, suiting action to meaning. The exact verbal correspondence, and absence of the original mode of playing, show that this version of the song, and consequently the rhymes of the pamphlet called "Mother Goose's Melodies," were not taken from the lips of Americans, but reprinted from English sources.

The version repeatedly printed in books for children is not truly popular. It has been remodelled by the recorder, and so the original idea has been disguised. We have, however, the pleasure of offering a genuine English version. We add fragments of American forms, and finally a curious text, for which Ireland is ultimately responsible. From these, taken together, the character of the old English game can be made out.

A.—Song of Charlestown Bridge, as printed (probably about 1786) in the chap-book, "Mother Goose's Melodies:"

Charlestown Bridge is broken down,
    Dance o'er my lady Lee;
Charlestown Bridge is broken down,
    With a gay lady.

How shall we build it up again?
    Dance o'er my lady Lee, etc.

Build it up with silver and gold,
    Dance o'er my lady Lee, etc.

Silver and gold will be stole away,
    Dance o'er my lady Lee, etc.

Build it up with iron and steel,
Dance o'er my lady Lee, etc.

Iron and steel will bend and bow,
Dance o'er my lady Lee, etc.

Build it up with wood and clay,
Dance o'er my lady Lee, etc.

Wood and clay will wash away,
Dance o'er my lady Lee, etc.

Build it up with stone so strong,
Dance o'er my lady Lee,
Huzza! 'twill last for ages long,
With a gay lady.

B.—London Bridge is broken down,
Dance over my lady Lee;
London Bridge is broken down,
With the gay lady.

How shall we mend it up again?
Dance over my lady Lee;
How shall we mend it up again
For the gay lady?

We will mend it up with gravel and sand,
Dance over my lady Lee;
We will mend it up with gravel and sand
For the gay lady.

But gravel and sand will wash away,
Dance over my lady Lee;
Gravel and sand will wash away
From the gay lady.

We will mend it up with iron and steel,
Dance over my lady Lee;
We will mend it up with iron and steel
For the gay lady.

But iron and steel will bend and break,
Dance over my lady Lee;
Iron and steel will bend and break,
With the gay lady.

We will mend it up with silver and gold,
Dance over my lady Lee;
We will mend it up with silver and gold
For the gay lady.

Silver and gold will be stolen away,
Dance over my lady Lee;
Silver and gold will be stolen away
From the gay lady.

We will put a man to watch all night,
Dance over my lady Lee;
We will put a man to watch all night
For the gay lady.

Suppose the man should fall asleep?
Dance over my lady Lee;
Suppose the man should fall asleep?
My gay lady!

We will put a pipe into his mouth,
Dance over my lady Lee;
We will put a pipe into his mouth,
For the gay lady.*

C.—London Bridge is falling down,
Falling down, falling down,
London Bridge is falling down,
My fair lady!

You've stole my watch and kept my keys,
My fair lady!

Off to prison she must go,
My fair lady!

Take the key and lock her up,
My fair lady!†

—*Boston, Mass.*

* From Prof. G. J. Webb, now of New York, who learned it from his mother, in the Isle of Wight, his birthplace.

† As the last verse is sung, the raised arms of the two directors of the game descend, and enclose the child who happens to be passing at the time. The prisoner is then led, still confined by the arms of her captors, to the corner which represents the prison. After this she must choose as described on page 204, and the two sides finally pull against each other. Our informant well remembers how seriously the matter was taken, and how disturbed and disgraced she felt when arrested and imprisoned.

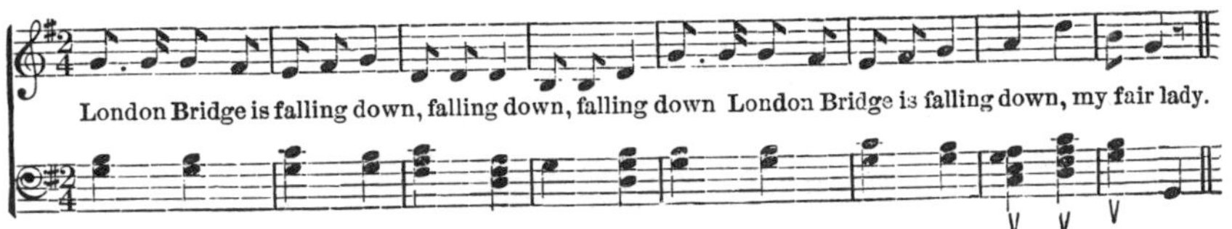

D.—London Bridge is falling down,
My fair lady!

What did the robber do to you?
My fair lady!

He broke my watch and stole my keys,
My fair lady!

Then off to prison she must go,
My fair lady!

—*Savannah, Ga.*

E.—Our last version is from the convent-school of Savannah, and, although recited by a girl of American birth, is of Irish origin:

London Bridge is falling down, etc.
My fair lady!

How shall we build it up again?—
Build it up with lime and stone.—
Stone and lime would wash away.—
Build it up with iron bars.—
Iron bars would bend and break.—
Build it up with gold and silver.—
Gold and silver would be stole away.—
Get a watch to watch all night.—
Suppose the watch should fall asleep?—
Get him a pipe to smoke all night.—
Suppose the pipe should fall and break?—
Get a dog to bark all night.—
Suppose the dog should get a bone?—
Get a cock to crow all night.—
Suppose the cock should fly away?—
What has this poor prisoner done?—
He's broke my box and stole my keys.—
A hundred pounds will set him free.—

A hundred pounds he has not got.—
Off to prison he must go,
*My fair lady!**

As to the origin of this remarkable game, our citations have already made clear that one of its features consists in a representation of the antagonism of celestial and infernal powers, and the final decision by which each soul is assigned a place on the one side or the other. It was universally believed in the Middle Ages, that the soul, separated from the body, had to cross a dangerous bridge, and subsequently undergo a literal weighing in the balance, according to the result of which its destiny was decided. It is in the nature of things that children, conversant with these ideas, should have dramatized them in their sports. We see no

* We have obtained a nearly identical, but more fragmentary version from Waterford, Ireland, with a refrain that seems a corruption of that belonging to the ordinary English song; thus—

London Bridge is broken down,
Fair lady!
How shall we build it up again?
Grand says the little dear.

We have also, from an Irish domestic, a most curious account of the use of the latter version in the town named. Agreeing, as it does, in essential respects with the character which the European game now possesses, and which the English game once evidently possessed, we do not doubt its general correctness; but we have had no opportunity to verify the statement of the somewhat inconsequent informant.

An actual bridge was built up with sticks and boards, and surrounded by the ring of players, dressed in costume; without stood the Devil. Little girls in variously colored dresses represented the angels.

The repeated fall and rebuilding of the bridge was acted out, as described in the verses of the song; this fall was ascribed to the malice of the Devil, who ruined it *during the night* (watching it, said the narrator, from the top of an ash-tree during the day).

The imprisonment of the child enclosed by the arms of the leaders was acted out as described in the note on page 208, but in a noteworthy fashion. A chain was taken, and wrapped round the child, in the form of a serpent (for the Devil *is* a serpent, said the reciter); the captive was taken to a hut (representing apparently the entrance to the Inferno) built by the sea. Meantime, the rest of the train called on their leader for help; but he answered, "the Devil has five feet, and thirteen eyes, and is stronger than I!" The performance lasted five hours; and the name of the edifice was the Devil's Bridge.

In this Irish game, tests were employed to determine whether the captive should belong to the Devil or not. One of these was the ability to walk on a straight line drawn on the ground.

On the windows of French mediæval churches devils may be seen surrounding the condemned with a great chain, which they use to drag them into their clutches.

reason, with the German writers, to go back to ancient Northern mythology; nor do we find any ground for believing that our game is more likely to be of Teutonic than Romance descent.

We suspect, however, that that part of the sport which relates to the warfare of good and evil powers does not belong to the original idea, but that a still more primitive game has taken on an ending which was common to many amusements in the Middle Ages. The central point of the whole is the repeated downfall of the structure. Now there is a distinct mythologic reason for such a representation. In early times no edifice was so important as a bridge, which renders intercourse possible between districts heretofore separated. Hence the sanctity attributed in mediæval times to the architects of bridges. The Devil, or (in more ancient guise) the elemental spirit of the land, who detests any interference with the solitude he loves, has an especial antipathy to bridges. His repeated and successful attempts to interfere with such a structure, until he is bought off with an offering like that of Iphigenia, are recorded in legends which attach to numerous bridges in Europe. It is on such supernatural opposition that the English form of the game appears to turn. The structure, which is erected in the daytime, is ruined at night; every form of material—wood, stone, and gold—is tried in vain; the vigilance of the watchman, or of the cock and the dog—guardian animals of the darkness—is insufficient to protect the edifice from the attack of the offended spirits.

The child arrested seems to be originally regarded as the price paid for allowing the structure to stand. In times when all men's thoughts were concerned about the final judgment, a different turn was given to the sport—namely, whether the prisoner should belong to the devils or to the angels, who wage perpetual warfare, and dispute with each other the possession of departed souls. Finally, in quite recent days, religious allusions were excluded, and the captive, now accused of mere theft, was sentenced to be locked up, not in the Inferno, but in a commonplace jail.

No. 151.

Open the Gates.

This game is a variation of the last, and is played similarly, ending with a "tug of war," as described on page 204.

Open the gates as high as the sky,
And let the King of Spain pass by;
Choose one,
Choose two,
Choose a pretty little girl like you.

More usual is a shorter rhyme, thus:

Open the gates as high as the sky,
And let King George and his troops* pass by.

No. 152.

Weighing.

Two children, linking hands, form a "basket" (each grasping with the left hand the right wrist of the other, and with the right hand his left wrist), in which another child is lifted, who embraces with his arms the necks of his bearers. He is then swung to and fro, and finally made to strike the wall. If he lets go his hold, he is called "Rotten egg," which is regarded as a highly ignominious name.

This title is also applied to the child who lets go in the "tug of war" in "London Bridge." A similar lifting in a basket (as we have been told by one who remembered so playing in youth) formed, in Philadelphia, part of the same game.

The original meaning of this exercise is made clear by an Italian counterpart, in which it is called "Weighing." The child after being lifted is made to jump over one of the lowered arms of his bearers, and if he escapes from their grasp is destined for *Paradise*, otherwise for the *Inferno*. The French usage is the same.† Weighing, to decide whether the child

* Or, his *wife*.

† À l'épayelle (that is, in the *basket*)
Tout du long de ciel,
Tout du long du paradis,
Saut'! Saut'! Saut souris!

should be angel or devil, sometimes forms part, also, of the German game corresponding to "London Bridge."

Another English game shows us a relic of this practice—namely, that called "Honey-pots," from which, as usual in children's sports, the original religious idea has disappeared. A child is lifted and swung until the hold is relaxed, when the *pot* is said to weigh so many pounds.*

Other tests used in German games to decide whether a child shall be an angel or not, are—tickling, in which a sober face must be kept; jumping over a cord, or measuring the height. These customs of play are surviving forms of usages once equally common in English sports.

No. 153.

Colors.

A.—A row of children, on the door-steps of a house, or against a chamber wall. Opposite each other stand two girls, representing, one the good, the other the bad, angel. Every child selects a color. The mother stands at the foot of the steps. The "Good Angel" knocks at the door (*i. e.*, the side of the flight of house-steps), and is answered by the mother:

"Who's knocking at the door?"
"The Angel with the Golden Star."
"What do you want?"
"Blue" (or any color).

The "Good Angel" names a color. If this color is represented among the children, the angel takes the child, but if the application is unsuccessful, must retire, whereon the "Bad Angel," or the "Angel with the Pitchfork," comes forward in like manner. When all the children are divided, a "tug of war" ensues, as in "London Bridge."

This form of the game is probably a recent translation from the German, by New York children.†

* See No. 154, E, and note.

† Game of New York German children: "Wer ist daraus?" "Der Engel mit dem goldenen Strauss." "Was will er?" "Eine Farbe." "Was für eine?" "Blau," etc. Then "Der Engel mit dem Feuerhaken" comes forward, and so on, "bis alle Farben fort sind."

B.—In the convent-school of Savannah, Ga., as we learn from a former pupil, birds instead of colors represented the children, and the formula was, "Barn, barn,* who comes here?" It was replied, "Good angel," or "Bad angel." The angels then "fought and tried to get the child."

C.—In Philadelphia there is a game in which the children, having received birds' names, are pursued by the mother, and, if captured, are put into the slop-bowl; otherwise, into the sugar-bowl.

Similarly, in a Swiss game, we have the mother and a bird-catcher. The latter endeavors to guess the titles of the children, who are called after birds or colors. When the name of a child is guessed, she takes flight, and if she can escape, returns to the mother; if caught, she belongs to the pursuer, and the game ends with a "tug of war."

Corresponding is the French game of "Animals." The devil and a purchaser are first chosen. The seller names the animals, and shuts them up in an enclosure. The devil, who has not heard the naming, comes up† and guesses the title of the beast. If he guesses right, the seller says "Go!" while the animal makes a circuit to return to his den. The devil must first buy (with so many taps on the palm of the hand of the dealer) the beast, before he can pursue. If he catches the latter, he marks him with three blows on the head and tail, and the animal becomes the devil's dog. The game finishes when all the animals have been so captured.

The conflict which ends this game is curious. In Switzerland, the angel who obtains a child carries it in his arms within his limit, and the devil similarly. After all the children are divided, a struggle begins, the devils defending themselves with claws, the angels with wings. In Austria the boundary between Heaven and Hell is marked out by a piece of wood, called "Fire." Each child grasps the waist of his predecessor with both arms, the leaders join hands over the "Fire," and the contest lasts until all are pulled to one side or the other.

These battles between opposing supernatural forces rest on a basis older than Christianity. The "Game of the Shell" is thus described by Pollux: "The shell-game; where the boys draw a line on the ground and choose sides, one side selecting the outside of a shell, the other the inside. One who stands on the line having thrown up the shell, which-

* An imitation of knocking. Italian, Din-din; French, pan! pan! etc.

† The dialogue is: "Pan! pan!" "Qui est-ce qui est là?" "C'est le diable avec sa fourche." "Que veut-il?" "Un animal." "Entrez."

ever face comes uppermost, those who belong to that give chase, and the other party turn and fly. Any fugitive who gets caught is called the *ass*. He who pitches the shell says, 'Night, day;' for the outside is smeared with pitch, and signifies night; whence this boys' game is also called the 'turning of the shell.'"

The word *ass* here means that the boy caught had to carry home his pursuer on his back.

Plato alludes to this game in the "Republic," saying of the efforts of the soul to pass from the realm of darkness to that of light, "it does not depend on the turn of a shell."

We thus see the successive mental conceptions of antiquity, the Middle Ages, and modern time reflected in the changes of children's sports.

No. 154.

Old Witch.

A.—Ten girls, a mother, a witch, and eight children—namely, Sunday, Monday, Tuesday, Wednesday, Thursday, Friday, Saturday, and the eldest daughter Sue. The mother, preparing to go out, addresses her children:

> Now all you children stay at home,
> And be good girls while I am gone;
> Let no one in*
> *   *   *   *   *
> Especially you, my daughter Sue,
> Or else I'll beat you black and blue.†

The witch knocks at the door, and is refused entrance by the children. She beguiles them by promises to admit her, which they finally do. She then holds out her pipe (a bit of stick), which she carries between her

* A line and a half are wanting.

† "I charge my daughters every one,
To keep good house while I am gone.
You and *you* [points] but specially *Sue*,
Or else I'll beat you black and blue."

From "Nursery Rhymes of England," where it is said to be a game of the Gypsy, who "during the mother's absence comes in, entices a child away, and hides her. This process is repeated till all the children are hidden, when the mother has to find them."

teeth, saying to Sue, "Light my pipe!" Sue refusing, she makes the same demand to each child, in the order of the days of the week, in which they are ranged. All refuse till she reaches the last, who consents and touches her pipe, whereupon the witch seizes her hand, and drags her out of the house to her "den."

The mother then returns, counts the children, and Sue is questioned and punished. This is played over until each child is taken, Sue last.

When the mother has lost all her children, the witch calls, and invites her to dinner. Upon going to the witch's door, she finds a table set for the meal, and the witch asks her to order a dish to suit her taste. She does so, whereupon the witch produces Sunday, and lays her upon the table, with considerable assistance from Sunday.

A very amusing dialogue now ensues between the witch and the mother. The former urges the mother to eat, with many blandishments, and the mother (recognizing her child) declines, with such excuses as any ingenious child can devise.

The mother, upon pretence of inability to eat the food, calls for another dish, and, when the witch leaves the room, hurries the child from the table and places her behind the chair. When the witch returns, she says that she found the dish so good that she ate it all, and calls for another.

Each child is produced in turn, with the same result. When all are arranged behind their mother, she calls for another dish, and when the witch leaves the room to get it, runs home with all her children.

Hartford, Conn.

Our second version (B) is from the lips of a little girl in New York city. The persons represented are the same, except that a servant instead of one of the daughters is left to take care of the children. Scene, the doorsteps, or "stoop," of a New York dwelling-house.

Mother [*sings*]. Chickany, chickany, crany, crow.
Went to the well to wash her great toe,
And when she came back her chicken was dead.*
[*To Servant*]. I am going out, and let nobody come in.
[*Exit. Enter presently, Witch.*

* This verse is borrowed from another game, No. 102. The drama opens with a foreboding. The prophetic soul of the mother uses the lament of a hen who has lost one of her brood.

Witch [*to Servant*]. Give me a match to light my pipe.

Servant. I haven't any.

Witch. Your kettle's boiling over.

Servant. No.

Witch. Your kettle is boiling over.

Servant [*goes to look*]. *Witch seizes a child and carries her off.* [*Re-enter Mother.*

Mother [*to servant*]. Where's my Monday?

Servant. Under the table.

Mother [*calls*]. Monday!

Servant. Up in the band-box!*

Mother. How to get up?

Servant. Put two broken chairs on a broken table.

Mother. Suppose I should fall and break my neck?

Servant. Good enough for you.

Mother beats servant, but recovering from her loss, goes out again. Witch enters as before, and carries off successively all the children, and at last the servant. Witch then puts the children in a row, cooks them, and makes them into pies, naming them apple-pie, peach-pie, etc. Mother goes out to buy pies.

Mother [*to Witch*]. Have you any pies?

Witch. Yes, some very nice apple-pies, which you will like.

Mother [*tastes*]. This tastes like my Monday. [*Re-animates Monday.*] Monday, who brought you here? [*Beats her, and sends her home.*]

The mother proceeds in the same manner, and brings to life the other children.

C.—The name of the witch in this variation is "Old Mother Cripsy-crops," and the game begins by playing No. 89. When the mother goes out, the children call after her, "Old mother, the kettle boils." She answers, "Take a spoon and stir it." "We haven't got any." "Buy one." "We have no money." "Borrow," says the mother. "People won't lend," reply the children.

The witch comes in, and entices Sunday away by fine promises. When the mother comes back, she inquires, "Where's my Sunday?" The children make some excuse, as, "Perhaps he has gone down cellar," etc. She tells Tuesday to take care of Monday, as she had previously placed Monday in charge of Sunday, and goes out again, when the same scene is repeated, until all the children have been carried off.

* Or any elevated position. Also, *in heaven.*

The mother now calls at the witch's house, and asks to be let in. The witch refuses, saying, "No, your shoes are too dirty." "But I will take off my shoes." "Your stockings are too dirty." "Then I will take off my stockings." "Your feet are too dirty." "I will cut off my feet." "That would make the carpet all bloody." "But I must see my children, and you have got them." "What should I know about your children? But if you like you may call to-morrow at twelve."

The mother departs, and as soon as she is gone the witch goes to the children and renames them all. One she calls Mustard, another Pepper, another Salt, another Vinegar, etc. Then she turns their faces to the wall, and tells them to give these names if they are asked who they are. The mother calls again at the house of the witch, and this time is admitted. She asks the children what their names are, and they all answer as they were instructed by the witch. She then asks the first child to let her feel his toe. He puts up his foot, and when the mother feels it she says, "This is my Sunday! let your big toe carry you home;" whereupon he runs off. The same process is gone through with all the other children.

D.—To the mother (this time present), in the midst of her children, approaches the witch, who comes limping, leaning on a cane. The dialogue is between mother and witch.

> "There's old mother Hippletyhop; I wonder what she wants to-day?"
> "I want one of your children."
> "Which one do you want?"

The witch names any child of the row.

> "What will you give her to eat?"
> "Plum-cake" (a different delicacy for each child).

The witch carries off the child, and observes: "Walk as I do, or else I'll kill you." She takes the child home and kills her, then returns for another. When all are gone the mother goes out to look for her children. She goes to the witch's house, and finds all the children (presumed to be dead) against the wall, making the most horrible faces. She points to a child, and asks, "What did [Mary] die of?" "She died of sucking her thumbs" (naming the child's gesture). Suddenly all the children come to themselves, and cry out, "Oh, mother, we are not dead!"

Portsmouth, N. H.

E.—In a fifth version, which we have failed to obtain in full, the witch changed the children into birds; and the mother, in order to recover them, must guess the name of the bird. Colors, instead of birds, were also used to represent the children.

F.—We have already spoken of the old English game of "Honey-pots" as an imitation of "Weighing." This trait, however, as might be supposed from its insignificant character, is a mere fragment of the original. In London (as we learn from an informant of the laboring class, who remembers taking part in the amusement), a child as market-woman arranges the rest in a row to indicate honey-pots, each with its specific flavor. While she is busy at one end of the row, a thief comes in and steals a pot from the other end. This process is repeated, until all the pots are taken. The dealer then goes out to buy honey-pots, and recognizes her own by the flavor, so recovering the stolen goods.

This game without doubt is the most curious of our collection, both on account of its own quaintness, and because of the extraordinary relation in which it stands to the childs' lore of Europe. We have, in a note, endeavored to show that our American versions give the most ancient and adequate representation now existing of a childish drama which has diverged into numerous branches, and of which almost every trait has set up for itself as an independent game. Several of these offshoots are centuries old, and exist in many European tongues; while, so far as appears, their original has best maintained itself in the childish tradition of the New World.

Among a great number of German forms, only one (from Suabia) nearly corresponds to ours, with the exception of a corrupted ending.

In this childish drama a mother has many children, who sleep. In her absence comes "Old Urschel" with her two daughters, the "Night-maidens" (a sort of fairies), who steal three children, and carry them off to their cave (hiding them behind their extended dresses). The mother visits Urschel's abode to complain of the theft, but the "Night-maidens," with deprecating gestures, deny any knowledge of the lost. The action is then repeated, the eldest daughter (who plays the same part as in our first version) being taken last.

When the mother's complaints are useless, she becomes a witch. The next day Urschel takes her stolen family for a walk. The mother comes up and pulls the dress of a child; by her magic art all feel it at the same time, and cry to Urschel, "Oh, mother, somebody is pulling my gown!" The latter replies, "It must be a dog." The mother then asks and obtains leave to join the party, but endeavors to bewitch (or disenchant) her children, who cry, "The Witch of London!" and scatter, but are captured by the latter and turned into witches.*

In Sweden the mother is called "Lady Sun." An old woman enters, propped on a cane, goes to Lady Sun's house and knocks. "Who is that knocking at my door?" "An old woman, halt and blind, asks the way to Lady Sun; is she at home?" "Yes." The old woman points out a child, and asks, "Dear Lady Sun, may I have a chicken?" She is refused at first, but by piteous entreaties obtains her wish, and returns, until all the "chickens" are carried off. "She was not so lame as she made believe," says Lady Sun, looking after her.

The antiquity of our game is sufficiently attested by the wide diffusion of many of its comparatively recent variations. We remark, further, that the idea of the child-eating demon, so prominently brought forward in our American versions, is a world-old nursery conception. The ancients were well acquainted with such feminine supernatural beings. "More fond of children than Gello," says Sappho, referring to an imaginary creature of the sort. The most ancient view of this passion for stealing children was, that it was prompted by the appetite. Tales of ogres and ogresses, who carried off and devoured young children, must have been as familiar in the Roman nursery as in our own.

The trait of *limping*, characteristic of "witches" in games, is equally ancient. That such demons are defective in one foot is expressed by the ancient Greek name "Empusa" (literally One-foot), to whom was attributed an ass's hoof, a representation which contributed to the mediæval idea of the devil. A child's game, in which a boy, armed with a knotted

* This Urschel is a mythologic character. When the children of Pfüllingen climb the Urschelberg, where she lives, each child deposits on a certain stone two or three horn buttons as an offering. On returning, they observe whether she has not taken them away; and, even if the buttons remain, they are sure that she has taken pleasure in them. When they pass a certain slope they roll down perforated stones (called "suns"), and the child whose "sun" rolls farthest says with pride, "Urschel liked my present best."

Urschel passes for an enchanted maiden, whose original name was Prisca. Every four centuries she plants a beech-tree for the cradle of the youth whose love is at last to release her. The chosen shepherd sees her sitting by the roadside, in the shape of an old woman, dressed in green gown and red stockings. But none has ever dared to wed her for the sake of the castle and treasure she offers.

handkerchief, pursues his comrades, hopping on one foot, is known in France as "The Limping Devil."* This game existed also in ancient Greece.

The reanimation and recovery of the children, with which the American performance closes, is a familiar trait of ancient nursery tales.

No. 155.

The Ogree's Coop.

Half a century since, in eastern Massachusetts, it was a pastime of boys and girls for one of the number to impersonate an *Ogree* † (as the word was pronounced), who caught his playmates, put them in a coop, and fattened them for domestic consumption. From time to time the Ogree felt his captives to ascertain if they were fat enough to be cooked. Now and then a little boy would thrust from between the bars of his cage a stick instead of a finger, whereupon the ogree would be satisfied of his leanness.

No. 156.

Tom Tidler's Ground.

A boundary line marks out "Tom Tidler's Ground," on which stands a player. The rest intrude on the forbidden precinct, but if touched must take his place. The words of the challenge are—

> I'm on Tommy Tidler's ground,
> Picking up gold and silver.

Or, dialectically, "*Tickler's* not at home."

This Eldorado has many different local names — *Van Diemen's land* in Connecticut; *Dixie's land* in New York, an expression which antedates the war; *Judge Jeffrey's land*, in Devonshire, England; *Golden Pavement*, in Philadelphia.

* "Le Diable Boîteux."

† "An Ogree is a giant with long teeth and claws, with a Raw Head and Bloody Bones, and runs away with naughty boys and girls, and eats them all up."—Story of the "Sleeping Beauty," as given in an old chap-book.

In the Southern States, "Tommy Tidler's Ground" is the name of the spot where the rainbow rests, and where it is supposed by children that a pot of gold is buried. A highly intelligent Georgian assures us that as a boy he has often searched for the treasure, but could never find the spot where the rainbow touched the ground.

"Tommy Tidler" represents the jealous fairy or dwarf who attacks any who approach his treasure.

No. 157.

Dixie's Land.

This is a variety of the last game, in which a monarch instead of a fairy is the owner of the ground trespassed upon. A line having been drawn, to bound "Dixie's Land," the players cross the frontier with the challenge:

> On Dixie's land I'll take my stand,
> And live and die in Dixie.

The king of Dixie's Land endeavors to seize an invader, whom he must hold long enough to repeat the words,

> Ten times one are ten,
> You are one of my men.

All so captured must assist the king in taking the rest.

The word "man" seems to be used in the ancient sense of subject, as in the Scotch formula, where one boy takes another by the forelock (a reminiscence of serfdom), saying,

> Tappie, tappie, tousie, will you be my man?

The game is played in much the same manner in Germany, with a rhyme which may be translated:

> King, I'm standing on your land,
> I steal your gold and silver-sand.

No. 158.

Ghost in the Cellar.

One of the children represents a ghost, and conceals himself in the cellar. Another takes the part of a mother, who is addressed by one of her numerous family:

"Mother, I see a ghost."
"It was only your father's coat hanging up."

Mother goes down with a match. Ghost appears. Terror and flight. Whoever is caught becomes the ghost for the next turn.

A similar game is played in London, called (we are told) "Ghost in the Copper."

The original of the "ghost" appears in the corresponding German game, where we find in his stead the "evil spirit," who haunts the garden.

No. 159.

The Enchanted Princess.

This interesting European game, though never naturalized in this country, has been occasionally played as a literal translation from the printed French. A little girl raises above her head her frock, which is sustained by her companions, who thus represent the tower in which she is supposed to be confined. The "enemy" comes up, and asks, "Where is pretty Margaret?" The answer is, "She is shut up in her tower." The "enemy" carries off one by one the stones of the tower (leads away, that is, the girls who personate stones), until one only is left, who drops the frock, and flies, pursued by Margaret, who must catch some one to replace her.

The celebrated French song begins, "Where is fair Margaret, Ogier, noble knight?"* "Ogier" is none other than Olger the Dane, hero of mediæval romance. The childish drama is one form of the world-old history of a maiden who is delivered by a champion from the enchanted castle. In the territory of Cambrai, she who is shut up in the tower is

* Où est la belle Marguerite,
Ogier, beau chevalier?

said to be "the fair one with the golden locks." We consider the following number to be a variation of the same theme.

No. 160.

The Sleeping Beauty.

About fifty years since, in a town of Massachusetts (Wrentham), the young people were in the habit of playing an exceedingly rustic kissing-game. A girl in the centre of the ring simulated sleep, and the words were—

There was a young lady sat down to sleep;
She wants a young gentleman to wake her up;
Mr. —— —— shall be his name.

The awakening was then effected by a kiss.

The same game comes to us as a negro sport from Galveston, Texas, but in a form which shows it to be the corruption of an old English round:

Here we go round the *strawberry bush*,
  This cold and frosty morning.

Here's a young lady sat down to sleep,
  This cold and frosty morning.

She wants a young gentleman to wake her up,
  This cold and frosty morning.

Write his name and send it by me,
  This cold and frosty morning.

Mr. —— his name is called,
  This cold and frosty morning.

Arise, arise, upon your feet,
  This cold and frosty morning.

Some unintelligible negro rhymes follow.

The refrain of the last version indicates that it is of old English origin, and was used as a May-game.

It would appear, from the character of the round, that various names are proposed to the sleeping girl, which she rejects until a satisfactory one is presented. At all events, this is the case in a Provençal game which we take to be of the same origin as ours. In this game it is explained that the girl is not asleep, but counterfeiting death. "Alas! what shall we give our sister? N. N. to be her husband."

A favorite French round describes the maiden as asleep "in the tower." The pretty song represents her as awakened by the rose her lover has left upon her breast. Though there is no very close resemblance between this and the Provençal game, the same idea of deliverance from enchantment appears to underlie both.

We infer, therefore, that the game, apparently so natural an invention, originally represented some form of the world-wide story of the "Sleeping Beauty." If this be so, to explain its history would lead us to write of Northern lay and mediæval legend; we should have to examine the natural symbolism of primitive religions, and the loves of ancient gods. The kissing-romp of a New England village would be connected with the poetry and romance of half the world.

In any case, this interlinking of the New World with all countries and ages, by the golden net-work of oral tradition, may supply the moral of our collection.

XVI.

AFTERMATH.

No. 161.

Tread the Green Grass.

(See No. 4.)

Tread, tread the green grass,
  Star, star, star;
Come on, you pretty fair maid,
  And walk along with me.

If you be a fair maid,
  As I suppose you be,
I'll take you by the lily-white hand,
  And lead you across the sea.

Maryland.

Of this pretty song American versions are incomplete, and British all more or less corrupt (see the Scottish variant, p. 50). From the manner of playing, as described by Mrs. Gomme, it appears that a *chassez* formed part of the movement, with alternate song, similar to American courtship rhymes, including formulas of invitation and refusal. The march, which in America seems to have made the principal feature, has in Great Britain been preserved only in Lanarkshire, where, half a century ago, as we are told, "the children sung with rather mincing and refined voices, evidently making an effort in this direction. They walked, with their hands clasped behind their backs, up and down the road. Each child was crowned with rushes, and also had sashes or girdles of rushes." The game was formerly played by a row of boys on one side and girls on the other; while singing, each boy selected a girl.

In the use of rushes we have a survival of the old custom by which dancers would be crowned and garlanded; while, as the verse indicates, the scene is the greensward, where the players, not children, but marriageable youth, moved in the mating season. It is pretty to see that the Maryland singers retained the poetic feeling of earlier centuries, and felt the word "star" more appropriate to the flowery mead than the corruption "dust."

No. 162.

Walking on the Green Grass.

Walking on the green grass,
  Walking side by side,
Walking with a pretty girl,
  She shall be my bride.

And now we form a round ring,
  The girls are by our sides;
Dancing with the pretty girls
  Who shall be our brides.

And now the king upon the green
Shall choose a girl to be his queen;
  Shall lead her out his bride to be,
  And kiss her, one, two, three.
Now take her by the hand, this queen,
And swing her round and round the green.

Oh, now we'll go around the ring,
And every one we'll swing.
  Oh, swing the king and swing the queen,
  Oh, swing the king and swing the queen,
  Oh, swing 'em round and round the green.
  Oh, swing 'em round the green.

This dance, belonging to young men and women as well as to children, is described by the recorder as follows:

The men select their partners as if for a dance, and, thus paired, promenade as in a school procession, singing the first verse, "Walking on the green grass." The procession then resolves itself into a ring, youths and maidens alternating, all singing: "And now we form a round ring." During the singing of this stanza the ring has kept moving. It is next broken into two lines, one of maidens, the other of youths, facing each other as for a reel. The song is resumed with the words, "And now the king upon the green," and each of the actions described in the verse is performed by the couple at the head of the lines. Having thus called out, saluted, and swung his partner, the man begins with the second woman, and thence down the line, swinging each of the women dancers in turn, the example being followed by his partner with the men, the song continuing, "Oh, now we'll go around the ring, and every one we'll swing." These words are sung over and over, if necessary, until all the dancers have been swung. Thereupon the king and queen take their places at the foot of the lines, and become the subjects of another couple, song and action beginning with the verse, "And now the king upon the green," etc. After all the couples have played at royalty, the promenade is resumed, and the game begun again, generally with change of partners.

This song is unrecorded in Great Britain; but its antiquity and status as a portion of a dance of which "Tread the Green Grass" is also a fragment seem to me sufficiently attested by correspondence with the third verse of the following rhyme, given by Mrs. Gomme:

Here we come up the green grass,
  Green grass, green grass,
Here we come up the green grass,
  Dusty, dusty, day.

Fair maid, pretty maid,
  Give your hand to me,
I'll show you a blackbird,
  A blackbird on the tree.

We'll all go roving,
  Roving side by side;
I'll take my fairest ——,
  I'll take her for a bride.

No. 163.

Walking on the Levy.

(See No. 63.)

I'm walking on the levy,
For you have gained the day.

Go in and out the windows,
For you have gained the day.

Stand up and face your lover,
For you have gained the day.

I measure my love to show you,
For you have gained the day.

I kneel because I love you,
For you have gained the day.

It breaks my heart to leave you,
For you have gained the day.

The players form a ring with a lad (or young man) in the centre. The ring moves around during the first verse. At the second verse, the words of which are identical in the two songs, the ring stands still and the player in the centre winds in and out under the clasped hands of the singers, which are raised for that purpose.

This dance is a variant of "Go Round and Round the Valley" (p. 128), in which the refrain is, "As we are all so gay."

A "levy" (also written "levee") is the embankment of a river, or that part of the bank on which is piled the freight of a steamer. Judging from the rhyme, the levy seems to have been locally popular as a promenade. "Levy" is plainly a substitute for "valley"; making the change, we have "Walking in the Valley"; the theme, therefore, is the same as that of "Walking on the Green Grass." The play belongs to the group of courtship dances, so that the Florida refrain cannot be considered as a corruption, but expresses the victory of the suitor who at last has gained the "flowers of May."

British versions are many but inferior. The initial line is "Round and round the village," where "village" is (in my opinion) a corruption of "valley." The refrain also is vulgarized, and even repulsive—"As you have done before"—and suggests a polygamy of which the mediæval singers, I think, would have been quite incapable.

As to movement, it is of interest to compare the account of Mrs. Gomme:

"The children join hands and form a ring with one child standing outside. The ring stands perfectly still throughout this game and sings the verses, the action being confined to at first one child, and then to two together. During the singing of the first verse the outside child dances round the ring on the outside. When the ring commences to sing the second verse the children hold up their hands to form arches, and the child who has been running round outside runs into the ring under one pair of joined hands, and out again under the next pair of arms, continuing this "in and out" movement until the third verse is commenced. The child should try and run in and out under all the joined hands. At the third verse the child stops in the ring and stands facing one whom she chooses for her lover, until the end of the verse; the chosen child then leaves the ring, followed by the first child, and they walk round the ring, or they walk away a little distance, returning at the commencement of the next verse." Kissing is sometimes the finale.

In a Kent version love is measured out with a handkerchief three times, and, after kneeling in the road, the chosen partner follows round the ring and reverses for the return.

It will be seen that in all these courtship dances the march changes to a ring.

Mr. Babcock supplies a rude rhyme, obviously the reduction of this pretty dance. The play begins, "Bounce around, my sugar-lump," and proceeds, "Lower the window," "Hoist the window," "Don't miss a window," the player accosted being always addressed as "sugar-lump." The game seems to continue until a window is missed.

"Sugar-lump" is British also, but I have not elsewhere noticed as term of endearment "cinnamon," which occurs in a Florida dance resembling the "Virginia Reel" (No. 20). The first man leads his partner to the foot of the ladies' line, himself proceeds to the top of the men's line, and turns each lady, as his partner does each man, the couple themselves turning after each of the others, to the melody:

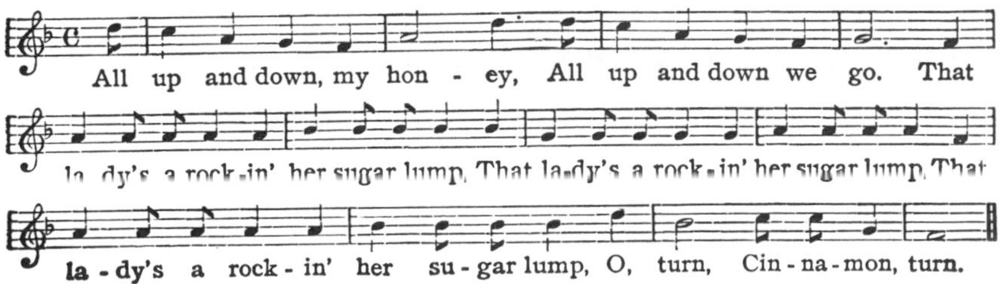

No. 164.

Swine-herders.

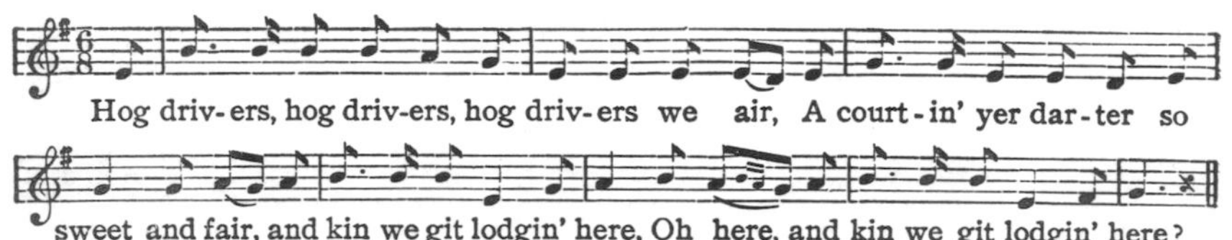

A.—"Hog-drivers, hog-drivers, hog-drivers we air,
A-courtin' your darter so sweet and fair;
And kin we git lodgin' here, O here—
And kin we git lodgin' here?"

"Now this is my darter that sets by my side,
And no hog-driver can get 'er fer a bride;
And you kain't get lodgin' here, O here—
And you kain't git lodgin' here."

"Yer darter is pretty, yer ugly yerself,
So we'll travel on further and seek better wealth,
And we don't want lodgin' here, O here—
And we don't want lodgin' here."

"Now this is my darter that sets by my side,
And Mr. ——— kin git 'er fer a bride,
And he kin git lodgin' here, O here—
And he kin git lodgin' here."

Come under, come under,
My honey, my love, my heart's above—
Come under, come under,
Below Galilee.

We've caught you as a prisoner,
  My honey, my love, my heart's above—
We've caught you as a prisoner,
  Below Galilee.

Then hug 'er neat, and kiss 'er sweet,
  My honey, my love, my heart's above—
Then hug 'er nice, and kiss 'er twice,
  Below Galilee.

B.—"Swine-herders, swine-herders, swine-herders we are,
A-courting your daughter so neat and so fair,
Can we get lodgings here, O here—
Can we get lodgings here?"

"Swine-herders, swine-herders, swine-herders ye are,
A-courting my daughter so neat and so fair,
And ye can't get lodgings here, O here—
And ye can't get lodgings here."

"You have a fair daughter, you're ugly yourself,
We'll travel on farther and seek better wealth,
And we don't want lodgings here, O here—
And we don't want lodgings here."

"I have a fair daughter, she sits by my knee,
And some young man can get her from me,
And he can get lodgings here, O here—
And he can get lodgings here."

North Carolina.

From the communication of the recorder is given the following account of the manner of playing: A man, generally an older man, and a girl sit side by side on two chairs in the middle of a room, so placed as to face in opposite directions; another man and a girl walk around hand in hand, and sing, "Naow this is my darter," etc. The "Hog-drivers" retort with the second verse, after which the father sings the third verse, in which he names as partner of his daughter any man whom the girl selects. The latter and her chosen swain then join hands and withdraw, another girl sits beside the father, and the performance is repeated until all players are paired. Then the last girl and the father stand up, and by joining hands make a bridge; they sing, "Come under," etc., while the other couples pass through. On a second attempt at passage, the first couple is captured by the father and his companion, who sing, "We've caught you as a prisoner," etc. The imprisoned man kisses his partner twice, the two are released, and the game continues with another couple. In the Hickory Gap region, some twenty miles from Asheville, the game is popular with old and young. These mountaineers consider dancing immoral, but gather from far and wide whenever a "fuss" is on foot.

In regard to the music, the recorder remarks that none of the intervals are absolutely correct, and that the impression made on the hearer curiously resembles that caused by songs of North American Indians. The intervals could be accurately reproduced only by a violin, but in singing the effect may be gained by flatting the crossed intervals.

In the mountains the game would be designated as "comic," such appellation being bestowed on any song which cannot be termed "sacred."

North Carolina Mountains (near Asheville, N. C.).

This dance is only a reduction of that which follows.

No. 165.

Three Kings.

(See No. 2.)

Three suitors approach a mother and daughter, and say, suiting the action to the words:

"Here come three sweeps,
And at your door they bend their knees.
May we have lodgings here, O here,
May we have lodgings here?"

The mother replies, "No." The suitors recede, and then approach again, saying:

"Here come three bakers,
And at your door they bend their knees.
May we have lodgings here, O here,
May we have lodgings here?"

The mother replies, "No." They recede a second time, and again advance, saying:

"Here come three kings,
And at your door they bend their knees.
May we have lodgings here, O here,
May we have lodgings here?"

The mother relents, and answers:

"Yes; here is my daughter all safe and sound,
And in her pocket a thousand pound,
And on her finger a guinea-gold ring,
And she's quite fit to walk with the king."

She hands over the daughter, for whom the suitors pretend to search. Then they bring her back to the mother and say:

"Here is your daughter, safe and sound,
And in her pocket no thousand pound,
And on her finger no guinea-gold ring;
She's not fit to walk with the king."

They run, and the mother runs after them. If she catches one, the latter becomes the mother for the next game.

Washington, D. C.

Mr. Babcock, who has recorded this version, observes that he has never witnessed the game, but obtained it from the recitation of a child.

British versions answer to American; the suitors, coming "three by three," appear as "sailors" (our A.) or "sweeps" (our B.); for the second line the variants show, "To court your daughter, a fair lady," "To court your daughter, fair and fair," or "Down by your door they bend the knee." The daughter accompanies the kings, who take her a little way apart, pretend to rob her of money, ring, and clothes, and return her to the mother. Finally, the suitors are chased by mother and daughter, and on repetition sides are changed.

The dance belongs to a group including several courtship games (Nos. 1-3, 161-165). It is true that the games exhibit variations; thus in some versions of No. 3 the address is made directly to the damsels, while variants preserve the older type in making the mother manage the negotiation; again, in No. 1 the lady is called Jane (only the generic name of a beauty), yet here also there is a choice. The changes seem no more than in any traditional song must arrive in course of time, and these courtship plays should, I think, be considered to belong together as fragmentary survivals of a single mediæval dance.

No. 166.

Knots of May.

(See No. 26.)

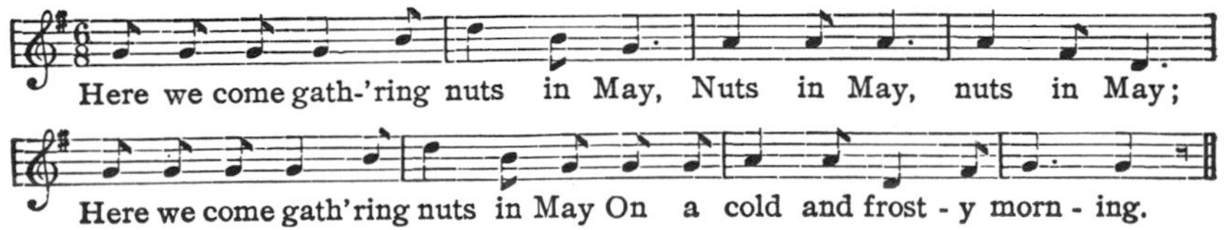

Here we come gath'ring nuts in May,
  Nuts in May, nuts in May;
Here we come gath'ring nuts in May,
  On a cold and frosty morning.

Toronto, Canada.

In England this is the most common of all singing games. Mrs. Gomme shows that we ought to read "Knots of May"—that is to say, bunches of the May or hawthorn; the maids are likened to such sprays, to be gathered by the lads and brought home as their "May." The manner of playing was probably the same as in Great Britain, where two children join hands and try to pull each other over a mark; the captured player joins the conqueror, and so on until all are selected. Mrs. Gomme shows that boys were once chosen to bring in the girls, who were expected to resist.

Mrs. Gomme considers the game to depend on "marriage by capture." If only ultimate origins are to be taken into account, the suggestion may be accepted; but, as in all dances of the courtship group, we have now only a fragment of an elaborate and stately mediæval predecessor; the metaphor which likens the chosen bride to a flower of the May has already been encountered in the beautiful lines of the betrothal dance (No. 3).

No. 167.

Jail-keys.

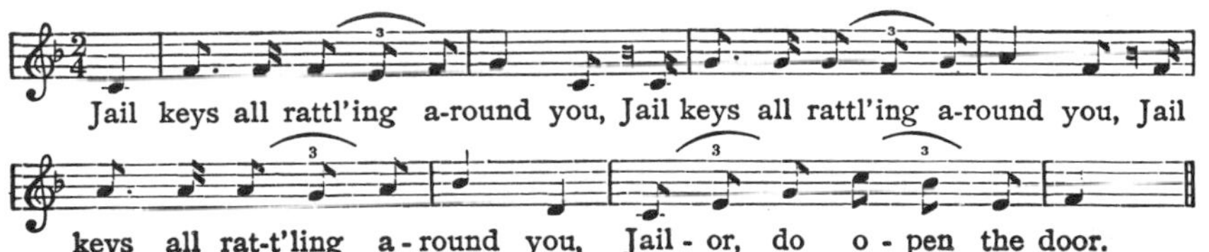

Jail-keys all rattling around you,
Jailer, do open the door!

The manner of playing has not been obtained, and there is no British equivalent. I suspect it belonged to the "Cushion Dance" (see the game of "Pillows and Keys," p. 62), in which a player kneels on a pillow and asks a kiss. The action of this dance is set forth by Mrs. Gomme, from whose account it appears that the youth who led locked the door, putting the key in his pocket; it seems likely that he transmitted the key to the next youth chosen, who may therefore have been designated as the "Jailer." The song would then be chanted by the ring of seated players. Formerly the girl selected was expected to offer a mock resistance.

No. 168.

Sailing at High Tide.

(See No. 45.)

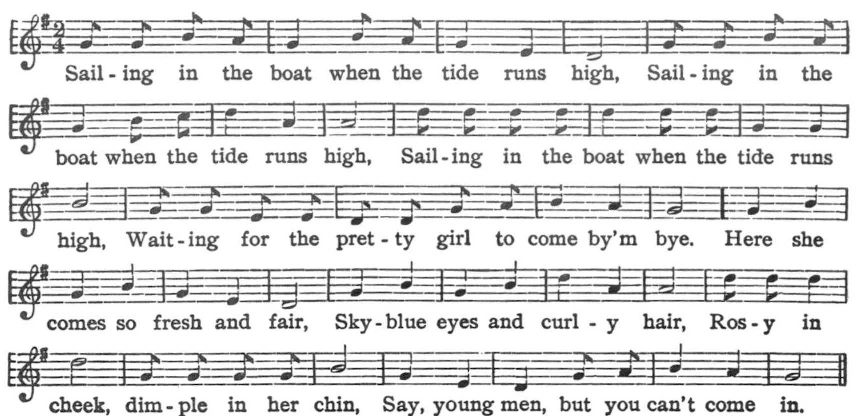

Sailing in the boat when the tide runs high [*thrice*]
Waiting for the pretty girl to come by'm by.
  Here she comes so fresh and fair.
  Sky-blue eyes and curly hair,
Rosy in cheek, dimple in her chin,
Say, young men, but you can't come in.

Rose in the garden for you, young man, [*twice*]
Rose in the garden, get it if you can,
But take care and don't choose a frost-bitten one.

Choose your partner, stay till day, [*thrice*]
Never mind what the old folks say.

Old folks say 'tis the very best way, [*thrice*]
To court all night and sleep all day.

Ashford, Conn. (1865).

The recorder (see note) remarks concerning this game and others from the same neighborhood that they were played as late as the year

1870, at the so-called "Evening Party." About midnight were served refreshments, and the singing and dancing kept up until about four o'clock in the morning, when the young men huddled about the door, and as the girls came out each offered his arm to the maid of his choice, with the words, "Can I see you home?" After which they separated, and went in the dark, often across fields, to their scattered homes, perhaps two miles away. At the door of the fair one there was always a final hug and kiss. Of flirting there was not much; when a girl had acquired the name of "liking the boys" (which meant receiving questionable attentions from more than one) she herself, and the young men who would "wait on her," were considered as of doubtful character, and likely no more to be accepted as escorts by those on whom no reproach rested.

No. 169.

Green Grows the Willow-Tree.

Green grows the willow-tree, [*thrice*]
Up steps a lady with a rose in her hand.

Bargain, bargain, you young man;
You promised to marry me long time ago;
You promised to marry me—you sha'n't say no.

Up steps a lady with a rose in her hand.

The children circle in a ring, singing the first verse; a girl steps into the middle, thus far vacant, and sings the second verse; the third is chanted in chorus. All stoop; the last down has to name her "beau" as a forfeit. *Washington, D. C.*

Mr. Babcock, from whose collection this game is taken, gives another round, in which the forsaken maid is represented as sitting under the willow, appropriate to pining lovers. The action, no doubt, originally showed the return of the absent friend and an embrace.

No. 170.

Marriage.

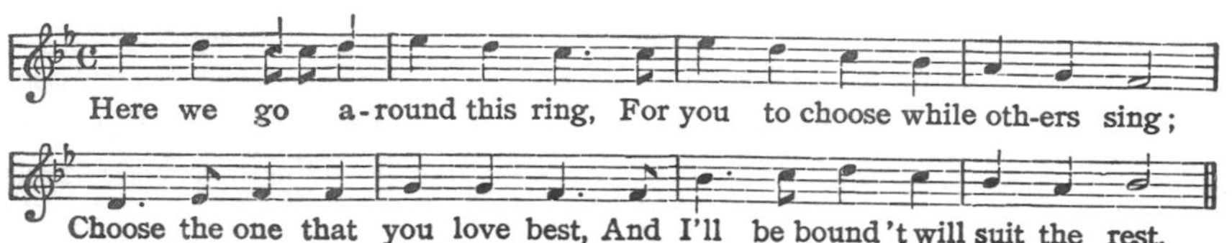

Here we go around this ring,
For you to choose while others sing;
Choose the one that you love best,
And I'll be bound 'twill suit the rest.

Now you're married you must be good,
Be sure and chop your husband's wood;
Live together all your life,
And be a good and faithful wife.

Connecticut (1865).

The line concerning wood-chopping has previously been given (p. 82) in connection with the game "Oats, Pease, Beans, and Barley Grows" (No. 21). It now appears that this game, as well as the mention of wood-chopping, are still familiar in the rural districts of England; furthermore, we have the same variations, by which the labor is put on the shoulders of the man or the wife, as the case may be.

A round under the name of "Marriage," already included (No. 10, 1), reduces to the simplest elements the description of separation and reunion. Equally crude romances are found in Great Britain, where a young lady named Isabella has attained a national repute as the heroine of such a history.

To the question what degree of antiquity can be ascribed to petty rounds of this character, only a hypothetical answer can be returned. From such indications as we possess, it seems probable that in the Middle Ages dances usually had a considerable length, which would not invite frequent repetition on the same occasion. In the course of time these became reduced to a brevity which permitted the same words to be repeated over again and again. Under such conditions, it was necessary to provide a second couple in place of the pair whose courtship had been represented; as a convenient method of choice, one player was allowed to retire, while the other was permitted to select a substitute. The solitary player was then regarded as a lover separated from the mate by absence or (supposed) death, and therefore assumed an attitude of mourning; the dancer chosen to replace the former was made to represent the returned "true love," and the mourner was consoled by reunion and kisses. Sometimes the appearance of sorrow (as in Nos. 13 and 15) was described as (love) sickness (No. 16), or as sleep (No. 160), always with the same result; the reappearing friend would make the only effective physician (No. 10, 5), or would revive the fainting lady with a kiss. Such representations are sufficiently explained as arising from the necessities of the dance.

At the same time, we have examples of kissing games apparently recent in language yet outgrowths of old roots (*e. g.*, No. 186); so that no general rule can be given.

No. 171.

The Needle's Eye.

(See No. 29.)

The following additional version is given for the sake of the melody:

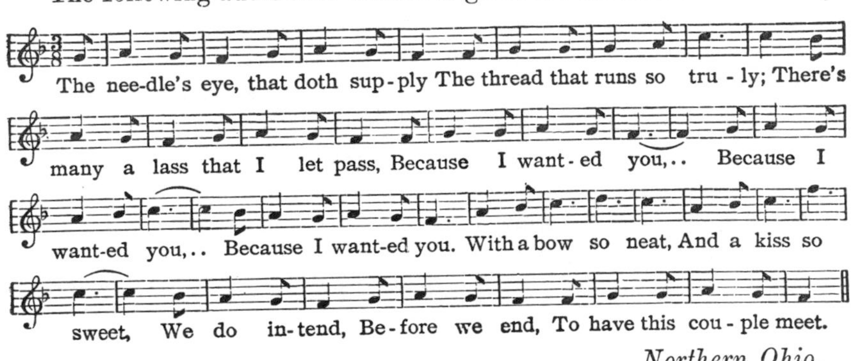

Northern Ohio.

The recorder observes that sometimes the players are sent through the arch in couples, when the captured pair kiss.

Mrs. Gomme shows that in England the game has in different localities been played on particular days of the year by young persons of both sexes, who danced through the streets, collecting numbers as they went, and finally attempted to encircle the village church with joined hands. Her versions show a connection with "London Bridge," of which this game may perhaps be a reduction.

No. 172.

Green Gravel.

(See No. 15.)

Green gravel, green gravel,
  The grass grows so green,
The fairest of ladies
  Is fit to be seen.

Dear ——, dear ——,
  Your true love is dead;
He sent you a letter
  To turn back your head.

Toronto, Canada.

Mr. Babcock gives a version by which it appears that in Washington the dancer, as the proper line is sung, turns her head over her shoulder; the process is repeated until all the children have so turned.

Turning the head is a sign of sorrow; in some British versions the game is continued by another in which the lost lover appears, and the dancers, who have all turned about, are one by one made to face the ring; as Miss Burne suggests, I think that "Green Gravel" was meant to receive such continuation.

In this case the absent lover has gone to the war, and the letter announcing his death in battle comes, I should think, from his officer (the king, p. 71). I do not now regard the game as the reduction of a ballad.

No. 173.

Under the Lily-white Daisies.

Johnny is his first name,
His first name, his first name—
Johnny is his first name,
Among the lily-white daisies.

——— is his second name—

Emma is her first name—

——— is her second name—

And now poor Johnny's dead and gone,
Dead and gone, dead and gone,
And now poor Johnny's dead and gone,
Among the lily-white daisies.

A single player stands in the centre of the ring, and before or during the singing of the last verse lies down as if dead. While singing, the children move round hand in hand.

Washington, D. C.

No. 174.

Miss Jenny Jones.

(See No. 11)

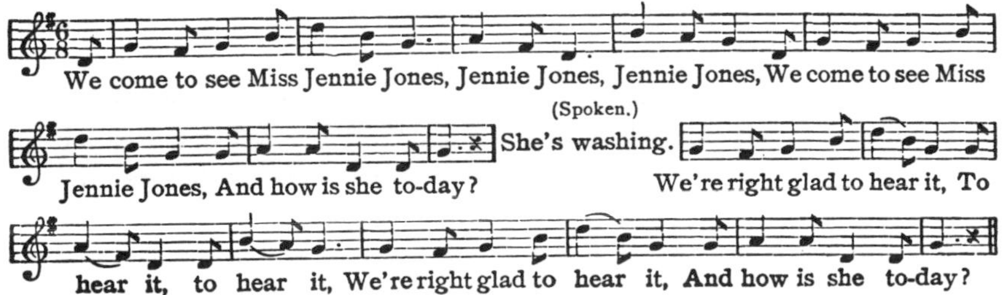

A.—"We come to see Miss Jenny Jones,
And how is she to-day?"

"She's washing."

"We're right glad to hear it,
And how is she to-day?"

"She's ironing."

"We're right glad to hear it,
And how is she to-day?"

"She's sick."

"We're right sorry to hear it,
And how is she to-day?"

"She's dead."

Maryland.

B.—Another melody:

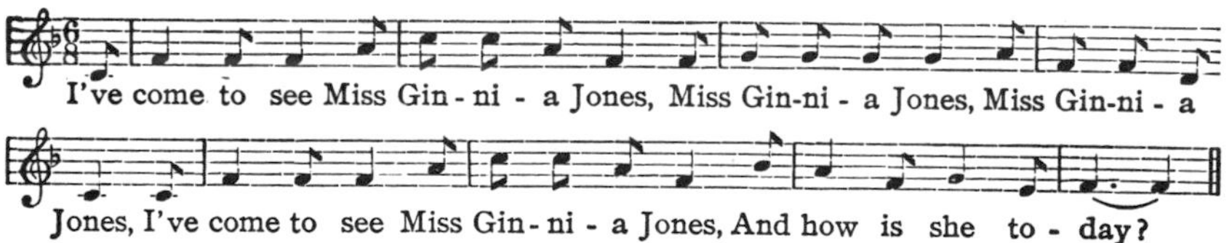

There is a wealth of British versions, of which some properly set forth that the white costume is to be worn, not by Janet, but by the maids who act as mourners.

As already remarked (p. 66), this drama was once a love-play, in which the heroine pines because her cruel parents refuse an offer for her hand. The relatives of the suitor, following the customary procedure, make successive visits to the house (as in the betrothal dance); but on this occasion there is no relenting. Miss Jones, despite her republican simplicity, is a lady of high degree, who is entitled to assume a title if she pleases; as is proper for a demoiselle of a noble house, she inhabits the upper story of the castle (the Scandinavian "high-loft"); superintendence of the household labors accomplished by her maidens is no more to her discredit than a like activity on the part of Nausicaa. Like Rosetina (p. 63), she dies of love, and her life, according to a belief older than the Æneid, passes into a flowering tree, below which, in after-years, her mournful and white-robed spirit is often to be seen. It is a strange example of the persistence of superstition that I have lately read a story in which the soul of a New England child, oppressed by a cruel guardian, similarly inhabits a shrub.

This particular play relates only to a maid; but variations of a game essentially the same apply to a male actor. The "Poor Johnny" of the preceding number, even in name, is the twin of Janet; and, examining the apparently absurd rhyme of No. 37, it will be seen to be no more than a variant. Originally the ghost would capture only a person of the other sex, and the names of Janet and John would be varied according to necessity.

No. 175.

My Pretty Pink.

My pretty little pink, I once did think
  That you and I would marry,
But now I've lost all hopes of that,
  I can no longer tarry.

I've got my knapsack on my back,
  My musket on my shoulder,
To march away to Quebec Town,
  To be a gallant soldier.

Where coffee grows on a white-oak-tree,
  And the rivers flow with brandy,
Where the boys are like a lump of gold,
  And the girls as sweet as candy.

East Tennessee.

The manner of playing has not been obtained. In another version, not gained in full, "Mexico" was substituted for "Quebec."

No. 176.

Quebec Town.

(See No. 59.)

We are marching down to Quebec town,
  Where the drums and fifes are beating;
The Americans have gained the day,
  The British are retreating.

The war's all over; we'll turn back
  To friends, no more to be parted:
We'll open our ring, and receive another in,
  To relieve this broken-hearted.

The manner of playing was as follows: The song was sung by the whole company as it marched around one person, who was blindfolded and seated in a chair placed in the centre of the room. He or she selected a partner by touching one of the ring with a long stick held for the purpose. The game concluded:

Put a hat on her head to keep her warm,
And a loving, sweet kiss will do her no harm.

North Carolina.

No. 177.

King William was King George's Son.

(See No. 17.)

A.—King William was King George's son,
  And from the royal blood he sprung;
  Upon his breast he wore a stowe,
  Which denotes the sign of woe.

  Say, young lady, will you 'list and go?
  Say, young lady, will you 'list and go?
  The broad-brimmed hat you must put on,
  And follow on to the fife and drum.

In this play a young man stands with a broad-brimmed hat in his hand. While the song proceeds he puts it on a girl's head, after which they march arm in arm, and finally she in turn puts it on the head of a young man, to continue as before. The play proceeds until all have been crowned with the hat, and march round the chimney in couples, singing with a will the words over and over.

Ashford, Conn. (1865).

The recorder observes that in the centre of the Colonial houses in which these games were played there was usually a large and old chimney, and that the rooms were connected by doors, so that it was possible to march around.

B.—King Charles he was King James's son,
And from the royal blood he sprung;
On his vest he wore a star,
Which he carried in time of war.

Of the second verse the informant only remembers the requirement to kneel "on this carpet" (the grass). (See p. 74.)

Dubuque Co., Iowa.

C.—King William was King James's son,
And on the royal race he run;
And on his breast he wore a star,
Which was carried in time of war.

Down on this carpet you must kneel,
As sure as grass grows on the field;
Go choose you east, go choose you west,
Go choose the one you love the best;
If she's not here to take your part,
Choose another with all your heart.

Washington, D. C.

Mrs. Gomme gives two versions, both more fragmentary than the American, and wanting the essential feature of the game, representing a call to arms.

It now appears to me that the Irish reciter whose account I have mentioned (p. 74) confused the game with some lines of a ballad, and that the suggestion as to derivation of the game (p. 75), founded on such information, is not maintainable.

That the final quatrain, though preserved only in New England, did make part of the old English game seems to be shown by the manner of playing in Sheffield, England, where, after the choice, the couples march inside the circle of players.

The song may receive the following explanation: A youth is chosen to enact the part of a prince who has been summoned to the field. While the dancers chant the first stanza, he marches within the ring after the manner of a soldier proceeding to war. On his way he meets a lady, on whom he fixes his affections; his suit is accepted, and, after the usual manner of May games, the couple kneel and kiss on the flowery sward. Unwilling to abandon his betrothed, the lover asks her to put on the attire of a soldier and accompany him; she accedes, and her assumption of the uniform is indicated; the pair now "follow the fife and drum." The play being ended, the man leaves the ring, and the maid is left to begin the second performance, in the course of which she is entitled to select a new partner.

No. 178.

Have You any Bread and Wine?

A.—"Have you any bread and wine,
My fairy and my fory?
Have you any bread and wine,
Within the golden story?"

"Yes, we have some bread and wine."
"May we have a pint of it?"
"Yes, you may have a pint of it."
"May we have a quart of it?"
"Yes, you may have a quart of it."
"May we have a gallon of it?"
"A gallon of it you shall not have."
"We are King William's fighting men."
"We are King George's fighting men."
"Are you ready for a fight?"

"Yes, we are ready for a fight,
My fairy and my fory;
Yes, we are ready for a fight,
Within the golden story."

Plymouth, Mass.

B.—A version given by Mr. Babcock, as played in Washington, D. C.:

"Have you got any blackberry wine,
Blackberry wine, blackberry wine,
Have you got any blackberry wine,
Mizzouri and Mizzauri?"

The reply being in the affirmative, the accosting party ask, "Will you lend me a pint of it?" and on refusal threaten successively to "break your dishes up," "send for the red-coat men," and for the "blue-coat men"; the other side is defiant, and preparations are made for a combat. The game is played in alternate song, with advance and retreat.

In England the game corresponds, and has a like imperfect refrain:

"Have you any bread and wine,
My Theerie and my Thorie?"

The assailants announce themselves as Prince Charlie's men, Romans, rovers, etc., while the defenders are King George's men, English, or guardian soldiers; such explanations, I should think, may be set down as modern additions. The participants divide into sides of about equal numbers and prepare for a contest.

No. 179.

Jamestown, Virginia.

The children form in two rows, facing each other, and a little apart. Two captains are chosen, usually by "speaking first." The first row advances, and a dialogue takes place:

"Here we come!"
"Where from?"
"Jamestown, Virginia."
"What's your trade?"
"Lemonade."
"Give us some."

The leader answers with initials which belong to some one child of his party, and which represent the first letters describing a particular trade (*e. g.,* "W. C.," for cutting wood), and his party proceeds to indicate by appropriate actions the craft in question. If the other side can guess, it chases the child who has been described, and, if caught, the latter belongs to his captors, and the successful party has another turn. If the initials are not guessed, the turn falls to the first side. The game ends when all the children of one side are caught.

This and No. 200 are the only games of a dramatic character played by children (girls from ten to twelve years) of the group to which the informant belongs. *St. Paul, Minn.* (1903).

The game is mentioned by Mr. Babcock as played in Washington, D. C., under the name of "New York." He does not mention giving initials of the occupation which is to be guessed. He observes that the name of any other place may be substituted for "New York."

In England Mrs. Gomme gives the game as "Trades." In France it has been played under the title of "Métiers."

No. 180.

Red Lion.

A.—Red Lion, Red Lion,
Come out of your den,
Whoever you catch
Will be one of your men.

The players count out to see who will be Red Lion, and the player chosen must retire to his den. When the words of defiance are sung, the Red Lion catches whom he can, and takes the prisoner to his den.

The others repeat the call, and the two come out together and catch another player; this is repeated until all are caught, and the first captured is Red Lion for the next game.

B.—The players choose a "chief," who calls "Loose!"—when the Red Lion rushes out; and, if he can catch a boy, must repeat "Red Lion" three times, after which both must hurry back to the den, in order to escape blows rained on them by the rest. If the chief exclaim "Cow-catcher!" the captive must be caught by putting interlocked arms over the head; if "Tight!" the pursuers must keep hands joined and catch by surrounding; if "Doubles!" the chasers must issue in twos.

Brooklyn, N. Y.

C.—"Red Line" is the name given to the running of the gantlet.

Washington, D. C.

It is evident that the latter form of the name is original, and that "Red Lion" is in the nature of a popular etymology; the appellation preserves the color of the British uniform. I do not find the name in Great Britain.

No. 181.

Violet Fights.

The recorder, Mrs. Fanny D. Bergen, writes:

"Armies of blue violets are annually sacrificed by little people in the 'Violet Fights.' Two children provide themselves with a goodly pile of these flowers, which they have purposely plucked with long stems. Each combatant holds his posy by the stem; the two spurs are interlocked; then the children simultaneously jerk the stems, and off comes one or the other violet head. Once in a great while the two heads fall, so evenly matched in resistance are they. Usually, however, one conquers the other; the flowerless stem is replaced by a fresh one from the pile, and the flower battle goes on. Occasionally a soldier is so valiant and successful as to lay low the heads of as many as a hundred or two of his enemies, but sooner or later he, too, is numbered with the beautiful slain. I am glad to have known of a few little girls who were too humane to take part in this ruthless play. The pastime is not only common among children throughout the United States and Canada, but is a familiar childish amusement in Japan, and a friend found that the same play was known to Indian children in the summer encampment at York Beach, Maine. The little red children say that the one whose violet conquers will be a great man. The Onandagas have a name for violets which, interpreted, means 'two heads entangled,' referring to the flower game."

No. 182.

Poppy-shows.

Mrs. Bergen further observes:

"The experience of what little girls call a 'poppy-show' was not numbered among my own personal joys. A friend once gave me the following account of these brilliant spectacles: 'I possessed two pieces of glass, very nearly of a size, between which I used to place fallen poppy petals, in lovely kaleidoscopic patterns. I had to hold the glasses together very tightly not to spoil the pattern by letting them slip. When several little girls had gathered their poppy-shows together on a board we used to chant when any one passed:

"Pinny, pinny, poppy-show,
Give me a pin and I'll let you know."

I don't know that any one ever accepted the enticing invitation. We varied the show at other seasons with different flowers—whole geranium blossoms or spiræa or apple-blossom petals, and many others—but we always called them poppy-shows and sang the same rhyme. Some girls carried their poppy-shows to school and passed them along under the desks. Other children gave their display in their barns, and one girl I knew had a tent in which her show was beautifully hidden from a pinless public. It was as exciting as going to a play to lift the flap and gaze upon the revealed splendors behind the screen."

In England the name is "Poppet-show," and by corruption "Poppy-show," or, because the usual charge was a pin, "Pinny-show." Mrs. Gomme says: "I remember well being shown how to make a peep or poppet show. It was made by arranging combinations of colors from flowers under a piece of glass, and then framing it with paper in such a way that a cover was left over the front, which could be raised when any one paid a pin to peep. The following words were said, or rather sung, in a sing-song manner:

"'A pin to see the poppet-show,
All manner of colors, oh!
See the ladies all below.'"

I should think likely that the show originally consisted of colored pictures or images of saints; it is popular etymology which has led to the use of poppies in America.

No. 183.

Rhyme for Jumping Rope.

The Bible is a holy and visible law,
I marry this Indian to this squaw,
By the point of my jack-knife
I pronounce you man and wife. *Virginia.*

Variations of the first line: "By the old Levitical law" (New England), or "By the holy evangels of the Lord."

Marriage by the knife is obviously a form of oath: "If I break this vow, may I perish by the edge of the sword."

No. 184.

London Bridge.

(See No. 150.)

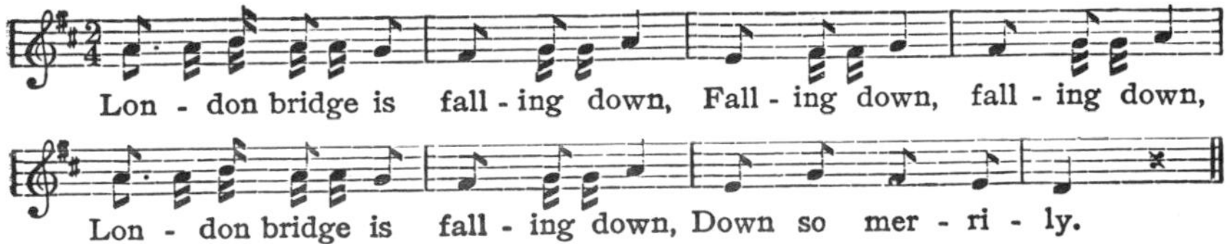

London Bridge is falling down,
Down, so merrily.

Here comes a candle to light you to bed.
Bed, so merrily.

Here comes a hatchet to chop off your head,
Head, so merrily.

Maryland.

In Great Britain there is at present no choice and "tug of war," as in the European and American versions; but that such was once the case is shown, I think, by the popularity of an offshoot which differs only in having dropped the mention of London Bridge as the scene of the play.

My explanation of the history involved in the game (p. 211) has been received with some favor. The account is not as conjectural as it appears, for the reason that any legend relating to the fall of a bridge is pretty sure to involve "foundation sacrifice." Till very lately it has been a general belief that bridges are objects of assaults by demons, from whom they can be defended only by immuring a living man in the foundation of the structure. The original idea seems to be that the soul of the victim becomes a guardian of the edifice. In case of an important construction, it was once thought necessary that choice should fall on an important personage (consequently a powerful soul, able to cope with demons). With economy due to experience, it was afterwards thought a pity to expend a precious life; perhaps a waif—a *filius nullius*—would answer, or a deposit of bones about the corner-stone would suffice.

The representation of the process would involve a long drama, of which in our modern rhyme we have but a pale remnant. Into the play would be introduced names of actors, who would vary from land to land, and the story would be made to apply to one bridge or another, as chance might direct, so that it is quite by accident that a particular name has found acceptance in English amusement; to suppose the invention of the game due to any particular historical incident is quite contrary to legitimate interpretation.

No. 185.

The Old Woman from Barbary.

(See No. 8.)

Here comes an old woman from Barbary, Barbary, Barbary,
Here comes an old woman from Barbary;
Oh, who'll take one of my daughters?
One can brew and one can spin,
And one can make a lily-white cake—
Oh, who'll take one of my daughters?

Now poor Nell has gone away, gone away, gone away;
In her pocket a thousand dollars,
On her hand a solid gold ring.
Good-bye, Nell, good-bye.

The "woman from Barbary" advances with her daughters on each side of her, all dancing in line towards a husband-elect, who stands-by himself. The mother sings, the children, as the recorder thinks, sometimes joining. After the first verse, the husband chooses and retains one, and the line dances back, singing the second verse. This is repeated until all have been chosen but one, who assumes the character of husband, and the child who before filled that rôle now becomes the old woman until all the daughters have been traded off again.

Washington, D. C.

In the course of remarks on this dance (p. 58 and in the Appendix, Note to No. 8), I expressed an opinion, based on comparison with European versions, that the game might be regarded as an offshoot of the witch drama (Nos. 154 and 190). British versions now explain the matter by showing that the player to whom the widow delivers her many children is not a husband, but a cruel mistress, who mutilates and devours the children; there is a close agreement in detail with versions of the witch game; my conjecture, therefore, seems to me substantiated.

No. 186.

The Rich Widow.

(See No. 8.)

I am a rich widow, I live all alone,
I have but one daughter, and she is my own;
Go, daughter, go daughter, and choose you a one,
Go choose you a good one, or else choose you none.

I've married off my daughter, I've given her away,
I've married off my daughter, she's bound to obey;
She's bound to obey and to never disagree,
So as you go round kiss her one, two, three.

This round is probably a reduction from the last number; the mother has given away (originally to the witch) all her daughters but one, whom she feels that she cannot spare, and therefore hesitates about yielding, till she is persuaded or compelled. In the present form the hypocritical sorceress is replaced by a lover; we have an example of a simple kissing round which has been evolved from a world-old drama of the most opposite character.

No. 187.

Pussy Wants a Corner.

The players outnumber the corners by one, and scramble for them, the unprovided child being " Pussy." She approaches one of the others, and announces, " Pussy wants a corner." " Ask my neighbor " is the reply. As " Pussy " passes on to repeat the petition before the next player, the girl just left tries to exchange places with her other neighbor, and " Pussy " hurries back to slip into one of the temporarily vacant corners. This is repeated until the effort is successful. The girl or boy left out becomes " Pussy " in her stead.

Washington, D. C.

The game is known as "Puss in the Corner." The girls in the corners beckon to each other, calling, "Puss! Puss!" as each tries to change places with a neighbor. *Cambridge, Mass.*

In Lancashire, England, the child in the middle chants, "Poor puss wants a corner"; the others beckon with the forefinger, and, calling, "Puss, Puss," run from point to point.

The game is European, and alike in Sweden and Sicily we find the same reply—"Go to my neighbor." In the former country the question is, "Can I borrow fire?" In Italy, a fifth player approaches one of the four stationed in the corners on pretence of having a candle to light. If the dialogue of the witch game is compared, it will be seen that we are now dealing with an offshoot of the latter, and that "Puss" is a transformation of the witch who comes to steal children.

No. 188.

Birds.

There are a row of "birds," a namer, and an angel. The namer, unheard by the angel, whispers a special name, such as "blue-bird," "red-bird," or "yellow-bird," to each one of the birds, then stands in front, facing them. The angel comes up and touches her on the back.

Namer. Who is that?
Angel. It's me.
Namer. What do you want?
Angel. I want some birds.
Namer. What color?
Angel. Blue [*for example*].
Namer. Run, blue.

The angel having guessed the color chosen for one of them, a chase ensues. If the angel touches blue-bird before the latter reaches a certain spot, blue-bird becomes an angel and the angel becomes a bird. If the blue-bird gains the asylum, she goes back to her place in the row, and the angel must try again. If the angel does not guess the color of any bird, the namer answers, "I haven't got any." If this occurs three times, the namer exclaims, "Go back and learn your A B C's!" The angel then withdraws to her original post, but soon comes forward to try again. This continues until she has guessed correctly and caught a bird.

"Ribbons" is played in the same manner, with this change of name for the row, except that there is a devil as well as an angel, who alternate in their guessing *Washington, D. C.* (Mr. Babcock.)

The game is a variant of "Colors" (No. 153). (That the angel, if his guess is correct, resigns his function and becomes a bird is a local variation.)

In England the game of "Ribbons" is nearly identical, a "minder" performing the office of the "namer." There is the same requirement to "Go and learn your A B C's," and the "angel" and "devil" figure.

In these games there is no "tug of war" at the end, as in "Colors" (No. 153), but that feature has evidently dropped out, being essential to any play making mention of angels and demons.

The games seem to be divergent forms of the witch drama, referring to that stage of the story in which the mother, in some forms of the legend, is obliged to guess back her stolen children. (See Note, 154, 6.)

No. 189.

Black Spider.

The children choose a Mother, Nurse, and Black Spider; the rest are the children, all of them flies; they are named after as many species of flies as the children can remember—Horse-fly, Dragon-fly, Day-fly, etc.

The Black Spider keeps out of sight. The Mother prepares to go out. She charges the Nurse to be very careful of her children, and not let the Black Spider get them. She then goes away.

The Black Spider now appears; she coaxes, wheedles, and frightens the children, until she finally drags one away.

The Mother, returning, exclaims, "Where is my Day-fly?" (or whatever may be the name of the child she misses).

The Nurse replies, "The Black Spider has it."

Again the Mother goes out, and repeats her former caution. The same thing is repeated until finally she comes back and finds that all are gone, even the Nurse. She cries aloud and laments, then searches for the Black Spider. Finding her, she demands her children. The Black Spider, however, will not give them up.

At last the Spider says, "What will you give me for such a one?" naming one of the flies. The mother offers cake, candy, houses, land—anything she can think of. After a great deal of haggling a bargain is struck and the fly purchased. This scene is repeated until all are restored, when the Mother goes off in triumph. *Holyoke, Mass.*

The game is a variant of the following.

No. 190.

Old Witch.

I give additional versions of this remarkable game.

G.—The persons represented are a Witch, Mother, Nurse named Sunday, and children called Monday, Tuesday, Wednesday, Thursday, Friday, and Saturday. Scene, the steps of a porch, on which the children sit in a row.

Mother [*to Nurse*]. I'm going out, and I advise you to take good care of the children, and not let any one come into the house.

[Enter Witch, in the character of an infirm old woman (not costumed), and desires to be let in; when admitted, she begs for medicine or cordial (*e. g.*, whiskey), which may relieve her ailments. While the Nurse has gone to get it, the Witch carries off a child, whom she takes to a corner supposed to represent her "store," and calls by a new name, of a character answering to her stock in trade, as, for example, "Lemon candy." Sunday re-enters, and cries to the absent Mother (who is supposed to be within call).

Sunday. Mother, mother, the tea-kettle is boiling over!

Mother. Take a spoon and stir it.

Sunday. I can't reach it.

Mother. Take a chair to stand on.

Sunday. I can't lift the chair.

Mother. Well, I suppose I've got to come home.

[The Mother returns, looks over the children, discovers that one is missing, and blames Sunday. The latter excuses herself, alleging that the lost child has gone to see a friend or is in the garden; at last she confesses.

Sunday. Oh, the Old Witch took her!

[Mother whips Sunday. The action is repeated, in successive visits of the Witch, until all the children are gone. The Witch returns for the last time, and carries off Sunday.

Witch. Well, since your mistress has been so bad to you, I'll take you myself.

[The Mother, finding the house empty, sets off in search of her children, and arrives at the store of the Witch.

Mother. What kind of a store is this?

Witch. A (candy) store.

Mother. I'd like to come in.

Witch. Your rubbers are too dirty.

Mother. I'll take them off.

Witch. Your shoes are too dirty.

Mother. I'll take them off.

Witch. Your stockings are too dirty.

Mother. I'll take them off.

Witch. Your blood will stain the carpet.

Mother. I'll tie them up in rags.

Witch. They'll leak through.

Mother. I'll put on glass slippers.

Witch. They're not good enough.

Mother. I'll put on diamond slippers.

Witch. You can come in.

Mother. Have you any (lemon candy)?

[Witch produces the child called Lemon Candy, and offers her to the Mother, who pretends to taste.

Mother. It's too sour. [Witch puts on sugar.

Mother. Why, this tastes like my child!

[The Mother sends the child home, and in a similar manner recovers her remaining children. After all have been regained, the game is ended, and may be renewed with a new Witch, Mother, and Nurse, the former actors becoming children for the next turn.

St. Paul, Minn. (1903).

H.—The persons represented are a Mother, many children, and the Old Witch, who is always lame, must carry a stick, and wears a cloak.

The Mother, who is blind, goes out to work, giving each child a piece of sewing, to be done in her absence, represented by the hem of her dress, and which she calls a stint. She bids the children be good, and not let the Old Witch get them. As soon as she leaves, the Old Witch knocks at the door, and asks for fire to light her pipe, saying, "If you don't give it to me, I'll kill you." As the eldest daughter turns to get the fire, the Witch seizes one of the children, and runs away. When the Mother comes back, the children kneel before her, and she puts her hands on their heads, calling them in turn—Monday, Tuesday, Wednesday, etc. One of the children, slipping down to the end of the line and stooping, simulates the youngest child, who is gone.

This process is repeated until all are gone but one, who can no longer keep up the pretence of representing others in addition to herself. The Mother calls out: "Oh, the Old Witch has taken all my children! Let us go back for them." She and her daughter go forth, and come to the place where the Old Witch is giving a party. She invites the Mother in. The children are kneeling on the floor, with aprons or dresses over their heads. The Old Witch invites the Mother to taste, saying, "This is Ice-cream," etc., until she comes to a child which she says is Cherry-pie. The Mother exclaims, "Why, this tastes like my Monday; how did you get here, child?" The child replies, "My great big toe brought me here"; whereupon all the children start up and run, pursued by the Mother and the Witch. The one whom the Mother catches plays the part of Mother in the next turn, and the one caught by the Witch becomes the new Witch. *Newburgh, N. Y.*

I.—Of a curious version, printed in the *Journal of American Folk-Lore,* I give only the substance:

The eldest daughter is called "Fairest of the Fair." The Mother goes out, crossing her fingers to bless the house. In the Mother's absence the Witch enters, and asks, "Give me fire; I'm cold." When refused, she takes out a necklace, and says, "All for one lighted sod and one fat child." Fairest of the Fair tries on the necklace, and says, "Take them" (two or three children are often taken at once). On her return the Mother observes the loss of the child, and rebukes Fairest, saying: "The children are gone, and where did you get the necklace?" "I bought it." "And what did you give for it?" "A lighted sod and one fat child." Mother beats Fairest, and says, "I told you not to give anything from the house." "I didn't; I sold it." The Mother scolds her, and the children are put to bed. On a second occasion Fairest of the Fair gives a child for a bracelet, and on the third exchanges another. When the Mother finds that all her children are gone she beats Fairest out of the house with contumely, forbidding return until she has brought back the children and gotten rid of the ill-gotten jewels. Fairest goes out, finds the house where the Witch lives, enters in her absence, seizes a lighted sod and one fat child, and drops her necklace in the place where the child stood. A game of tag follows, in which the children try to be touched by Fairest of the Fair, while the Witch endeavors to prevent them. Finally the children are all recovered, and the game is ended, the Mother saying, "Now you are again Fairest of the Fair."

The game is of long duration, and played with many variations and original additions. *Boston, Mass.*

British variants closely correspond, and often show additional traits, evidently archaic. Thus in Dromfield the Witch stands near the corner of a wall, so that she can peep round (as she watches an opportunity to steal in). In London, on her way to the house of the Witch, the Mother meets the latter in disguise, who endeavors to dissuade her from approach by accounts of the fierce animals in the path. The children, after they have been taken by the Witch, are placed in a crouching attitude behind chairs; the Mother tastes a child, and is told that it is a barrel of pork. In a version from Deptford, the Witch bribes the daughter left in charge by offer of a ribbon (compare the last version). In Cornwall, at the end, the Mother and children chase the Witch, and, when caught, bind her hand and foot, throw her on a pile, and burn her, the children fanning with their pinafores imaginary flames.

In a whole class of versions the Mother is represented as going out to wash.

In this drama the Witch secures admission on pretext of seeking a light; in days not far removed in actual time, though remote in custom, when the household fire went out the easiest way of rekindling was to obtain coals from a neighbor. In the case of a stranger such application would be suspicious, since the possession of so important an object of domestic use would enable an enchanter to cast a spell on the inmates. Hence a fear of giving away fire, which survives in Ireland as respects May-day, when in former days all fires were allowed to expire, and relighted by a sod brought from the priest's house. To quote Mr. Mooney: "None will be given out of the house on this day for any consideration, as such an act brings all kinds of ill-fortune upon the family, and especially enables the borrower to steal all the butter from the milk, so that any one who should ask for the loan of a lighted sod of turf on May-day would be regarded as a suspicious character, whom it would be just as well to watch. To give out either fire or salt on this day is to give away the year's luck." The request makes apparent the sinister purpose of the visitor; but the trait is no more primitive than numerous others belonging to the game.

As the continuing interest of the witch-play is shown by vivacity and persistence, so its ancient currency is attested by unexampled variation; as already observed (p. 219), almost every trait has attained independent existence in the form of games so divergent as to resemble neither one another nor the parent.

Fondness for referring human acts to animal performers appears in a multiplicity of names; the children are presented as chickens, lambs, pigs, geese, or flies; the Witch figures as kite, fox, wolf, or spider. Prohibition of exit by the departing Mother has created childish expressions of mockery or defiance (Nos. 89, 114, 123). The avoidance on the part of successive children of the arriving Witch is represented in the most familiar of parlor games (No. 187). The promenade of the family in quest of a lost child is attended by a meeting with the disguised Witch (No. 102), or else this march is considered as an attempt to hire out or marry daughters (No. 185). The desire of the Mother to retain one daughter makes a kissing-round (No. 186). Her efforts to recover the butchered infants furnish suggestion for a whole series of games; she may be described as a purchaser who desires to recover stolen goods (No. 154, F., and Note), or the action may be put in the form of a guessing contest, in which angel and devil replace the original performers (Nos. 153, 188). In this manner it requires (according to my estimate) thirteen numbers of my gathering to exhibit the offshoots of this single drama.

By an adequate investigation it would be possible to elucidate the witch-play, but such a task is beyond the limits of this book. It will be sufficient to affirm that, in tracing the history, we should find the actors originally divine or demonic, at last plebeian. The declension is progressive: holy rite, courtly dance, childish play. The stair which seemed likely to end in the lumber-room conducts to the cupola of the dome.

APPENDIX

COLLECTIONS OF CHILDREN'S GAMES.

THE following is a list of collections of popular games of children, or collections containing such, consulted in preparing the present volume, and referred to in the notes by the names of the editors:

BRAND, J. Popular Antiquities of Great Britain. With corrections and additions by W. Carew Hazlitt. (Lond. 1870, 3 vols.) The same, arranged and revised by Henry Ellis. (Lond. 1813, 2 vols.; new ed. 1849.)

CHAMBERS, R. Popular Rhymes of Scotland. (New ed. Edinb. 1870; 1st ed. 1842.)

HALLIWELL [PHILLIPS], J. O. The Nursery Rhymes of England. (6th ed. Lond. 1860; 1st ed. 1842; 2d ed. 1843.)

Popular Rhymes and Nursery Tales. (Lond. 1849.)

STRUTT, J. The Sports and Pastimes of the People of England. (Lond. 1801.)

BELÈZE, G. Jeux des Adolescents. (Paris, 1873.)

BUJEAUD, J. Chants et Chansons Populaires des Provinces de l'Ouest. (Niort, 1866, 2 vols.)

CELNART, MADAME. Manuel Complet des Jeux de Société. (2d ed. Paris, 1830.)

CHABREUL, MADAME DE. Jeux et Exercises des Jeunes Filles. (2d ed. Paris, 1860.)

DUMERSAN, M. Chansons et Rondes Enfantines. (Paris, 1858.)

DURIEUX, A., and BRUYELLE, A. Chants et Chansons Pop. du Cambresis. (Cambrai, 1864–68, 2 vols.)

GAGNON, E. Chansons Pop. du Canada. (Quebec, 1880.)

GAIDOZ, H., and ROLLAND, E. Mélusine. Recueil de Myth., Lit Pop., Trad., et Usages. (Paris, 1878.)

KUHFF, P. Les Enfantines du Bon Pays de France. (Paris, 1878.)

PUYMAIGRE, T. J. B. DE. Chants Pop. Rec. dans le Pays Messin. (Paris, 1865; 2d ed. 1881.)

TARBÉ, P. Romancero de Champagne. (Reims, 1843, 5 vols.)

ARBAUD, D. Chants Pop. de la Provence. (Aix, 1862, 2 vols.)

MONTEL, A., and LAMBERT, L. Chants Pop. du Languedoc. (Paris, 1880.)

COELHO, F. A. Romances Pop. e Rimas Infantís Portuguezes. (Zeit. f. Rom. Phil. vol. iii. 1879.)

MARIN, F. R. Cantos Pop. Españoles, Tomo 1. Rimas Infantiles. (Sevilla, 1882.)

MASPONS Y LABRÓS, F. Jochs de la Infancia. (Barcelona, 1874.)

VILLABRILLE, F. Los Juegos de la Infancia. (Madrid, 1847.) Contains little of a popular character.

BERNONI, G. Guiochi Pop. Veneziani. (Venezia, 1874.)

CORAZZINI, F. I Componimenti Minori della Letteratura Pop. Ital. (Benevento, 1877.)

DALMEDICO A. Ninne-nanne e Guiochi Infantili Veneziani. (Venezia, 1871.)

FERRARO, G. Canti Pop. di Ferrara, etc. (Ferrara, 1877.)

Cinquanta Guiochi Fanciulleschi Monferrini. In Archivio per lo Studio delle Trad. Pop. G. Pitrè, S. Salomone-Mario. Fasc. I., II. (Palermo, 1882.)

GIANANDREA, A. S. Saggio di Guiochi e Canti fanciulleschi delle Marche. In Vol. I. of Rivista di Letteratura Pop., G. Pitrè, F. Sabatini. (Roma, 1877.)

IMBRIANI, V. Canti Pop. Avellinesi. (Bologna, 1874.)

Canzonetti Infantili Pomiglianesi. In Vol. X. of Il Propugnatore. (Bologna, 1877.)

IVE, A. Canti Pop. Istriani. In Vol. V. of Canti e Racconti del Pop. Ital., D. Comparetti and A. D'Ancona. (Torino, 1877.)

PITRÈ, G. Canti Pop. Siciliani. (Palermo, 1870–71, 2 vols.)

COUSSEMAKER, C. E. DE. Chants Pop. des Flamands de France. (Gand, 1856.)

HOFFMANN VON FALLERSLEBEN, A. H. Horae Belgicae. (2d Aus. Hannover, 1866.)

LOOTENS, A., and FEYS, J. Chants Pop. Flamands rec. à Bruges. (Bruges, 1879.)

WILLEMS, J. F. Oude Vlaemsche Liederen. (Gent, 1848.)

Aus dem Kinderleben, Spiele, Reime, Räthsel. (Oldenburg, 1851.)

Baslerische Kinder- und Volks-Reime. (Basel, 187–.)

BIRLINGER, A. Nimm mich mit! Kinderbüchlein. (Freiburg, 1871.)

DUNGER, H. Kinderlieder und Kinderspiele aus dem Vogtlande. (Plauen, 1874.)

FEIFALIK, J. Kinderreime und Kinderspiele aus Mähren. (Zeit. f. deutsch Myth., Vol. IV.)

FIEDLER, E. Volksreime und Volkslieder in Anhalt Dessau. (Dessau, 1847.)

FRISCHBIER, H. Preussische Volksreime und Volksspiele. (Berlin, 1867.)

HANDELMANN, H. Volks- und Kinder-Spiele aus Schleswig-Holstein. (Kiel, 1874.)

KEHREIN, J. Volkssprache und Volkssitte im Herzogthum Nassau. (Weilburg, 1862, 2 vols.)

MANNHARDT, W. Germanische Mythen. (Berlin, 1858.)

MEIER, E. Deutsche Kinderreime und Kinderspiele aus Schwaben. (Tübingen, 1851.)

MUELLENHOFF, K, Sagen, Märchen, und Lieder d. Herzogthümer Schleswig - Holstein und Lauenburg. (Kiel, 1845.)

PETER, A. Volksthumliches aus Oesterreichish-Schlesien. (Troppau, 1867, 2 vols.)

ROCHHOLZ, E. L. Alemannisches Kinderlied und Kinderspiel. (Leipzig, 1857.)

SCHUSTER, F. W. Siebenbürgisch- Sächische Volkslieder. (Herrmannstadt, 1865.)

SIMROCK, K. Das deutsche Kinderbuch. (Frankfurt am Main, 1857.)

STOEBER, A. Elsassisches Volksbüchlein. (Strasburg, 1842.)

Vernaleben, T., and Branky, F. Spiele und Reime der Kinder in Oesterreich. (Wien, 1873.)
Wiegenlieder, Ammenreime und Kinderstuben-Scherze in plattdeutscher Mundart. (Bremen, 1859.)
Zeitschrift für deutsche Myth. und Sittenkunde, I.–IV. (Göttingen, 1853–59.)
Zingerle, J. V. Das deutsche Kinderspiel im Mittelalter. (2d ed. Innsbruck, 1873.)

Arwiddson, A. I. Svenska Fornsånger. (Stockholm, 1842, 3 vols.)
Djurklou, G. Ur Nerike's Folksprak och Folklif. (Örebro, 1860.)
Dybeck, R. Runa, En Skrift för fädernes-landets fornvänner. (Stockholm, 1842–49.)
Grundtvig Svend. Gamle Danske Minder i Folkemunde. (Copenhagen, 1854. New Series, 1857.)
Danske Folkeminder. (Copenhagen, 1861.)
Hammershaimb, V. U. Faeröiske Skikke og Lege. (Antiquarisk Tidsskrift, Copenhagen 1849–51.)
Thiele, J. M. Danske Folkesagn. (Copenhagen, 1820–23, 4 vols.)
Wigstrom, Eva. Folkdiktning. (Copenhagen, 1880.)

Bezsonoff, A. Dyetskia Pyesni. Songs of (Russian) Children. (Moscow, 1868.)
Mozarowski, A. Svyatochnoia Pyesni. Christmas Games of the Government of Kazan (Kazan, 1873.)
Vrčević, V. Sprske Narodne Igre. Servian Popular Games (Belgrade, 1868.)

Neus, H. Ehstnische Volkslieder. (Reval, 1850.)

Babcock, W. H. Games of Washington Children. (Amer. Anthropologist, Vol. I. Washington, D. C., 1888.)
Backus, E. S. Song-Games from Connecticut. (Jour. of Amer. Folk-Lore, Vol. XIV. Boston, Mass.)
Bolton, H. C. The Counting-out Rhymes of Children, their Antiquity, Origin, and Wide Distribution. (London, 1888.)
Culin, S. Street Games of Boys in Brooklyn, N. Y. (Jour. Amer. Folk-Lore, Vol. IV. Boston, 1891.)
Gomme, A. B. The Traditional Games of England, Scotland, and Ireland. (London, 1894 and 1898, 2 vols. 8vo.) ("List of Authorities," vol. i. pp. xi.-xiv.)
Krehbiel, H. E. Southern Song Games. (New York Tribune, July 27 and August 4, 1902.)
Maclagan, R. C. The Games and Diversions of Argyleshire. (Publications of the Folk-Lore Society, XLVII. London, 1901.)

COMPARISONS AND REFERENCES.

The object of the following notes is to exhibit, in a clear manner, the extent of the correspondence between the games of American children and those belonging to children in other countries. This volume is not intended to include all games of children, but (with some exceptions in favor of certain amusements which possess interest as folk-lore) only such as are played with words or quaint formulas. Of games of this class, we find in the collections very few known to children in Great Britain, and possessing European diffusion, which are not represented in this series by independent American versions (see No. 160, note, end). With these exceptions, the British game-formulas to which American usage does not offer equivalents are local and of trifling interest. The references given below may, therefore, be considered as a comparative account of English children's games in general.

The coincidence which this comparison shows to exist between English and German games is very close. Taking three German collections—belonging respectively to Switzerland (Rochholz), to Suabia (Meier), and to Schleswig-Holstein (Handelmann)—and leaving out of account songs and ballads, we have about eighty games played with rhymes or formulas. Of this number, considering only cases of obvious identity, we estimate that forty-five have equivalents in the present series, and thirty-three are not so paralleled. But of the latter class, six are known to have been played in Great Britain, while thirteen others appear to be variations of types represented in this collection. Of the small number remaining, few seem to be ancient, it being impossible to point out more than three or four really curious games which are not played also in an English form. This agreement cannot be explained by inheritance from a common stock, a theory which research has also discredited in other branches of folk-lore. The relationship is only a degree less near in other countries; thus, in a collection of Spanish games belonging to Catalonia (Maspons y Labrós), we find that, out of thirty-eight games, twenty-five have English equivalents.

NOTES TO INTRODUCTION.

CAROL, p. 9. Middle Latin *Choraula*, from *choreola*. The word *coraula* is still used to denote the ring-dance in Switzerland; also *coreihi*, to leap (choreare), Rochholz, p. 371. Russian *chorom*, a round of children, Bezsonoff, p. 190.

MAY-GAMES, pp. 16–19. Tarbé, "Romancero de Champagne," ii. 61. Puymaigre, p. 201, "Trimazos." A. Rivinus, "De Majumis," etc., in Graevius, Syntagma (Utrecht, 1702).

GAMES CITED BY FROISSART (pp. 34, 35).—The passage here rendered (with the omission of two or three obscure names of amusements) is from "L'Espinette Amoureuse," l. 143–338, 35–47. Many of the games mentioned cannot now be recognized from the titles given. Others, however, can be identified; thus, *Queue loo loo* (keuve leu leu) is No. 106 of the present collection; *Oats* (avainne), No. 21; *Scorn* or *Derision* (risées), perhaps No. 61; *King who does not lie*, perhaps No. 55; *Grasses* (erbelette), No. 42; *Cligne-musette* (Cluignette), No. 105; *Pince-merine*, according to Menagier de Paris, lxxvii., the same as *Pince-sans-rire*, No. 77, C. *Playing with nuts*, No. 144; *Throwing pence*, etc., No. 144, B. *Pebbles* (picrettes), No. 137, or No. 148. *Hook* (havot), perhaps *Hockey*, No. 136. *Mule*, a kind of leap-frog, still played in Italy, *Salta-muletta*, Gianandrea, No. 30. A species of this game in Philadelphia is now called *Saults*. Replies (réponniaux), a sort of *Hide and seek*, No. 105, in which the concealed person indicates his whereabouts in answer to a call; see same poem, l. 2653. *Astonishment* (esbahi), a game which consisted in imitating that emotion; thus, when the horses of a party have given out unexpectedly—"I should think we were playing at Astonishment," says one of the cavaliers, looking at the faces of the rest (Dict. of La Curne de Sainte-Palaye, art. "Esbahi"). On the whole, the impression which the catalogue gives us, is that the sports of a child in the Middle Ages were very similar to those of to-day, or, perhaps we should rather say, of yesterday.

LOVE-GAMES (p. 39).—This is an old name for games representing or offering opportunity for courtship, as "love-songs" is for ballads. We have heard both expressions in New England, from the lips of aged persons, in whose youth they were current. See the Gentleman's Magazine, Feb. 1738.

NOTES TO GAMES.

No. 1. English versions are numerous. Halliwell, Nurs. Rh. (6th ed.), Nos. 332, 333. Pop. Rh., pp. 123, 124. Chambers, p. 143; p. 141, "Janet jo." Notes and Queries, 1st ser. VI. 241; 5th ser. IV. 51, 157. — *German*, Meier, p. 107 (cited), 109; Handelmann, p. 62. Vernaleken, p. 55, etc. — *Swedish*, Arwiddson, iii. 175 f.—*Icelandic*, Arwiddson, iii. 182. Lyngbye, Faeröiske Quaeder, p. 37, introd. note.—*Faroese*, Antiq. Tids., 1849–51, p. 310, "Princes riding," compare No. 3.—*Italian*, Bernoni, p. 43, "L'Imbasciatore." Gianandrea, No. 23, "Il bel Castello."—*Spanish* (Catalan), Maspons y Labrós, p. 47, "La Conversa del rey Moro."—*French*, Ch. du Cambresis, i. 80.

2. A variety of No. 1. Corresponding is the *Faroese* version referred to, in which the suitors, after rejection as thralls, smiths, etc., are finally accepted as princes, with the expression "tak vid" (literally "take with"), be welcome, which may explain the peculiar use of the word "take" in our rhyme.

3. Also a variety of No. 1. Folk-lore Record, iii. 170. Chambers, p. 139 (cited). "I am a lusty wooer" (the version referred to, p. 49, note) is said to have been

played by Charles II. See the Gentleman's Magazine, Feb. 1738; Nurs. Rh., No. 491.

4. Henderson, Folk-lore of the Northern Counties (Lond. 1879), p. 27. Compare French round in Celnart, p. 24.
5. Nurs. Rh., No. 479. Compare No. 31.
6. Nurs. Rh., No. 466, "The Keys of Canterbury." Chambers, p. 61, "The Tempted Lady."
7. *French*, Celnart, p. 15, sixth round, presents verbal correspondence.
8. These versions belong to a game, widely diffused through Europe, in which a "rich" mother begs away, one by one, the daughters of a "poor" mother, until she has secured them all.—*German*, Frischbier, No. 657.—*French*, Chabreul, p. 175, "Riche et Pauvre." Celnart, p. 382, "Olivé Beauvé et la voisine." Ch. du Camb., i. 77, "La Boiteuse." The celebrated song "Giroflé Girofla" is of the same origin. In the Canadian round (Gagnon, p. 149), and in the English rhyme, for the sake of the dance, the mother whose daughters are begged away or stolen is turned into a mother whose object is to marry her many daughters; so the *Swedish* (Arwiddson, iii. 203), which presents verbal correspondence to the English song of our collection. Arwiddson, iii. 167, game of "Rich and Poor Birds." The first comes in limping, leaning on a cane, and with piteous gestures begs the train of the other. By comparing No. 154, and note, it will be seen that all the above games make up a single branch of the numerous outgrowths of a primitive root, which is responsible for no small part of the amusements of youth in Europe. Compare Nurs. Rh., No. 343.
10. Connected is a European game representing courtship—meeting, saluting, parting, etc.—*German*, Frischbier, No. 674.—*Swedish*, Arwiddson, iii. 257.—*Flemish*, Looten and Feys, No. 113. A different but related game is *French*, Celnart, p. 14 (cited). Chabreul, p. 157. Gagnon, p. 151.—*Italian*, Corazzini, p. 84.—The words "Rowe the boat" begin a waterman's roundel, A.D. 1453; see Chappell's Pop. Music of the Olden Time, p. 482.—(4.) *French*, Ch. du Camb., i. 221 (cited).
11. Chambers, p. 140, "Janet jo." Folk-lore Record, iii. 171, "Jenny Jones." See Coussemaker, p. 100, Flemish "Maiden's Dance."—Bernoni, Cant. Pop. Venez. xi. 2, "Rosetina."—Roxburghe Coll. i. 186–189, Ballad of "The Bride's Buriall."
12. Compare N. and Q., 3d ser. VII. 353.
13. Halliwell, Pop. Rh., p. 133. Henderson, Folk-lore, p. 26.
15. N. and Q., 5th ser. III. 482.—French round cited, Ch. du Camb., ii. 58. Gagnon, p. 303 (cited, p. 8). Bugeaud, i. 202.
16. Chambers, p. 118.—*French*, Ch. du Camb., ii. 42.
17. *Danish* and *Swedish* ballads, Sv. Grundtvig, Danmarks Gamle Folkeviser, Nos. 180, 181.
18. Child, Eng. and Scot. Ballads, 1857, iii. 136.
19. Child, ii. 154.
20. *Swedish*, Arwiddson, iii. 196.
21. *French*, Celnart, p. 21, etc.—*Provençal*, see Fauriel, Hist. de la Poésie Prov., ii. 87. —*Spanish* (Catalan), Mila y Fontanals, Romanc. Cat., p. 173.—*Italian*, Bernoni, p. 37. (Sicily) Pitrè, ii. 33.—*German*, Meier, pp. 136, 137.—*Swedish*, Arwiddson, iii. 326.— Rounds of a similar type, Chabreul, p. 146, "Salade." Bugeaud, i. 48, "Plantons la Vigne."

22. *German*, Dunger, pp. 184–186. Mullenhoff, p. 484, No. 2. "Aus dem Kinderleben," p. 33.—*Finnish*, Neus, p. 387.
23. Halliwell, Pop. Rh., p. 127. Chambers, p. 134.
25. A variation of 23, 24. Halliwell, Pop. Rh., p. 130. Chambers, p. 135.—*French*, Gagnon, p. 99. Chabreul, p. 141, etc.—*Spanish*, Marin, i. 96, "Thus do the Shoemakers."
26. Folk-lore Rec., iii. 170. Compare French game, Ch. du Camb., i. 223.
28. Nurs. Rh., No. 287.
29. Folk-lore Rec., iii. 169. For French game referred to, see Laisnel de la Salle, ii. 151.—*French*, Celnart, p. 53, "L'Anguille Enfilée."
30. Compare Provençal nurse-songs, in Chants Pop. du Languedoc, "Chants énumeratifs," especially p. 432.
31. Compare No. 5.
32. Halliwell, Pop. Rh., p. 119, "Mary Brown." N. and Q., 6th ser. II. 248.—*Swedish*, Arwiddson, iii. 233.—*Finnish*, Neus, p. 388.—*Italian*, Comparetti, iv. 263.—*French*, Mélusine, p. 542.
33. Chambers, p. 25. N. and Q., 4th ser. II. 274. — *Flemish, Dutch, German*, Hor. Belg., ii., Nos. 143, 145.—*French* (Canada), Gagnon, p. 129.
34. Nurs. Rh., No. 290. To this class of jests belongs the German tale, Grimm, No. 119, "Die sieben Schwaben."
35. Chambers, p. 344. Halliwell, Pop. Rh., p. 218, quotes the first lines of this rhyme from Aubrey's Miscellanies, ed. 1696.
36. Compare Chambers, p. 137, "A Courtship Dance."—*French*, Celnart, p. 19.—Canadian song of Perrette, Gagnon, p. 286.
38. For way of playing, compare No. 22.
40. Chappell, Pop. Music of the Olden Time, p. 589.—*French* (Canada), Gagnon, p. 223.—*Swedish*, Arwiddson, iii. 369.
42. *German* usages, Rochholz, pp. 172–174. Meier, p. 93.—In Middle Ages, Zingerle, pp. 32, 33. —*Italian*, Corazzini, pp. 93, 94.—Drawing lots by spires of grass is probably the "Erbelette" of Froissart; see Celnart, p. 105, "L'Herbette Joliette."—*Spanish*, Marin, i. 123.
43. *German* usages, Rochholz, pp. 174–183.
45. Compare French of Gagnon, p. 147.
46. *French*, Ch. du Camb., i. 119, etc.—*German*, Peter, p. 49, etc.—*Flemish*, Willems, p. 522.—*Breton*, Mélusine, p. 462.
47. *French*, Rabelais, Gargantua, ch. xxii. Laisnel de la Salle, ii. 156.
48. Halliwell, Pop. Rh., pp. 263–265. Chambers, p. 31.—*German*, Rochholz, pp. 156–170; he refers to the Rigsmál of the poetic Edda. Schuster, p. 364, etc.—*Provençal*, Ch. Pop. du Languedoc, p. 517, "Las Bestios."
50. Nurs. Rh., No. 278. Compare Finnish game, Neus, p. 417.
52. *German*, Vernaleken, p. 94. Meier, p. 135.—*French*, Chabreul, p. 183.—*Swedish*, Arwiddson, iii. 400.
53. Strutt, p. 294. Brand, ii. 287. — *German*, Vernaleken, p. 86, "Ritterschlagen." Rochholz, p. 435.—*French*, "Les Ambassadeurs," Celnart, p. 131. Old English game of "Questions and Commands," Gent.'s Mag., Feb. 1738; Rochholz, p. 413.
55. Perhaps the "Roi qui ne ment" of Froissart, which he mentions as a game of his childhood (see p. 34), and also as played by great personages.

56. *French*, Celnart, p. 125.
57. Similarly, in a French game, "Le Roi Dépouillé" (Celnart, p. 139), the player must say "Oserais-je?" at every movement.
58. See the round in Chappell, Pop. Mus., p. 77.
60. Perhaps connected with No. 154. Compare German, Vernaleken, p. 52, No. 8.
61. Very likely the "Derision" (Risées) of Froissart.
62. *German*, Rochholz, p. 183. Vernaleken, p. 47, etc.—*Provençal*, "Lou brandet de Roso," Ch. Pop. du Languedoc, p. 577.
64. *German*, Dunger, p. 176, played also in New York. The rhyme in the text seems a recent translation.
68. Nurs. Rh., No. 352. Chambers, p. 137.—*French*, Celnart, p. 19.—*Spanish*, Maspons y Labrós, p. 100, "Jan petit."
71. Nurs. Rh., No. 218.
74. Chambers, p. 139, "Curcuddie."—*French*, Celnart, p. 353, "Les Jarcotons."—Among games of motion might have been mentioned the familiar "Puss in the Corner," Gent.'s Mag., Feb. 1738.—*French*, Celnart, p. 57, "Les Quatre Coins," etc.
75. Halliwell, Pop. Rh., p. 128.—*Danish*, Grundtvig, Dansk. Folk., 2d ser. p. 142.—*Italian*, Bernoni, p. 19, No. 18.—*Spanish*, Marin, i. 52, No. 84.
76. Halliwell, Pop. Rh., p. 112.—*French*, Chabreul, p. 8, "Petit bonhomme vist encore, car il n'est pas mort."—*German*, Handelmann, p. 31, "Little man still lives."—The *High-German* formula is, "Stirbt der Fuchs, so gilt der Balg." Like the English phrase is a Danish game, "Do not let my master's bird die, Syv, "Adagia Danica," p. xlvii.—*Russian* (Kazan), Mozarowski, p. 88, "Kurilka lives, she is not dead."
77. (a) *German*, Vernaleken, p. 89.—*French*, Celnart, p. 307 —(b) Nurs. Rh., No. 282.—*German*, Vernaleken, p. 88, "Vater Eberhard."—(c) *German*, Rochholz, p. 430, No. 50.—*French*, Rabelais, Gargantua, ch. xxii. Celnart, p. 124, "Pince-sans-rire."
79. Compare finger-game in Chambers, p. 116. Italian finger-game referred to, Bernoni, p. 22, No. 25.
81. Strutt, p. 290, "Hammer and Block.
83. *French*.—Celnart, p. 162, "Le Chevalier Gentil."
86. Nurs. Rh., Nos. 297, 307.—*German*, Meier, p. 138; Handelmann, p. 40.—*French*, Mélusine, p. 198.
87. *Italian* (the game, not the rhyme), Ferraro, G. Monfer., No. 10.—*Spanish*, Marin, i. 48, No. 71. Compare Nurs. Rh., No. 293; Chambers, p. 159.
88. Celnart (2d ed., A.D. 1830) gives sixty kinds of "pénitences," consisting in kissing, as then usual in French society (see p. 6).—*French*, Celnart, p. 302, "Les Aunes d'Amour," the same as "Measuring yards of tape."—*German*, Frischbier, p. 201, "Aus dem Brunnen erretten," equivalent to "I'm in the well." Redeeming forfeits in Germany," Frischbier, p. 199.
89. With the dialogue at the end of the second version, compare No. 154, B. An Italian game, Corazzini, p. 104, has a similar theme.
90. Spectator, No. 268.—*German*, Rochholz, p. 440.
91. Strutt, p. 386. "Even or Odd." A universal game.—*Ancient Egyptian*, Wilkinson, ii. 416.—*Ancient Greek*, Aristotle, Rhet. iii. 5. The formula is ἄρτια ἤ περισσά.—*Latin*, "par impar."—*German*, "grad oder ungrad," or "effen oder uneffen."—*Spanish*, Marin, i. 51, "Pares ó Nones" ("par est, non est").

92. The similar *Italian* game begins, "Galota, galota," whence, no doubt, our "*Hul gul*," Gianandrea, No. 20.—*Ancient Greek*, Scholiast to Aristophanes, Plut. 1057, πόσα ἐν χερσὶν ἔχω; "How many have I in my hands?" Suidas (10th century), Lexicon, under παιδιά, writes: "There is a game of the following character among the Athenians: Having taken up a number of nuts and holding out his hand, one asks, 'How many have I?' And if [the other] guesses the number, he takes as many as he has in his hand; but if he fails to guess, he loses as many as the asker holds in his hand."—*Latin*, given by Helenius Acron (4th century), "quot in sunt?" See Marin, note to preceding game.—*German*, Meier, p. 123, "Wie viel sollen Kerner in meiner Hand sein?" Handelmann, p. 35, etc.

93. A child rests his head in the lap of another, while a third claps the back of the first, keeping time to the words of the rhyme, and finally raises a certain number of fingers; if the kneeling child can guess the number, he takes the other's place. —*Spanish*, Marin, i. 51, No. 81. The rhyme closely resembles the English given in the text.—*Italian*, Imbriani, No. 30, where the question is, "How many horns do I hold up?"—*German*, Meier, pp. 135, 136, where it is asked, "Wie viel Hörner hat der Bock?" This allusion to the goat (as a leaping animal) refers to the usual practice of riding on the back of the stooping child while putting the question. —*German*, Rochholz, p. 434.—*Dutch*, Hor. Belg., vi. 182. The formulas differ. Tylor, Primitive Culture, i. 67. The Latin formula of Petronius is curiously translated by F. Nodot, A.D. 1694: "Étant â cheval sur luy, il luy donna plusieurs coups du plat de la main sur les épaules, disant tout haut en riant, Quatre cornes dans un sac, combien font-ils? ce jeu fini," etc. Nodot remarks of his free translation, that it is still a boys' game in France.

94. Halliwell, Pop. Rh., p. 116, "Handy-Dandy."—*German* (Austria), Vernaleken, p. 41. The formula is the exact counterpart of the English: "Windle, wandle, in welchen Handle, oben oder unt?" Handelmann, p. 35 (Schleswig-Holstein), "Where dwells the smith? Above or below?"—*Spanish*, Marin, p. 50, No. 77.

95. *German*, Meier, p. 124, "Under which finger sits the hare?"

97. Halliwell, Pop. Rh., p. 125, "My Lady's lost her diamond ring."—*Low-German* formulas exactly correspond to our "Hold fast what I give you." Thus the North Frisian, "Biwari wel, wat ik di du," Handelmann, p. 38. Corresponding to "Button, button, who's got the button?" is the *Italian* "Anello, anello, chi ha mi anello?" Gianandrea, No. 14.—*Spanish*, Maspons y Labrós, p. 86.

98. Halliwell, Pop. Rh., p. 133.

99. *German*, Frischbier, p. 195.

100. A universal game.

101. Halliwell, Nurs. Rh., Nos. 328, 357; Pop. Rh., p. 118; Chambers, p. 123, "The King and Queen of Cantelon."—*German*, Rochholz, p. 414, No. 32.

102. Halliwell, Pop. Rh., p. 132, "The Old Dame," like our B. The Scotch of Chambers, p. 130, "Gled Wylie" (wily hawk) corresponds to our first version.—*German*, Mullenhoff, p. 488; Handelmann, p. 76, etc.—*Swedish*, Arwiddson, iii. 164.—*Italian*, Bernoni, p. 34, No. 40, here a game of a witch like our second version.—*Finnish*, Neus, p. 418, begins like the Scotch.—*Russian*, Bezsonoff, p. 195, probably borrowed from the German.

103. The name, "Tag," in Gent.'s Mag., Feb. 1738.—*German*, Handelmann, p. 66, "Eisen anfassen;" "Eisenzech" in Berlin; "Eisenziggi" in Switzerland.—*Italian*,

Bernoni, p. 62, "Toca fero."—"Squat-tag" is also *Spanish*, Maspons y Labrós, p. 81.

105. *Ancient Greek*, Pollux, ix. 117, Ἀποδιδρασκίνδα, "Game of Running Away."—*German*, Vernaleken, p. 89, "Verstecherlspiel," "Einschauen."—*Italian*, Bernoni, p. 61, "Chi se vede, eh!"—*French*, Celnart, p. 55, "Cligne-musette" or "Cache-cache."

106. *French*, Chabreul, p. 1, "La Queue Leuleu," mentioned by Froissart.—*German*, Rochholz, p. 408, etc.; Schuster, p. 392, a game of wolf and geese; so *Russian*, Bezsonoff, p. 205.

107. *Spanish*, Marin, i. 169. The seeker must wait until the hiders, who go off one by one as they are counted out, cry "Jilo blanco, jilo negro," etc. Hence, probably, the cry "Blanca-lilo, etc., of the English game. The rest proceeds like No.105. In the Spanish sport, a player reaching goal must spit three times; this seems to have been originally a conjuration against the Evil Spirit, whom the seeker represented.

108. *Ancient Greek*, Pollux, ix. 113, 123. The game is universal. See Handelmann, p. 71. Child, Eng. and Scot. Pop. Bal., 1882, i. 67.

109. *German*, Handelmann, p. 65, "Die Hexe." The games are identical; yet the children, from whom the version in the text was learned, imagined that they had "made it up!"

110. Strutt, p. 61.—*German*, Vernaleken, p. 63, "Das Barlaufen."—*French*, Celnart, p. 58, "Les Barres."—*Italian*, Bernoni, p. 87. The French word *barres* is probably only a false interpretation of an older word *bar*, a form of our base, meaning goal; so Swiss "Bahre," Basle. Kindr., p. 30.—*Flemish*, in Hor. Belg., vi. 181.

111. N. and Q., 2d ser. VIII. pp. 70, 132. Brand, ii. 316.—*German*, Handelmann, p. 81, "Die Katzen von dem Berge." The phrase is "Cat, cat, off my hill!"—*French*, Belèze, p. 42, "Le Roi Détroné."

113. Chambers, p. 122, "Hickety Bickety."—*German*, Aus dem Kinderleben, p. 24. Rochholz, p. 442.

114. Folk-lore Rec., iii. 169; Chambers, p. 36. See No. 89.

115. *German*, Vernaleken, p. 74, "Weinbeer-Schneiden."—*Italian*, Bernoni, p. 50. This is a variation of No. 156; compare Frischbier, p. 186.

116. Chambers, p. 127, "Scots and English."

117. This number includes the remains of two ancient games: (a) *Ancient Greek*, σχοινοφιλίνδα, Pollux, ix. 115, in which a player must be whipped round the ring with the cord he has dropped at the back of another.—*German*, in 14th century, Mone, Anzeiger, 1839, p. 395.—*Spanish*, Maspons y Labrós, p. 22.—*French*, Celnart, p. 55. (b) Strutt, p. 285, "Cat and Mouse, or Kiss in the Ring," where a player pursues another round and through the circle.—*French*, Celnart, p. 39, "Le Chat et la Souris."—*Italian*, Gianandrea, No. 6.—*German*, Handelmann, p. 78.

122. Variation of No. 121. The name connects it with the old English game of "Frog in the Middle," Strutt, p. 293; the ancient Greek, χυτρίνδα, "pot-game," see p. 31, note.

123. *German*, Vernaleken, p. 75. Handelmann, p. 80. Meier, p. 105. See No. 89.

124. *French*, Chabreul, p. 22, "La Toilette de Madame."

125. Nurs. Rh., No. 131.

127. *German*, Rochholz, p. 430, No. 50. See Nos. 77, 152, 153.

128. "Marble-day" in Sussex is Good Friday, N. and Q., 5th ser. XII. 18. "Times" of German sports, Basle. Kindr., p. 30. Meier, p. 92, 8.

129. Brand, ii. 302, "Camp." Strutt, p. 78.—*Ancient Greek*, Pollux, ix. 104.—*Icelandic* and *Low-German*, Weinhold, Altnord. Leben, p. 292. Egils Saga, ch. 40.

130. Games of ball played with the hand are, of course, universal.

131. Strutt, p. 381 (new ed.). Strutt, p. 76. Bradford's History of Plymouth (ed. by Ch. Deane, Boston, 1856), p. 112. Ducange, under Pelota. Wirt Sikes, British Goblins, p. 272.

132. *German* (Austria), Vernaleken, p. 2. (Schleswig-Holstein), Handelmann, p. 88, "Stehball." (Switzerland), Rochholz, p. 388.

136. Jamieson gives Scotch name as "Shinty."—*Italian*, Ferraro, G. Monfer., No. 38.

137. *German*, Vernaleken, p. 9.—*French*, Celnart, p. 69.—*Italian*, Ferraro, G. Monfer., No. 23, "Le Pietruzze."

138. *German*, Vernaleken, p. 10. Rochholz, p. 389.

139. *German*, Vernaleken, p. 11. Rochholz, p. 399.

140. *German*, Vernaleken, p. 15.—The American word "Cat" ("one old cat," "two old cat," etc.) is explained by the Flemish "Caetsen, Ketsen," the common name of the game of ball in the Netherlands, Hor. Belg., vi. 177.

141. *German*, names of "marbles." "Schnell-Kügelchen" (15th century), "Schusser," "Löper," also "Marmeln," the latter when made of marble. A MS. of the 15th century mentions "the yellow glass used for the little yellow balls with which schoolboys play, and which are very cheap," Rochholz, p. 421.—Playing marbles (*kluckern*) in the streets was forbidden on pain of torture, by the Reformers in Zurich, A. D. 1530.—The general name in North Friesland is "Rollkugle," "rollballs."—*French* name, "*billes;*" see Celnart and Belèze for description of games. The game of Roman boys with nuts, from which marbles is probably derived, is still played in the Netherlands, Hor. Belg., vi. 182. Nuts are also used instead of marbles in Italy, Gianandrea, No. 20.

142. Strutt, p. 86, "Tip-cat." Brand, ii. 303, "Kit-cat." The game, which is played in *Hindostan*, N. and Q., 4th ser. IV. 93, may probably have made its way into Europe from the East.—*German*, Handelmann, p. 89, "Kipseln." Vernaleken, p. 29, "Titschkerln."—*Italian*, Bernoni, p. 81; p. 82, "Chiba e Cheba."

143. Brand, ii. 305.

144. (a) *German*, Rochholz, p. 426. Vernaleken, p. 25.—*French*, Celnart, p. 379, "La Fossette aux Noyaux," played with cherry-stones or plum-stones. The fillip given to the stone is called *poquer*, poke. Froissart appears to allude to this game. (b) Also ancient.—*Italian*, Gianandrea, No. 20, "Battemuro."

145. *German*, Handelmann, p. 92, "Kaak."—*Italian*, Gianandrea, No. 17, "La Checca."

146. Strutt, p. 266. Brand, ii. 330, "Scotch-hoppers" mentioned A.D. 1677.—*German*, Vernaleken, p. 38, "Tempelhupfen."—*Italian*, Bernoni, p. 84, "El Campanon."—*French*, Celnart, p. 379, "La Marelle."—*Hindostan*, N. and Q., 4th ser. IV. 93.

147. *German*, Handelmann, p. 96, "Stickmest."

148. Though played in Great Britain, the game is not (so far as we know) mentioned by writers.—*French*, Celnart, p. 375 f., "Les Osselets."—*Spanish*, Marin, pp. 80–95, 150–159, "Juego de las Chinas," "Game of the Stones."—*German*, Meier, p. 145.—*Japanese*, Tedama, "Hand-balls."

149. Rhymes for counting out are used throughout Europe, and examples could be cited of types corresponding to most of the English forms, and sometimes evident-

ly related. Peculiar is the usage in Spain, where the syllables are told off alternately on the closed hands of a player, who holds a pebble; if the last syllable falls on the hand containing the stone, the lad proving his fortune is free, and so on until only one child remains. The custom has given a proverb to the language. Marin, i. 117. A like usage (without the rhymes) we have found to be the usual way of selection in a town of Pennsylvania (Bethlehem).

150. First printed in Ritson's "Gammer Gurton's Garland." Other original versions: (1) Gent.'s Mag., Sept. 1823; (2), (3) The Critic, Jan 15, 1857, and (4) Feb. 2, 1857. The last mentioned is nearly identical with our B. The communicator of (1) refers it, through an aged informant, to a lady born in the reign of Charles II.; it has several more verses than the last, generally agreeing with our E, but lacks the ending. The rhyme, in England, appears at present to be known as a song only. The European rhyme is properly a dialogue, the verses being sung alternately by the warders and the approaching party; the former, whose joined and lowered arms represent the fallen bridge, do not elevate them until the negotiations are concluded. The game is, no doubt, that mentioned under the name of "Coda Romana," by G. Villani, Istorie Fiorent., A.D. 1328, ch. xcvi., as played by the boys of Florence, in which the question put to the imprisoned player is said to have been, "Guelf or Ghibelline?"—*German*, Meier, p. 101 (cited), etc. Mannhardt in Zeitschr. f. d. Myth., iv. 301–320, gives twenty-seven versions, including *Slavic, Hungarian, Scandinavian.* — *Swedish*, Arwiddson, iii. 250. — *French*, Chabreul, p. 117, "Le Ciel et l'Enfer." Celnart, p. 52, "Le Pontlevis." — *Italian*, Bernoni, p. 46, "Le Porte." Corazzini, pp. 90–93; p. 87 (a mixed form with No. 154).—*Spanish*, A. de Ledesma, A.D. 1605, beginning "Fallen is the bridge." See Marin, i. 166–168.—For the English rhyme, see also N. and Q., 1st Ser. II. p. 338.

The name "Lady Lee" in the song may imply a legend. We read in Nature, June 15, 1871, p. 118: "It is not, for example, many years since the present Lord Leigh was accused of having built an obnoxious person—one account, if we remember right, said eight obnoxious persons—into the foundation of a bridge at Stoneleigh." The communicator of version (2) (The Critic, Jan. 15, 1857) spelt the name *Leigh*, and took "the Lady Leigh of the song to be the wife of Sir Thomas Leigh, who was Lord Mayor of London in 1558, . . . ancestor of the noble family of Leigh of Stoneleigh, Warwickshire." Compare the ballad of "The Bridge of Arta," Passow, Pop. Carmina Græciæ Recent., No. 511; Tommaseo, Cant. Pop. Toscani, iii. 174 f.; F. Liebrecht, Zur Volkskunde, 1879, p. 284.

151. A variation of No. 150.—*Italian*, Corazzini, pp. 91–93, beginning, "Open, open the gates." Gianandrea, No. 3, "Le Porte del Paradiso." The dialogue ends, "Let the King of France with all his soldiers pass."

152. *Italian*, Bernoni, p. 54.—*French*, Ch. du Camb. i. 133.—*German*, Vernaleken, p. 55.

153. *German*, Meier, p. 117, "Farben aufgeben," etc. —*Italian*, Bernoni, p. 51, "I colori." This version is identical with the German and our A, as is also the *Spanish* (or Catalan), Maspons y Labrós, p. 91. The game of "Los Colores" is mentioned by A. de Ledesma, A.D. 1605.—*French*, Belèze, p. 40 (cited).

Intermediate between this number and the following are games of *selling birds*, Frischbier, p. 184; of *catching birds*, Rochholz, p. 449.

Greek game of the shell, *'Οστρακίνδα*, Pollux, ix. 111.

154. The following is our classification of the numerous games (not before noticed as connected) belonging to this cycle of childish tradition:

(1.) Versions preserving the original idea of the child-stealing witch (as in our A, B, and C).—Halliwell, Pop. Rh., p. 131 (cited).—*German,* Meier, p. 117 (cited). —*Italian,* Corazzini, p. 110, a fragment.

(2.) Versions in which (as in our D) the mother is represented as present, and the game becomes one of *begging* instead of *stealing* children. This is the case in most *German* versions. The tests described in No. 152 are introduced and become the leading feature of the game.—*German,* Frischbier, p. 183. Rochholz, p. 436, and p. 444, where the mother is called "Maria, mother of God," and the game "Getting Angels." Mullenhoff, p. 486, No. 7.—*Swedish,* Arwiddson, iii. p. 437 (cited). Mannhardt, Germanische Mythologie, pp. 273–321, gives fourteen versions, with a long discussion of this game, and concludes (p. 297) that the last girl of the row (who in our A is the eldest daughter, but here represents the "Mother Rose") "personates the goddess Freya cherishing in or behind the clouds the souls of the dead, who, renewed through the heavenly waters (the fountain of youth), are destined to return to earth at new birth as the souls of children!"

It is very curious to observe that several Prussian versions contain traits only explained by the American games, the form of which they thus imply as more original. Thus the mother is *invited to a meal* by the witch, Frischbier, p. 182, and the person invited sends *excuses* (see our A).

(3.) The mother and children are represented in childish fashion as a hen and her brood (see our B, and No. 101). Hence the game of the "Rich and Poor Birds;" see references in No. 8, note.—*Italian,* Corazzini, pp. 86–88. Gianandrea, No. 19, "Madonna Pollinara."

(4.) The children are denoted by the names of leaves or flowers.—*German,* Vernaleken, p. 58, "Die Grossmutter." The visitor begs for a leaf as balsam to heal her injury, and the girls are gathered under the name of leaves. So Frischbier, p. 181. Feifalik, No. 81.—*Spanish,* Maspons y Labrós, pp. 87–89, game of "Pulling Leeks."

(5.) The game has become a representation of selling pottery.—*German,* Frischbier, p. 183. Mannhardt, p. 284.—*Swedish,* Arwiddson, iii. 169, "Selling Pots," a dance, has become a mere mercenary transaction.—The English game of "Honeypots" is a version of this, where the weighing feature is to be explained as in No. 152.—*Italian,* Bernoni, p. 57, "I Piteri," where the original idea reappears. The purchaser advances *limping* (a characteristic of witches), and the game is one of stealing and recovery (like our London version E).—*Italian,* Gianandrea, No. 19. The first part of the game is played as in (3). The "pots" are weighed, as in the English game mentioned. Ferraro, G. Monfer., No. 43, where the purchaser is the devil, and the game thus passes over into the form of No. 153.—*Spanish,* Maspons y Labrós, p. 87, "Las Gerras."

(6.) A game of stealing or measuring cloth.—*German,* Rochholz, p. 437, "Tuch anmessen." In this game, mentioned by the mother of Goethe (Düntzer, Frauenbilder aus Goethe's Jugendzeit, p. 506), the children are arranged against the wall to represent cloth, which the dealer measures and names by the color of the stockings of the children. A thief steals the cloth bit by bit, which the dealer must recover by guessing the color, a task of some difficulty, the stockings having been taken off in the interval. A very curious Low-German version, Brem. Wiegenlieder, p. 61, removes any doubt as to the relation of the amusement to the original game. In this version the colored cloths are only names for children. There are verbal coincidences with forms given in the text, the dialogue beginning "Mother, the broth is boiling over!" (as in our version B), put (as in our version C) into the mouth of the watcher left in charge by the absent mother; so Aus dem Kinderleben, p. 39, "Leinendieb." The remainder of the first paragraph of C will be found almost word for word in Handelmann, p. 57, No. 80, "Frau Rosen," a version of the form (2). — *Italian*, Bernoni, p. 55, "I Brazzi de Tela," "the measures of cloth." The thief advances *limping*, the owner having departed, steals the cloth, but is pursued, and the goods recovered, as in the game of pots described above. Ferraro, G. Monfer., No. 3. — *French*, Celnart, p. 43, "La Toile," has become a kissing romp of grown people.

(7.) Finally, to the same root belong various rounds and dances which represent a mother who wishes to marry her many daughters, or of a poor widow who has but one daughter; see our No. 8, and note.

155. *German*, Grimm, No. 15, "Hansel und Grethel."

156. Gent.'s Mag., Feb. 1738, "Fryar's Ground."—*Spanish*, Maspons y Labrós, p. 92.—*French*, Celnart, p. 53, "Château du Corbeau;" "Je suis dans ton château, corbeau, et j'y serai toujours."—*German*, Meier, p. 98, "Ist der Kukuk zu Haus?" see No. 115, note. German games based on this idea are numerous. Vernaleken, p. 77, "The Black Man;" p. 62, "Dead man, arise;" p. 73, "Wassermannspiel." The child representing the Water-spirit lies in the dry bed of a brook and pretends to sleep. The rest approach to tease him, when he endeavors to seize one without leaving the brook or pit. The first so caught must assist him to capture the rest. The superstition about a treasure buried at the foot of the rainbow is also Swiss, see Lütolf, Sagen, etc., Von Lutzern, p. 384.

157. A variation of 156.—*German*, Meier, p. 121. Rochholz, p. 415.

158. *German*, Meier, p. 102, "Der Böse Geist."

159. *French*, Celnart, p. 365, etc.—*German*, Vernaleken, p. 52, etc. See Mannhardt, Germ. Myth., pp. 492–511, who gives twenty-three versions, including a Spanish (Catalan) one. He imagines, as usual, a good deal of mythology in the game. The mythologic character belongs, not to the details of the children's rounds, but to the cycle of traditions on which these are founded. The name in Suabia is "Prinzessin erlösen," "to disenchant the princess."

160. *Provençal*, Arbaud, ii. 207.—*French*, Puymaigre, p. 334. Bugeaud, i. 126. Tarbé, ii. 178.

161. Communicated by Miss Anne Weston Whitney, Baltimore, Md., Secretary of the Baltimore Folk-Lore Society. Gomme, "Green Grass."

162. Krehbiel, from record of Mrs. Louisa Clarke Pyrnelle. Rhyme cited, "Here we come up the green grass," Gomme, i. 159, 160.

163. As described by the recorder, the action of the game continues in the following manner: At the third verse the actor in the ring chooses his partner, and the two stand facing each other; at the fourth he puts his hands together, then throws them apart, measuring whatever distance he wishes to have looked upon as indicating the extent of his affection; at the fifth he places his hand on his breast in the cardiac region, and then extends it

towards the chosen one, repeating the gesture in time to the music till the verse is ended; at the refrain he leads the lassie to the centre of the ring; at the beginning of the sixth verse he kneels before her, still holding her hand, but at the end he leaves her and takes his place in the ring; during the seventh verse the lassie remains alone in the ring. The song is then resumed from the beginning, and the lassie chooses her lover from among the lads. Krehbiel, from Mrs. Pyrnelle. Babcock, p. 255. Gomme, "Round and round the village." "Sugar-lump," Babcock, p. 256. "Turn, cinnamon, turn," Krehbiel, from Mrs. Pyrnelle.

164. (A) Krehbiel, from record of Mrs. James W. Morrisson, Chicago, Ill., and from information of Mrs. Laura C. Gaston, Richmond, Ind. (B) Backus, Jour. Amer. Folk-Lore, xiii. 104.
165. Babcock, p. 259. Gomme, "Three Sailors," Compare Gomme, "Three Dukes," "Knights of Spain," and numerous variant or connected rhymes.
166. A. F. Chamberlain, Worcester, Mass. Jour. Amer. Folk-Lore, viii. 253. Gomme, "Nuts in May."
167. Krehbiel. Compare Gomme, "Garden Gate," "Bull in the Park."
168. Backus, p. 296.
169. Babcock, p. 249. Compare rhymes, p. 246 and p. 249.
170. Backus, p. 297. For the formula "Now you're married," etc., compare Gomme, "Oats and Beans and Barley," "Three Bachelors," etc.
171. Communicated by Mr. Krehbiel. Gomme, "Thread the Needle" and "Through the Needle Eye, Boys."
172. Chamberlain, *loc. cit.* Babcock, p. 244. Gomme, "Green Gravel."
173. Babcock, p. 244.
174. (A) Miss Whitney. (B) Communicated by Mr. Krehbiel. Gomme, "Jenny Jones." Related is No. 37, Babcock, p. 245; Gomme, "Old Roger is Dead."
175. J. Mooney. Jour. Amer. Folk-Lore, ii. 104.
176. N. C. Hoke. Jour. Amer. Folk-Lore, v. 118.
177. (A) Backus, p. 299. (B) Communicated by Washington Matthews, Major and Surgeon, U. S. A., Washington, D. C. (C) Communicated by Mrs. Washington Matthews. Gomme, "King William."
178. (A) Mrs. C. H. Toy, Cambridge, Mass., as heard in Plymouth, Mass., where the game is said to have been introduced by a child from Washington, D. C. (B) Babcock, p. 261. Gomme, "We are the Rovers." Compare Gomme, "Barbarie."
179. From recitation of a girl twelve years of age, a connection of my own.
180. Culin, No. 14.
181. Mrs. F. D. Bergen, Boston Transcript, April 6, 1895; copied in Jour. Amer. Folk-Lore, viii. 151.
182. Bergen, *loc. cit.* Gomme, "Pinny-show."
183. Mary O. Clarke, Jour. Amer. Folk-Lore, iii. 290. Babcock, p. 267.
184. Miss Whitney. Gomme, "London Bridge."
185. Babcock, p. 260. Gomme, "Lady of the Land."
186. (A) Backus, p. 298. Mrs. A. M. L. Clarke, Lancaster, Mass., Jour. Amer. Folk-Lore, x. 325. Gomme, "Soldier," "Widow," "Poor Widow," "Silly Old Man (or Maid)."

187. Babcock, p. 277. Gomme, "Puss in the Corner."
188. Babcock, p. 281. Gomme, "Angel and Devil," "Fool, Fool, Come to School," "Namers and Guessers."
189. Julia D. Whiting, Jour. Amer. Folk-Lore, ii. 235.
190. (G) From the reciter of No. 177. (H) Mary H. Skeel, Newburgh, N. Y., Jour. Amer. Folk-Lore, iii. 315. (I) Jour. Amer. Folk-Lore, iii. 141. Gomme, "Gipsy," "Keeling the Pot," "Mother, mother, the pot boils over," "The Witch." Compare, also, Gomme, "Shepherd and Sheep," "Steal the Pigs," "Who goes round my stone wall?" "Wolf." Related games: No. 102, Gomme, "Chicamy," "Fox and Goose," "Hen and Chicken," "Gled-wylie," "Old Dame," "Chicken Come Clock," "Old Cranny-crow." No. 114, Gomme, "Milking-pails." (Connection with the witch-game indicated by the quality of the mother as a laundress.) No. 89, Gomme, "Basket." Gomme, No. 123, "Mother, mother, may I go out to play?" (Connection indicated only by the cumulative form.) W. W. Newell, "Game of the Child-stealing Witch," Jour. Amer. Folk-Lore, iii. 139–148. In this article are given two variants from London, not reprinted by Mrs. Gomme; these were obtained, respectively, from recitation of Miss Glover, Chantrey Road, Brixton, and Rev. Mr. Spears, Gascoyne Road, Victoria Park. The first answers to (B), the second to (D). No comparative study has been made further than that contained in the note to No. 154; I believe that a full inquiry will justify the classification of European games given in this note.

THE END

INDEX.

NOTE: The names Newell uses for American and British songs and games are listed, as well as the first lines of American and British songs, rhymes, and game formulas. No attempt has been made to index comparative material translated from other languages, nor to collate Newell's titles and first lines with other collections, nor to index exhaustively all the fascinating topics he discusses. The earlier editions (1883 and 1903) had no index.

Game titles are in CAPITALS. First lines are in *italics*; the first lines of counting out formulas are gathered together under the entry Counting Out Rhymes. When an asterisk (*) follows a game title, the accompanying first line is identical with the title and is not repeated.

A CATALOG OF SELECTED

DOVER BOOKS

IN ALL FIELDS OF INTEREST

A CATALOG OF SELECTED DOVER BOOKS IN ALL FIELDS OF INTEREST

CONCERNING THE SPIRITUAL IN ART, Wassily Kandinsky. Pioneering work by father of abstract art. Thoughts on color theory, nature of art. Analysis of earlier masters. 12 illustrations. 80pp. of text. 5⅜ × 8½. 23411-8 Pa. $3.95

ANIMALS: 1,419 Copyright-Free Illustrations of Mammals, Birds, Fish, Insects, etc., Jim Harter (ed.). Clear wood engravings present, in extremely lifelike poses, over 1,000 species of animals. One of the most extensive pictorial sourcebooks of its kind. Captions. Index. 284pp. 9 × 12. 23766-4 Pa. $11.95

CELTIC ART: The Methods of Construction, George Bain. Simple geometric techniques for making Celtic interlacements, spirals, Kells-type initials, animals, humans, etc. Over 500 illustrations. 160pp. 9 × 12. (USO) 22923-8 Pa. $8.95

AN ATLAS OF ANATOMY FOR ARTISTS, Fritz Schider. Most thorough reference work on art anatomy in the world. Hundreds of illustrations, including selections from works by Vesalius, Leonardo, Goya, Ingres, Michelangelo, others. 593 illustrations. 192pp. 7⅛ × 10¼. 20241-0 Pa. $8.95

CELTIC HAND STROKE-BY-STROKE (Irish Half-Uncial from "The Book of Kells"): An Arthur Baker Calligraphy Manual, Arthur Baker. Complete guide to creating each letter of the alphabet in distinctive Celtic manner. Covers hand position, strokes, pens, inks, paper, more. Illustrated. 48pp. 8¼ × 11. 24336-2 Pa. $3.95

EASY ORIGAMI, John Montroll. Charming collection of 32 projects (hat, cup, pelican, piano, swan, many more) specially designed for the novice origami hobbyist. Clearly illustrated easy-to-follow instructions insure that even beginning papercrafters will achieve successful results. 48pp. 8¼ × 11. 27298-2 Pa. $2.95

THE COMPLETE BOOK OF BIRDHOUSE CONSTRUCTION FOR WOODWORKERS, Scott D. Campbell. Detailed instructions, illustrations, tables. Also data on bird habitat and instinct patterns. Bibliography. 3 tables. 63 illustrations in 15 figures. 48pp. 5¼ × 8½. 24407-5 Pa. $1.95

BLOOMINGDALE'S ILLUSTRATED 1886 CATALOG: Fashions, Dry Goods and Housewares, Bloomingdale Brothers. Famed merchants' extremely rare catalog depicting about 1,700 products: clothing, housewares, firearms, dry goods, jewelry, more. Invaluable for dating, identifying vintage items. Also, copyright-free graphics for artists, designers. Co-published with Henry Ford Museum & Greenfield Village. 160pp. 8¼ × 11. 25780-0 Pa. $9.95

HISTORIC COSTUME IN PICTURES, Braun & Schneider. Over 1,450 costumed figures in clearly detailed engravings—from dawn of civilization to end of 19th century. Captions. Many folk costumes. 256pp. 8⅜ × 11¾. 23150-X Pa. $10.95

STICKLEY CRAFTSMAN FURNITURE CATALOGS, Gustav Stickley and L. & J. G. Stickley. Beautiful, functional furniture in two authentic catalogs from 1910. 594 illustrations, including 277 photos, show settles, rockers, armchairs, reclining chairs, bookcases, desks, tables. 183pp. 6½ × 9¼. 23838-5 Pa. $8.95

AMERICAN LOCOMOTIVES IN HISTORIC PHOTOGRAPHS: 1858 to 1949, Ron Ziel (ed.). A rare collection of 126 meticulously detailed official photographs, called "builder portraits," of American locomotives that majestically chronicle the rise of steam locomotive power in America. Introduction. Detailed captions. xi + 129pp. 9 × 12. 27393-8 Pa. $12.95

AMERICA'S LIGHTHOUSES: An Illustrated History, Francis Ross Holland, Jr. Delightfully written, profusely illustrated fact-filled survey of over 200 American lighthouses since 1716. History, anecdotes, technological advances, more. 240pp. 8 × 10¾. 25576-X Pa. $11.95

TOWARDS A NEW ARCHITECTURE, Le Corbusier. Pioneering manifesto by founder of "International School." Technical and aesthetic theories, views of industry, economics, relation of form to function, "mass-production split" and much more. Profusely illustrated. 320pp. 6⅛ × 9¼. (USO) 25023-7 Pa. $8.95

HOW THE OTHER HALF LIVES, Jacob Riis. Famous journalistic record, exposing poverty and degradation of New York slums around 1900, by major social reformer. 100 striking and influential photographs. 233pp. 10 × 7⅞. 22012-5 Pa $10.95

FRUIT KEY AND TWIG KEY TO TREES AND SHRUBS, William M. Harlow. One of the handiest and most widely used identification aids. Fruit key covers 120 deciduous and evergreen species; twig key 160 deciduous species. Easily used. Over 300 photographs. 126pp. 5⅜ × 8½. 20511-8 Pa. $3.95

COMMON BIRD SONGS, Dr. Donald J. Borror. Songs of 60 most common U.S. birds: robins, sparrows, cardinals, bluejays, finches, more—arranged in order of increasing complexity. Up to 9 variations of songs of each species. Cassette and manual 99911-4 $8.95

ORCHIDS AS HOUSE PLANTS, Rebecca Tyson Northen. Grow cattleyas and many other kinds of orchids—in a window, in a case, or under artificial light. 63 illustrations. 148pp. 5⅜ × 8½. 23261-1 Pa. $3.95

MONSTER MAZES, Dave Phillips. Masterful mazes at four levels of difficulty. Avoid deadly perils and evil creatures to find magical treasures. Solutions for all 32 exciting illustrated puzzles. 48pp. 8¼ × 11. 26005-4 Pa. $2.95

MOZART'S DON GIOVANNI (DOVER OPERA LIBRETTO SERIES), Wolfgang Amadeus Mozart. Introduced and translated by Ellen H. Bleiler. Standard Italian libretto, with complete English translation. Convenient and thoroughly portable—an ideal companion for reading along with a recording or the performance itself. Introduction. List of characters. Plot summary. 121pp. 5¼ × 8½. 24944-1 Pa. $2.95

TECHNICAL MANUAL AND DICTIONARY OF CLASSICAL BALLET, Gail Grant. Defines, explains, comments on steps, movements, poses and concepts. 15-page pictorial section. Basic book for student, viewer. 127pp. 5⅜ × 8½. 21843-0 Pa. $3.95

BRASS INSTRUMENTS: Their History and Development, Anthony Baines. Authoritative, updated survey of the evolution of trumpets, trombones, bugles, cornets, French horns, tubas and other brass wind instruments. Over 140 illustrations and 48 music examples. Corrected and updated by author. New preface. Bibliography. 320pp. 5⅜ × 8½. 27574-4 Pa. $9.95

HOLLYWOOD GLAMOR PORTRAITS, John Kobal (ed.). 145 photos from 1926–49. Harlow, Gable, Bogart, Bacall; 94 stars in all. Full background on photographers, technical aspects. 160pp. 8⅜ × 11¼. 23352-9 Pa. $9.95

MAX AND MORITZ, Wilhelm Busch. Great humor classic in both German and English. Also 10 other works: "Cat and Mouse," "Plisch and Plumm," etc. 216pp. 5⅜ × 8½. 20181-3 Pa. $5.95

THE RAVEN AND OTHER FAVORITE POEMS, Edgar Allan Poe. Over 40 of the author's most memorable poems: "The Bells," "Ulalume," "Israfel," "To Helen," "The Conqueror Worm," "Eldorado," "Annabel Lee," many more. Alphabetic lists of titles and first lines. 64pp. 5³⁄₁₆ × 8¼. 26685-0 Pa. $1.00

SEVEN SCIENCE FICTION NOVELS, H. G. Wells. The standard collection of the great novels. Complete, unabridged. First Men in the Moon, Island of Dr. Moreau, War of the Worlds, Food of the Gods, Invisible Man, Time Machine, In the Days of the Comet. Total of 1,015pp. 5⅜ × 8½. (USO) 20264-X Clothbd. $29.95

AMULETS AND SUPERSTITIONS, E. A. Wallis Budge. Comprehensive discourse on origin, powers of amulets in many ancient cultures: Arab, Persian, Babylonian, Assyrian, Egyptian, Gnostic, Hebrew, Phoenician, Syriac, etc. Covers cross, swastika, crucifix, seals, rings, stones, etc. 584pp. 5⅜ × 8½. 23573-4 Pa. $12.95

RUSSIAN STORIES/PYCCKNE PACCKA3bl: A Dual-Language Book, edited by Gleb Struve. Twelve tales by such masters as Chekhov, Tolstoy, Dostoevsky, Pushkin, others. Excellent word-for-word English translations on facing pages, plus teaching and study aids, Russian/English vocabulary, biographical/critical introductions, more. 416pp. 5⅜ × 8½. 26244-8 Pa. $8.95

PHILADELPHIA THEN AND NOW: 60 Sites Photographed in the Past and Present, Kenneth Finkel and Susan Oyama. Rare photographs of City Hall, Logan Square, Independence Hall, Betsy Ross House, other landmarks juxtaposed with contemporary views. Captures changing face of historic city. Introduction. Captions. 128pp. 8¼ × 11. 25790-8 Pa. $9.95

AIA ARCHITECTURAL GUIDE TO NASSAU AND SUFFOLK COUNTIES, LONG ISLAND, The American Institute of Architects, Long Island Chapter, and the Society for the Preservation of Long Island Antiquities. Comprehensive, well-researched and generously illustrated volume brings to life over three centuries of Long Island's great architectural heritage. More than 240 photographs with authoritative, extensively detailed captions. 176pp. 8¼ × 11. 26946-9 Pa. $14.95

NORTH AMERICAN INDIAN LIFE: Customs and Traditions of 23 Tribes, Elsie Clews Parsons (ed.). 27 fictionalized essays by noted anthropologists examine religion, customs, government, additional facets of life among the Winnebago, Crow, Zuni, Eskimo, other tribes. 480pp. 6⅛ × 9¼. 27377-6 Pa. $10.95

THE BEST TALES OF HOFFMANN, E. T. A. Hoffmann. 10 of Hoffmann's most important stories: "Nutcracker and the King of Mice," "The Golden Flowerpot," etc. 458pp. 5⅜ × 8½. 21793-0 Pa. $8.95

FROM FETISH TO GOD IN ANCIENT EGYPT, E. A. Wallis Budge. Rich detailed survey of Egyptian conception of "God" and gods, magic, cult of animals, Osiris, more. Also, superb English translations of hymns and legends. 240 illustrations. 545pp. 5⅜ × 8½. 25803-3 Pa. $11.95

FRENCH STORIES/CONTES FRANÇAIS: A Dual-Language Book, Wallace Fowlie. Ten stories by French masters, Voltaire to Camus: "Micromegas" by Voltaire; "The Atheist's Mass" by Balzac; "Minuet" by de Maupassant; "The Guest" by Camus, six more. Excellent English translations on facing pages. Also French-English vocabulary list, exercises, more. 352pp. 5⅜ × 8½. 26443-2 Pa. $8.95

CHICAGO AT THE TURN OF THE CENTURY IN PHOTOGRAPHS: 122 Historic Views from the Collections of the Chicago Historical Society, Larry A. Viskochil. Rare large-format prints offer detailed views of City Hall, State Street, the Loop, Hull House, Union Station, many other landmarks, circa 1904-1913. Introduction. Captions. Maps. 144pp. 9⅜ × 12¼. 24656-6 Pa. $12.95

OLD BROOKLYN IN EARLY PHOTOGRAPHS, 1865-1929, William Lee Younger. Luna Park, Gravesend race track, construction of Grand Army Plaza, moving of Hotel Brighton, etc. 157 previously unpublished photographs. 165pp. 8⅞ × 11¾. 23587-4 Pa. $12.95

THE MYTHS OF THE NORTH AMERICAN INDIANS, Lewis Spence. Rich anthology of the myths and legends of the Algonquins, Iroquois, Pawnees and Sioux, prefaced by an extensive historical and ethnological commentary. 36 illustrations. 480pp. 5⅜ × 8½. 25967-6 Pa. $8.95

AN ENCYCLOPEDIA OF BATTLES: Accounts of Over 1,560 Battles from 1479 B.C. to the Present, David Eggenberger. Essential details of every major battle in recorded history from the first battle of Megiddo in 1479 B.C. to Grenada in 1984. List of Battle Maps. New Appendix covering the years 1967-1984. Index. 99 illustrations. 544pp. 6½ × 9¼. 24913-1 Pa. $14.95

SAILING ALONE AROUND THE WORLD, Captain Joshua Slocum. First man to sail around the world, alone, in small boat. One of great feats of seamanship told in delightful manner. 67 illustrations. 294pp. 5⅜ × 8½. 20326-3 Pa. $5.95

ANARCHISM AND OTHER ESSAYS, Emma Goldman. Powerful, penetrating, prophetic essays on direct action, role of minorities, prison reform, puritan hypocrisy, violence, etc. 271pp. 5⅜ × 8½. 22484-8 Pa. $5.95

MYTHS OF THE HINDUS AND BUDDHISTS, Ananda K. Coomaraswamy and Sister Nivedita. Great stories of the epics; deeds of Krishna, Shiva, taken from puranas, Vedas, folk tales; etc. 32 illustrations. 400pp. 5⅜ × 8½. 21759-0 Pa. $9.95

BEYOND PSYCHOLOGY, Otto Rank. Fear of death, desire of immortality, nature of sexuality, social organization, creativity, according to Rankian system. 291pp. 5⅜ × 8½. 20485-5 Pa. $7.95

A THEOLOGICO-POLITICAL TREATISE, Benedict Spinoza. Also contains unfinished Political Treatise. Great classic on religious liberty, theory of government on common consent. R. Elwes translation. Total of 421pp. 5⅜ × 8½. 20249-6 Pa. $7.95

MY BONDAGE AND MY FREEDOM, Frederick Douglass. Born a slave, Douglass became outspoken force in antislavery movement. The best of Douglass' autobiographies. Graphic description of slave life. 464pp. 5⅜ × 8½. 22457-0 Pa. $8.95

FOLLOWING THE EQUATOR: A Journey Around the World, Mark Twain. Fascinating humorous account of 1897 voyage to Hawaii, Australia, India, New Zealand, etc. Ironic, bemused reports on peoples, customs, climate, flora and fauna, politics, much more. 197 illustrations. 720pp. 5⅜ × 8½. 26113-1 Pa. $15.95

THE PEOPLE CALLED SHAKERS, Edward D. Andrews. Definitive study of Shakers: origins, beliefs, practices, dances, social organization, furniture and crafts, etc. 33 illustrations. 351pp. 5⅜ × 8½. 21081-2 Pa. $7.95

THE MYTHS OF GREECE AND ROME, H. A. Guerber. A classic of mythology, generously illustrated, long prized for its simple, graphic, accurate retelling of the principal myths of Greece and Rome, and for its commentary on their origins and significance. With 64 illustrations by Michelangelo, Raphael, Titian, Rubens, Canova, Bernini and others. 480pp. 5⅜ × 8½. 27584-1 Pa. $9.95

PSYCHOLOGY OF MUSIC, Carl E. Seashore. Classic work discusses music as a medium from psychological viewpoint. Clear treatment of physical acoustics, auditory apparatus, sound perception, development of musical skills, nature of musical feeling, host of other topics. 88 figures. 408pp. 5⅜ × 8½. 21851-1 Pa. $9.95

THE PHILOSOPHY OF HISTORY, Georg W. Hegel. Great classic of Western thought develops concept that history is not chance but rational process, the evolution of freedom. 457pp. 5⅜ × 8½. 20112-0 Pa. $8.95

THE BOOK OF TEA, Kakuzo Okakura. Minor classic of the Orient: entertaining, charming explanation, interpretation of traditional Japanese culture in terms of tea ceremony. 94pp. 5⅜ × 8½. 20070-1 Pa. $2.95

LIFE IN ANCIENT EGYPT, Adolf Erman. Fullest, most thorough, detailed older account with much not in more recent books, domestic life, religion, magic, medicine, commerce, much more. Many illustrations reproduce tomb paintings, carvings, hieroglyphs, etc. 597pp. 5⅜ × 8½. 22632-8 Pa. $9.95

SUNDIALS, Their Theory and Construction, Albert Waugh. Far and away the best, most thorough coverage of ideas, mathematics concerned, types, construction, adjusting anywhere. Simple, nontechnical treatment allows even children to build several of these dials. Over 100 illustrations. 230pp. 5⅜ × 8½. 22947-5 Pa. $5.95

DYNAMICS OF FLUIDS IN POROUS MEDIA, Jacob Bear. For advanced students of ground water hydrology, soil mechanics and physics, drainage and irrigation engineering, and more. 335 illustrations. Exercises, with answers. 784pp. 6⅛ × 9¼. 65675-6 Pa. $19.95

SONGS OF EXPERIENCE: Facsimile Reproduction with 26 Plates in Full Color, William Blake. 26 full-color plates from a rare 1826 edition. Includes "The Tyger," "London," "Holy Thursday," and other poems. Printed text of poems. 48pp. 5¼ × 7. 24636-1 Pa. $3.95

OLD-TIME VIGNETTES IN FULL COLOR, Carol Belanger Grafton (ed.). Over 390 charming, often sentimental illustrations, selected from archives of Victorian graphics—pretty women posing, children playing, food, flowers, kittens and puppies, smiling cherubs, birds and butterflies, much more. All copyright-free. 48pp. 9¼ × 12¼. 27269-9 Pa. $5.95

PERSPECTIVE FOR ARTISTS, Rex Vicat Cole. Depth, perspective of sky and sea, shadows, much more, not usually covered. 391 diagrams, 81 reproductions of drawings and paintings. 279pp. 5⅜ × 8½. 22487-2 Pa. $6.95

DRAWING THE LIVING FIGURE, Joseph Sheppard. Innovative approach to artistic anatomy focuses on specifics of surface anatomy, rather than muscles and bones. Over 170 drawings of live models in front, back and side views, and in widely varying poses. Accompanying diagrams. 177 illustrations. Introduction. Index. 144pp. 8⅜ × 11¼. 26723-7 Pa. $7.95

GOTHIC AND OLD ENGLISH ALPHABETS: 100 Complete Fonts, Dan X. Solo. Add power, elegance to posters, signs, other graphics with 100 stunning copyright-free alphabets: Blackstone, Dolbey, Germania, 97 more—including many lower-case, numerals, punctuation marks. 104pp. 8⅛ × 11. 24695-7 Pa. $7.95

HOW TO DO BEADWORK, Mary White. Fundamental book on craft from simple projects to five-bead chains and woven works. 106 illustrations. 142pp. 5⅜ × 8. 20697-1 Pa. $4.95

THE BOOK OF WOOD CARVING, Charles Marshall Sayers. Finest book for beginners discusses fundamentals and offers 34 designs. "Absolutely first rate . . . well thought out and well executed."—E. J. Tangerman. 118pp. 7¾ × 10⅝. 23654-4 Pa. $5.95

ILLUSTRATED CATALOG OF CIVIL WAR MILITARY GOODS: Union Army Weapons, Insignia, Uniform Accessories, and Other Equipment, Schuyler, Hartley, and Graham. Rare, profusely illustrated 1846 catalog includes Union Army uniform and dress regulations, arms and ammunition, coats, insignia, flags, swords, rifles, etc. 226 illustrations. 160pp. 9 × 12. 24939-5 Pa. $10.95

WOMEN'S FASHIONS OF THE EARLY 1900s: An Unabridged Republication of "New York Fashions, 1909," National Cloak & Suit Co. Rare catalog of mail-order fashions documents women's and children's clothing styles shortly after the turn of the century. Captions offer full descriptions, prices. Invaluable resource for fashion, costume historians. Approximately 725 illustrations. 128pp. 8⅜ × 11¼. 27276-1 Pa. $10.95

THE 1912 AND 1915 GUSTAV STICKLEY FURNITURE CATALOGS, Gustav Stickley. With over 200 detailed illustrations and descriptions, these two catalogs are essential reading and reference materials and identification guides for Stickley furniture. Captions cite materials, dimensions and prices. 112pp. 6½ × 9¼. 26676-1 Pa. $9.95

EARLY AMERICAN LOCOMOTIVES, John H. White, Jr. Finest locomotive engravings from early 19th century: historical (1804–74), main-line (after 1870), special, foreign, etc. 147 plates. 142pp. 11⅜ × 8¼. 22772-3 Pa. $8.95

THE TALL SHIPS OF TODAY IN PHOTOGRAPHS, Frank O. Braynard. Lavishly illustrated tribute to nearly 100 majestic contemporary sailing vessels: Amerigo Vespucci, Clearwater, Constitution, Eagle, Mayflower, Sea Cloud, Victory, many more. Authoritative captions provide statistics, background on each ship. 190 black-and-white photographs and illustrations. Intıoduction. 128pp. 8⅞ × 11¾. 27163-3 Pa. $12.95

EARLY NINETEENTH-CENTURY CRAFTS AND TRADES, Peter Stockham (ed.). Extremely rare 1807 volume describes to youngsters the crafts and trades of the day: brickmaker, weaver, dressmaker, bookbinder, ropemaker, saddler, many more. Quaint prose, charming illustrations for each craft. 20 black-and-white line illustrations. 192pp. 4⅜ × 6. 27293-1 Pa. $4.95

VICTORIAN FASHIONS AND COSTUMES FROM HARPER'S BAZAR, 1867–1898, Stella Blum (ed.). Day costumes, evening wear, sports clothes, shoes, hats, other accessories in over 1,000 detailed engravings. 320pp. 9⅜ × 12¼. 22990-4 Pa. $13.95

GUSTAV STICKLEY, THE CRAFTSMAN, Mary Ann Smith. Superb study surveys broad scope of Stickley's achievement, especially in architecture. Design philosophy, rise and fall of the Craftsman empire, descriptions and floor plans for many Craftsman houses, more. 86 black-and-white halftones. 31 line illustrations. Introduction. 208pp. 6½ × 9¼. 27210-9 Pa. $9.95

THE LONG ISLAND RAIL ROAD IN EARLY PHOTOGRAPHS, Ron Ziel. Over 220 rare photos, informative text document origin (1844) and development of rail service on Long Island. Vintage views of early trains, locomotives, stations, passengers, crews, much more. Captions. 8⅞ × 11¾. 26301-0 Pa. $13.95

THE BOOK OF OLD SHIPS: From Egyptian Galleys to Clipper Ships, Henry B. Culver. Superb, authoritative history of sailing vessels, with 80 magnificent line illustrations. Galley, bark, caravel, longship, whaler, many more. Detailed, informative text on each vessel by noted naval historian. Introduction. 256pp. 5⅜ × 8½. 27332-6 Pa. $6.95

TEN BOOKS ON ARCHITECTURE, Vitruvius. The most important book ever written on architecture. Early Roman aesthetics, technology, classical orders, site selection, all other aspects. Morgan translation. 331pp. 5⅜ × 8½. 20645-9 Pa. $8.95

THE HUMAN FIGURE IN MOTION, Eadweard Muybridge. More than 4,500 stopped-action photos, in action series, showing undraped men, women, children jumping, lying down, throwing, sitting, wrestling, carrying, etc. 390pp. 7⅞ × 10⅝. 20204-6 Clothbd. $24.95

TREES OF THE EASTERN AND CENTRAL UNITED STATES AND CANADA, William M. Harlow. Best one-volume guide to 140 trees. Full descriptions, woodlore, range, etc. Over 600 illustrations. Handy size. 288pp. 4½ × 6⅜. 20395-6 Pa. $5.95

SONGS OF WESTERN BIRDS, Dr. Donald J. Borror. Complete song and call repertoire of 60 western species, including flycatchers, juncoes, cactus wrens, many more—includes fully illustrated booklet. Cassette and manual 99913-0 $8.95

GROWING AND USING HERBS AND SPICES, Milo Miloradovich. Versatile handbook provides all the information needed for cultivation and use of all the herbs and spices available in North America. 4 illustrations. Index. Glossary. 236pp. 5⅜ × 8½. 25058-X Pa. $5.95

BIG BOOK OF MAZES AND LABYRINTHS, Walter Shepherd. 50 mazes and labyrinths in all—classical, solid, ripple, and more—in one great volume. Perfect inexpensive puzzler for clever youngsters. Full solutions. 112pp. 8⅛ × 11. 22951-3 Pa. $3.95

PIANO TUNING, J. Cree Fischer. Clearest, best book for beginner, amateur. Simple repairs, raising dropped notes, tuning by easy method of flattened fifths. No previous skills needed. 4 illustrations. 201pp. 5⅜ × 8½. 23267-0 Pa. $5.95

A SOURCE BOOK IN THEATRICAL HISTORY, A. M. Nagler. Contemporary observers on acting, directing, make-up, costuming, stage props, machinery, scene design, from Ancient Greece to Chekhov. 611pp. 5⅜ × 8½. 20515-0 Pa. $11.95

THE COMPLETE NONSENSE OF EDWARD LEAR, Edward Lear. All nonsense limericks, zany alphabets, Owl and Pussycat, songs, nonsense botany, etc., illustrated by Lear. Total of 320pp. 5⅜ × 8½. (USO) 20167-8 Pa. $5.95

VICTORIAN PARLOUR POETRY: An Annotated Anthology, Michael R. Turner. 117 gems by Longfellow, Tennyson, Browning, many lesser-known poets. "The Village Blacksmith," "Curfew Must Not Ring Tonight," "Only a Baby Small," dozens more, often difficult to find elsewhere. Index of poets, titles, first lines. xxiii + 325pp. 5⅜ × 8¼. 27044-0 Pa. $8.95

DUBLINERS, James Joyce. Fifteen stories offer vivid, tightly focused observations of the lives of Dublin's poorer classes. At least one, "The Dead," is considered a masterpiece. Reprinted complete and unabridged from standard edition. 160pp. 5³⁄₁₆ × 8¼. 26870-5 Pa. $1.00

THE HAUNTED MONASTERY and THE CHINESE MAZE MURDERS, Robert van Gulik. Two full novels by van Gulik, set in 7th-century China, continue adventures of Judge Dee and his companions. An evil Taoist monastery, seemingly supernatural events; overgrown topiary maze hides strange crimes. 27 illustrations. 328pp. 5⅜ × 8½. 23502-5 Pa. $7.95

THE BOOK OF THE SACRED MAGIC OF ABRAMELIN THE MAGE, translated by S. MacGregor Mathers. Medieval manuscript of ceremonial magic. Basic document in Aleister Crowley, Golden Dawn groups. 268pp. 5⅜ × 8½. 23211-5 Pa. $7.95

NEW RUSSIAN-ENGLISH AND ENGLISH-RUSSIAN DICTIONARY, M. A. O'Brien. This is a remarkably handy Russian dictionary, containing a surprising amount of information, including over 70,000 entries. 366pp. 4½ × 6⅛. 20208-9 Pa. $8.95

HISTORIC HOMES OF THE AMERICAN PRESIDENTS, Second, Revised Edition, Irvin Haas. A traveler's guide to American Presidential homes, most open to the public, depicting and describing homes occupied by every American President from George Washington to George Bush. With visiting hours, admission charges, travel routes. 175 photographs. Index. 160pp. 8¼ × 11. 26751-2 Pa. $10.95

NEW YORK IN THE FORTIES, Andreas Feininger. 162 brilliant photographs by the well-known photographer, formerly with *Life* magazine. Commuters, shoppers, Times Square at night, much else from city at its peak. Captions by John von Hartz. 181pp. 9¼ × 10¾. 23585-8 Pa. $12.95

INDIAN SIGN LANGUAGE, William Tomkins. Over 525 signs developed by Sioux and other tribes. Written instructions and diagrams. Also 290 pictographs. 111pp. 6⅛ × 9¼. 22029-X Pa. $3.50

PHOTOGRAPHIC SKETCHBOOK OF THE CIVIL WAR, Alexander Gardner. 100 photos taken on field during the Civil War. Famous shots of Manassas, Harper's Ferry, Lincoln, Richmond, slave pens, etc. 244pp. 10⅝ × 8¼.
22731-6 Pa. $9.95

FIVE ACRES AND INDEPENDENCE, Maurice G. Kains. Great back-to-the-land classic explains basics of self-sufficient farming. The one book to get. 95 illustrations. 397pp. 5⅜ × 8½. 20974-1 Pa. $6.95

SONGS OF EASTERN BIRDS, Dr. Donald J. Borror. Songs and calls of 60 species most common to eastern U.S.: warblers, woodpeckers, flycatchers, thrushes, larks, many more in high-quality recording. Cassette and manual 99912-2 $8.95

A MODERN HERBAL, Margaret Grieve. Much the fullest, most exact, most useful compilation of herbal material. Gigantic alphabetical encyclopedia, from aconite to zedoary, gives botanical information, medical properties, folklore, economic uses, much else. Indispensable to serious reader. 161 illustrations. 888pp. 6½ × 9¼. 2-vol. set. (USO) Vol. I: 22798-7 Pa. $9.95
Vol. II: 22799-5 Pa. $9.95

HIDDEN TREASURE MAZE BOOK, Dave Phillips. Solve 34 challenging mazes accompanied by heroic tales of adventure. Evil dragons, people-eating plants, bloodthirsty giants, many more dangerous adversaries lurk at every twist and turn. 34 mazes, stories, solutions. 48pp. 8¼ × 11. 24566-7 Pa. $2.95

LETTERS OF W. A. MOZART, Wolfgang A. Mozart. Remarkable letters show bawdy wit, humor, imagination, musical insights, contemporary musical world; includes some letters from Leopold Mozart. 276pp. 5⅜ × 8½. 22859-2 Pa. $6.95

BASIC PRINCIPLES OF CLASSICAL BALLET, Agrippina Vaganova. Great Russian theoretician, teacher explains methods for teaching classical ballet. 118 illustrations. 175pp. 5⅜ × 8½. 22036-2 Pa. $4.95

THE JUMPING FROG, Mark Twain. Revenge edition. The original story of The Celebrated Jumping Frog of Calaveras County, a hapless French translation, and Twain's hilarious "retranslation" from the French. 12 illustrations. 66pp. 5⅜ × 8½.
22686-7 Pa. $3.50

BEST REMEMBERED POEMS, Martin Gardner (ed.). The 126 poems in this superb collection of 19th- and 20th-century British and American verse range from Shelley's "To a Skylark" to the impassioned "Renascence" of Edna St. Vincent Millay and to Edward Lear's whimsical "The Owl and the Pussycat." 224pp. 5⅜ × 8½.
27165-X Pa. $4.95

COMPLETE SONNETS, William Shakespeare. Over 150 exquisite poems deal with love, friendship, the tyranny of time, beauty's evanescence, death and other themes in language of remarkable power, precision and beauty. Glossary of archaic terms. 80pp. 5$\frac{3}{16}$ × 8¼. 26686-9 Pa. $1.00

BODIES IN A BOOKSHOP, R. T. Campbell. Challenging mystery of blackmail and murder with ingenious plot and superbly drawn characters. In the best tradition of British suspense fiction. 192pp. 5⅜ × 8½. 24720-1 Pa. $5.95

THE WIT AND HUMOR OF OSCAR WILDE, Alvin Redman (ed.). More than 1,000 ripostes, paradoxes, wisecracks: Work is the curse of the drinking classes; I can resist everything except temptation; etc. 258pp. 5⅜ × 8½. 20602-5 Pa. $4.95

SHAKESPEARE LEXICON AND QUOTATION DICTIONARY, Alexander Schmidt. Full definitions, locations, shades of meaning in every word in plays and poems. More than 50,000 exact quotations. 1,485pp. 6½ × 9¼. 2-vol. set.
Vol. 1: 22726-X Pa. $15.95
Vol. 2: 22727-8 Pa. $15.95

SELECTED POEMS, Emily Dickinson. Over 100 best-known, best-loved poems by one of America's foremost poets, reprinted from authoritative early editions. No comparable edition at this price. Index of first lines. 64pp. 5³⁄₁₆ × 8¼.
26466-1 Pa. $1.00

CELEBRATED CASES OF JUDGE DEE (DEE GOONG AN), translated by Robert van Gulik. Authentic 18th-century Chinese detective novel; Dee and associates solve three interlocked cases. Led to van Gulik's own stories with same characters. Extensive introduction. 9 illustrations. 237pp. 5⅜ × 8½.
23337-5 Pa. $5.95

THE MALLEUS MALEFICARUM OF KRAMER AND SPRENGER, translated by Montague Summers. Full text of most important witchhunter's "bible," used by both Catholics and Protestants. 278pp. 6⅝ × 10. 22802-9 Pa. $10.95

SPANISH STORIES/CUENTOS ESPAÑOLES: A Dual-Language Book, Angel Flores (ed.). Unique format offers 13 great stories in Spanish by Cervantes, Borges, others. Faithful English translations on facing pages. 352pp. 5⅜ × 8½.
25399-6 Pa. $8.95

THE CHICAGO WORLD'S FAIR OF 1893: A Photographic Record, Stanley Appelbaum (ed.). 128 rare photos show 200 buildings, Beaux-Arts architecture, Midway, original Ferris Wheel, Edison's kinetoscope, more. Architectural emphasis; full text. 116pp. 8¼ × 11. 23990-X Pa. $9.95

OLD QUEENS, N.Y., IN EARLY PHOTOGRAPHS, Vincent F. Seyfried and William Asadorian. Over 160 rare photographs of Maspeth, Jamaica, Jackson Heights, and other areas. Vintage views of DeWitt Clinton mansion, 1939 World's Fair and more. Captions. 192pp. 8⅞ × 11. 26358-4 Pa. $12.95

CAPTURED BY THE INDIANS: 15 Firsthand Accounts, 1750–1870, Frederick Drimmer. Astounding true historical accounts of grisly torture, bloody conflicts, relentless pursuits, miraculous escapes and more, by people who lived to tell the tale. 384pp. 5⅜ × 8½. 24901-8 Pa. $7.95

THE WORLD'S GREAT SPEECHES, Lewis Copeland and Lawrence W. Lamm (eds.). Vast collection of 278 speeches of Greeks to 1970. Powerful and effective models; unique look at history. 842pp. 5⅜ × 8½. 20468-5 Pa. $13.95

THE BOOK OF THE SWORD, Sir Richard F. Burton. Great Victorian scholar/adventurer's eloquent, erudite history of the "queen of weapons"—from prehistory to early Roman Empire. Evolution and development of early swords, variations (sabre, broadsword, cutlass, scimitar, etc.), much more. 336pp. 6⅛ × 9¼. 25434-8 Pa. $8.95

AUTOBIOGRAPHY: The Story of My Experiments with Truth, Mohandas K. Gandhi. Boyhood, legal studies, purification, the growth of the Satyagraha (nonviolent protest) movement. Critical, inspiring work of the man responsible for the freedom of India. 480pp. 5⅜ × 8½. (USO) 24593-4 Pa. $7.95

CELTIC MYTHS AND LEGENDS, T. W. Rolleston. Masterful retelling of Irish and Welsh stories and tales. Cuchulain, King Arthur, Deirdre, the Grail, many more. First paperback edition. 58 full-page illustrations. 512pp. 5⅜ × 8½. 26507-2 Pa. $9.95

THE PRINCIPLES OF PSYCHOLOGY, William James. Famous long course complete, unabridged. Stream of thought, time perception, memory, experimental methods; great work decades ahead of its time. 94 figures. 1,391pp. 5⅜ × 8½. 2-vol. set.
Vol. I: 20381-6 Pa. $12.95
Vol. II: 20382-4 Pa. $12.95

THE WORLD AS WILL AND REPRESENTATION, Arthur Schopenhauer. Definitive English translation of Schopenhauer's life work, correcting more than 1,000 errors, omissions in earlier translations. Translated by E. F. J. Payne. Total of 1,269pp. 5⅜ × 8½. 2-vol. set.
Vol. 1: 21761-2 Pa. $10.95
Vol. 2: 21762-0 Pa. $11.95

MAGIC AND MYSTERY IN TIBET, Madame Alexandra David-Neel. Experiences among lamas, magicians, sages, sorcerers, Bonpa wizards. A true psychic discovery. 32 illustrations. 321pp. 5⅜ × 8½. (USO) 22682-4 Pa. $8.95

THE EGYPTIAN BOOK OF THE DEAD, E. A. Wallis Budge. Complete reproduction of Ani's papyrus, finest ever found. Full hieroglyphic text, interlinear transliteration, word-for-word translation, smooth translation. 533pp. 6½ × 9¼. 21866-X Pa. $9.95

MATHEMATICS FOR THE NONMATHEMATICIAN, Morris Kline. Detailed, college-level treatment of mathematics in cultural and historical context, with numerous exercises. Recommended Reading Lists. Tables. Numerous figures. 641pp. 5⅜ × 8½. 24823-2 Pa. $11.95

THEORY OF WING SECTIONS: Including a Summary of Airfoil Data, Ira H. Abbott and A. E. von Doenhoff. Concise compilation of subsonic aerodynamic characteristics of NACA wing sections, plus description of theory. 350pp. of tables. 693pp. 5⅜ × 8½. 60586-8 Pa. $13.95

THE RIME OF THE ANCIENT MARINER, Gustave Doré, S. T. Coleridge. Doré's finest work; 34 plates capture moods, subtleties of poem. Flawless full-size reproductions printed on facing pages with authoritative text of poem. "Beautiful. Simply beautiful."—*Publisher's Weekly*. 77pp. 9¼ × 12. 22305-1 Pa. $5.95

NORTH AMERICAN INDIAN DESIGNS FOR ARTISTS AND CRAFTS-PEOPLE, Eva Wilson. Over 360 authentic copyright-free designs adapted from Navajo blankets, Hopi pottery, Sioux buffalo hides, more. Geometrics, symbolic figures, plant and animal motifs, etc. 128pp. 8⅜ × 11. (EUK) 25341-4 Pa. $7.95

SCULPTURE: Principles and Practice, Louis Slobodkin. Step-by-step approach to clay, plaster, metals, stone; classical and modern. 253 drawings, photos. 255pp. 8⅛ × 11. 22960-2 Pa. $9.95